Japanese Perceptions of
Papua New Guinea

War, Culture and Society

Series Editor: Stephen McVeigh, Associate Professor,
Swansea University, UK

Editorial Board:
Paul Preston *LSE, UK*
Joanna Bourke *Birkbeck, University of London, UK*
Debra Kelly *University of Westminster, UK*
Patricia Rae *Queen's University, Ontario, Canada*
James J. Weingartner *Southern Illinois University, USA (Emeritus)*
Kurt Piehler *Florida State University, USA*
Ian Scott *University of Manchester, UK*

War, Culture and Society is a multi- and interdisciplinary series which encourages the parallel and complementary military historical and socio-cultural investigation of 20th and 21st century war and conflict.

Published:
The Testimonies of Indian Soldiers and the Two World Wars,
Gajendra Singh (2014)
The British Imperial Army in the Middle East, James E. Kitchen (2014)
South Africa's 'Border War', Gary Baines (2014)
Filming the End of the Holocaust, John J. Michalczyk (2014)
The Japanese Comfort Women and Sexual Slavery during the China and Pacific Wars,
Caroline Norma (2015)
Cultural Responses to Occupation in Japan, Adam Broinowski (2016)
Second World War British Military Camouflage, Isla Forsyth (2017)
Jewish Volunteers, the International Brigades and the Spanish Civil War,
Gerben Zaagsma (2017)
Women, Warfare and Representation, Emerald M. Archer (2017)
Prisoners of the Sumatra Railway, Lizzie Oliver (2017)
The Franco-Algerian War through a Twenty-First Century Lens,
Nicole Beth Wallenbrock (2020)
Picturing Genocide in the Independent State of Croatia, Jovan Byford (2020)
Japanese Perceptions of Papua New Guinea, Ryōta Nishino (2022)

Forthcoming:
Military Law, the State, and Citizenship in the Modern Age, Gerard Oram (2023)
Literature and Cultural Identity during the Korean War, Jerôme de Wit (2023)
The Lost Cause of the Confederacy and American Civil War Memory,
David J. Anderson (2023)

Japanese Perceptions of Papua New Guinea

War, Travel and the Reimagining of History

Ryōta Nishino

BLOOMSBURY ACADEMIC
LONDON • NEW YORK • OXFORD • NEW DELHI • SYDNEY

BLOOMSBURY ACADEMIC
Bloomsbury Publishing Plc
50 Bedford Square, London, WC1B 3DP, UK
1385 Broadway, New York, NY 10018, USA
29 Earlsfort Terrace, Dublin 2, Ireland

BLOOMSBURY, BLOOMSBURY ACADEMIC and the Diana logo are
trademarks of Bloomsbury Publishing Plc

First published in Great Britain 2022
Paperback edition published 2024

Copyright © Ryōta Nishino, 2022

Ryōta Nishino has asserted their right under the Copyright, Designs and
Patents Act, 1988, to be identified as Author of this work.

For legal purposes the Acknowledgements on pp. xv–xvi constitute an
extension of this copyright page.

Cover image: Sogeram River in Papua New Guinea © Getty Images.

All rights reserved. No part of this publication may be reproduced or transmitted in
any form or by any means, electronic or mechanical, including photocopying,
recording, or any information storage or retrieval system, without prior
permission in writing from the publishers.

Bloomsbury Publishing Plc does not have any control over, or responsibility for, any
third-party websites referred to or in this book. All internet addresses given in this
book were correct at the time of going to press. The author and publisher regret any
inconvenience caused if addresses have changed or sites have ceased to exist, but
can accept no responsibility for any such changes.

Every effort has been made to trace the copyright holders and obtain permission to
reproduce the copyright material. Please do get in touch with any enquiries or any
information relating to such material or the rights holder. We would be
pleased to rectify any omissions in subsequent editions of this
publication should they be drawn to our attention.

A catalogue record for this book is available from the British Library.

A catalog record for this book is available from the Library of Congress.

ISBN: HB: 978-1-3501-3900-8
PB: 978-1-3503-6926-9
ePDF: 978-1-3501-3901-5
eBook: 978-1-3501-3902-2

Series: War, Culture and Society

Typeset by Newgen KnowledgeWorks Pvt. Ltd., Chennai, India

To find out more about our authors and books visit www.bloomsbury.com
and sign up for our newsletters.

Contents

List of Illustrations	viii
Note to the Reader	ix
Preface	xii
Acknowledgements	xv

1 Introduction — 1
    An outline of the New Guinea campaign and varying legacies — 3
    Invisible chains of history — 7
    Travelling memory: Towards the third wave of the memory boom — 10
    Three narrative categories — 15
    Five historical interpretations — 18
    Part and chapter outline — 20
    Part 1: Memoirs of soldiers and army doctors — 21
    Part 2: Films and documentaries — 24
    Part 3: Travelogues — 26

Part 1   Memoirs of Soldiers and Army Doctors

2 To hell and back: The question of cannibalism in memoirs of the New Guinea campaign — 31
    Soldiers' opposition to cannibalism — 35
    Pragmatic adoption of survival egoism in cannibalistic hell — 42
    Ruminating before and after enacting survival egoism — 46
    Conclusion — 53

3 Army doctors' struggle with medical crises and self-discipline — 55
    Army doctors' roles, status and discipline through writing — 56
    Doctors' views of New Guinea as a zone of medical crisis — 58
    Doctors' views of combatants' fits of insanity — 61
    The medical gaze and self-discipline: Observing the self — 65
    The medical gaze and self-discipline: Sexual desire and appetite — 69
    Mercy killing — 73
    Conclusion — 76

Part 2 Films and Documentaries

4 Finding reasons for living and dying in a war zone: Cinematic adaptations of Katō Daisuke's *Minami-no-shima ni yuki ga furu* — 81
    Katō's memoir and war in Manokwari — 84
    The 1961 adaptation: Katō finds his *ikigai* — 86
    Residues of the empire in 'Shūchō no musume' (Chieftain's Daughter) — 89
    A curtailed debate on *sange* and *nanshi* — 91
    The last glimpse of snow — 92
    The 1995 adaptation: Clashes between *sange* and *nanshi* — 94
    The Japanese flag in the nationalist theatre — 97
    The final confrontation — 99
    Conclusion — 102

5 Documentaries as co-performative partnership: Framing and presenting testimonies of painful memories — 105
    Yukiyukite Shingun: Excessive rage impeding engagement with painful memories — 107
    Senjō no onna tachi/Sensō Daughters: Co-performing victimhood and self-advocacy — 112
    Ushiyama Jun'ichi: Countering the victim narrative by collecting New Guineans' voices — 120
    Conclusion — 128

Part 3 Travelogues

6 From a soldier to a best friend forever? Manga artist Mizuki Shigeru and the villagers of New Britain Island — 133
    Phase 1: Wartime – between hell and heaven — 136
    Phase 2: Paradise revisited — 142
    Phase 3: The end of Mizuki's long wartime: A pickup truck in three narratives — 147
    Phase 4: Closing the circle — 155
    Conclusion — 158

7 Vicarious consumer travel and the performance of emotional awakening in travelogues — 161
    The war that never leaves us — 165
    Tangible reminders of an intangible presence — 169

	Photography as occupation and its imaginary reoccupation	172
	An inner journey	174
	A *sarariiman* abroad: From ignorance to action	179
	Travelling in the footsteps of fallen heroes	182
	Conclusion	184
8	Conclusion: The road behind and ahead	187

Glossary	199
Notes	201
Select Bibliography	229
Index	243

Illustrations

Figures

2.1	A pictorial scroll of hell	34
6.1	Mizuki reflects on the death of Emperor Hirohito	150

Maps

1	Historical territories and names of Papua New Guinea	x
2	New Guinea Island and its adjacent islands	xi
3	Areas under Japanese occupation, 1942	4
4	The South Sepik River area	123

Tables

1.1	Wartime and Post-war Generations and Phases of Transmission of War Stories	14
1.2	Travelling Memories and Media	22
6.1	Four Phases of Mizuki's Travelogues	136
6.2	Mizuki Shigeru's War and Travel-Related Books	139
6.3	Mizuki's Narratives of Gifting the Pickup Truck	148
7.1	Profiles of the Travel Writers	163

Note to the Reader

This book follows the Japanese naming convention of the surname first followed by the given name when referring to Japanese (-born) people. Exception apply to the authors who mainly or exclusively publish in English. When transliterating Japanese names and words, the book uses macrons to indicate the lengthening of vowels. Notable exceptions are words that entered the English lexicon and names well recognized outside Japan. *Tōfu* in Japanese becomes *tofu* in English. The Japanese pronounce Kyōto and Tōkyō, but the common English spelling has them as Kyoto and Tokyo. Unless otherwise noted, all translations from Japanese into English are mine. The terms 'Japan' and 'Japanese' often carry assumptions of homogeneity that can lead to exclusionary and hierarchical rhetoric and practices. My usage of these two terms does not endorse such assumptions, rhetoric or practices.

The names authors use to refer to the political entities and the peoples may cause confusion. The name of the independent nation we know today as Papua New Guinea went through several changes throughout history (Map 1). Before 1942, the eastern half of New Guinea Island was divided into Papua in the southeast and New Guinea in the northeast. Also under the Territory of New Guinea was the Bismarck Archipelago lying to the east of New Guinea Island. In 1942, the Australian military administration amalgamated Papua and New Guinea into a combined Territory of New Guinea. In 1971, the name changed to Papua New Guinea, which has been the official name adopted upon independence in 1975. The western half of New Guinea Island was a Dutch colony of Dutch New Guinea; it is now part of Indonesia, also known as West Papua. Naming the peoples comes with attendant complications. Most use specific geographical locations. Some sources adopt the categories of the Papuans and the New Guineans in the respective colonial territories, and Papua New Guineans. I use Papua New Guineans and its abbreviation PNG when the text refers to today's independent nation of Papua New Guinea, or when the authors make a general statement that applies to today's PNG.

Japanese-language sources broadly follow the historical changes that led to today's PNG and follow the official name *Papua Nyūginia* as it is transliterated in Japanese. In Japan, *Nyūginia sensen* refers to the New Guinea campaign across

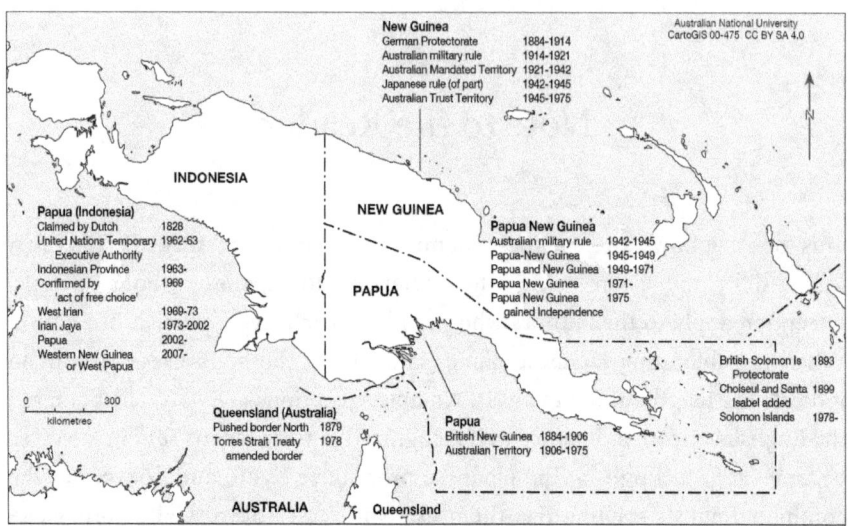

Map 1 Historical territories and names of Papua New Guinea. Map reproduced with the permission of CartoGIS Services, ANU College of Asia and the Pacific, The Australian National University.

the entire New Guinea Island plus the Bismarck Archipelago and the former Dutch New Guinea. Authors who write about the New Guinea campaign tend to conflate Papua and New Guinea, which follows the merger by the Australians in 1942. While *Nyūginia* (New Guinea) and *Nyūginia-jin* (New Guineans) are the most common term Japanese authors use, many name individual islands such as Bougainville, New Britain and New Ireland. Some use Papua and *Papuan-jin* (Papuans) when they refer to the territory and the people of the former Papua (Map 2).

The military engagements that occurred between Japan and the Allies in today's PNG form part of the war that many call the Pacific War or the Second World War. This book uses the term Asia-Pacific War (*Ajia-Taiheiyō Sensō*). It lags in recognition and circulation compared with the other two descriptors, but is gaining acceptance among historians and scholars in associated disciplines in both Japanese- and English-speaking circles today. The term Asia-Pacific War is seen as preferable for several reasons. The use of the Second World War implies the centrality of the European theatres and campaigns. A more salient term in the United States is the Pacific War, which highlights the Pacific Island campaigns. The Asia-Pacific War conveys the multiplicity of campaigns the Japanese fought in Asia and the Pacific. Furthermore, in Japan the names of the war changed. The wartime government used *Daitōa Sensō* (The Greater East Asian War). Its

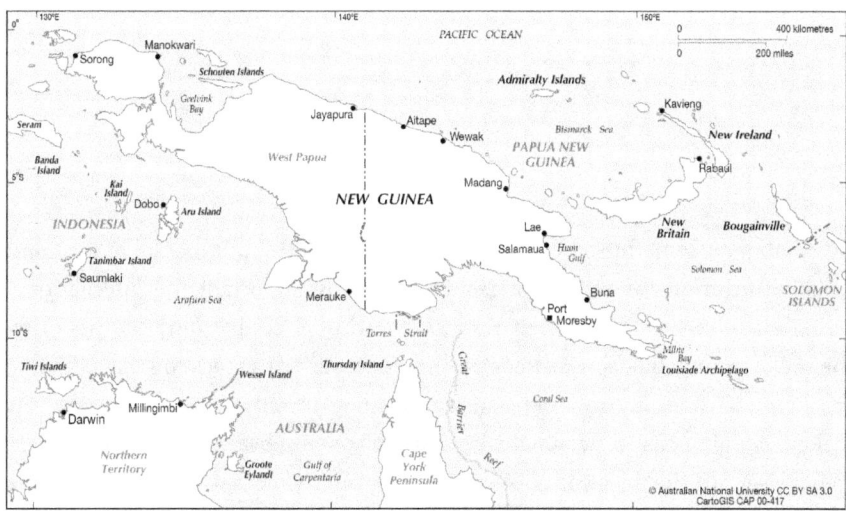

Map 2 New Guinea Island and its adjacent islands. Map reproduced with the permission of CartoGIS Services, ANU College of Asia and the Pacific, The Australian National University.

association with the wartime ideology to liberate Asia from Western imperial control jarred with the American-led occupiers who insisted on *Taiheiyō Sensō* (the Pacific War). It recast the Americans as the main adversaries and diverted attention from the Asian continent where the largest number of combatants and civilians died. *Taiheiyō Sensō* practically reduced Japan's war in China into a precursor and moved the beginning of the war from the Marco Polo Bridge Incident of 1937 to the bombing of Pearl Harbor in 1941. An alternative term *Jūgonen Sensō* (The Fifteen Year War) gained wider recognition from the 1970s. It sets the beginning of the war at the Mukden Incident of 1931, thus winding the clock back even further than 1937 and 1941. The weakness of *Jūgonen Sensō* is the muting of geographical reference. *Taiheiyō Sensō* still remains the most widely used and recognized. In less formal contexts, many Japanese call the war *ano sensō* (that war) or simply *sensō* (war).[1] One could say that the euphemistic undertone blunts the specific reference to the Asia-Pacific War and the suffering and aggression. These words illustrate Yoshikuni Igarashi's observation about the 'absent presence of [Japan's] war memories' that persists despite popular sentiment and efforts to sanitize the history of defeat.[2]

Preface

Readers may sometimes be curious about the identity of a book's author and their motivation for writing it. Authorship was important for international relations scholar and historian E. H. Carr who advised: 'Study the historian before you study the facts.'[1] I imagine that Carr was not suggesting that personal background was the only determinant shaping the historian's work. He was acknowledging that a personal biography has some bearings on what she or he does. With this in mind, I offer this preface to what has brought me to the writing of this book.

Ever since I can recall, the Asia-Pacific War has been a historical event that was both close to and far away from my consciousness. Close because it features in newspapers, magazines, news programmes and even in conversations. I have watched war-themed films and television programmes, read manga dealing with aspects of the war, and learnt about it at school. At the same time, the war is also distant from me. I was born almost three decades after Japan's defeat. What added to the distance from the war was my family history and circumstances. It was after I left Japan for the first time in 1994 on a high school exchange programme to Canada that I became acutely aware of how little I knew of the war. In Canada, I took a course on twentieth-century world history. The depth and the coverage of the Second World War, including the Asia-Pacific War, far exceeded the scant overview of it that the crowded curricula in Japan could ever afford to teach.

As far as I can trace, all my great grandparents, grandparents and my parents are of Japanese descent. Both my parents were born in 1952 in small rural villages in Niigata prefecture and moved to Yokohama in the 1970s. I was born in 1976; my brother in 1979. During my childhood, we paid an average of one visit a year to our grandparents and relatives. Typically, on these visits, we spent much of our time playing with our cousins. Wartime stories from our grandparents or relatives hardly featured. The only person in my extended family that was conscripted and sent to battle during the war was the brother of my maternal grandmother. All she told us was that he was a private and died in a battle in China, and she knew little else about his death. Both of my grandfathers were eligible for conscription, but neither went to the

Asia-Pacific War. My maternal grandfather (1925–2007) failed the physical examination on account of his poor eyesight. My paternal grandfather (1923–2006) also failed the physicals. He had lost three fingers on his dominant hand in a threshing machine. The examining doctor deemed him unfit for military service because he could not pull the trigger. I believed these stories without any doubt. Years later I came to learn that many youths had deliberately severed their fingers or harmed themselves to evade conscription.[2] I could not ascertain whether my grandfather's accident was a calculated move or truly a coincidence.

As my grandfathers had not participated in the war, I, as a grandson, grew up without direct input of war stories from close family members. Similarly, our parents gave me and my brother little insight into the war. Both my parents' families had little advanced education to equip them with the cultural capital and idiom to process and articulate their memories. Furthermore, the demands of farm labour and my grandfathers' seasonal work away from Niigata left them with little time or inclination to talk much, least of all about the painful wartime past. In this respect, my upbringing was different from some of my peers. They might have had grandfathers who had fought in the war and told their stories. Their parents might also have relayed their parents' wartime experiences.

Following my high school exchange, I have experienced how the past catches and confronts me unawares, especially when I travelled abroad. People asked me about the war, and the standard answers that I gave were 'I don't know much, because my grandparents did not go to war' and 'My teachers didn't teach us much about it'. On some occasions, my answers led me to explain how my grandfathers did not go to war and how Japanese schools taught history. However, it took me years to realize that my ignorance came partially from the disrupted intergenerational transfer of wartime stories. The more severe lesson was the disconnect between my understanding of history as an intellectual pursuit and everyday practice or even appreciation of it. Coming to the South Pacific in 2011 amplified this lesson. It spurred me to learn more about the south western Pacific campaigns of which I knew little. While planning a book-length project, I narrowed down my focus to the New Guinea campaign.

My previous ignorance was not the fault of my grandparents or my parents. It was too late when I felt compelled to ask my grandparents about their experience of the wartime in rural Japan. After I began teaching myself about the Asia-Pacific War, I realized more acutely that I could not change my family history or my past. But what I can change and overcome is my perception: that I lacked such opportunities and exposure to war history and its legacy. Interacting with history and acknowledging its legacy enables us to remind ourselves of how the contemporary world turned out to be the way it has, and also how history and interpretations of it continue to influence the personal and the collective identities of today's global citizens.

Acknowledgements

No book is a work completed in isolation. Many people and institutes generously shared their precious time, wisdom and resources with me. Here I wish to thank the following individuals and organizations in this limited space. A sabbatical I won in 2016 from the University of the South Pacific, Fiji, laid the foundation of this book project. During the sabbatical, Vicki Luker at the Australian National University, Stacey Steele at Melbourne Law School, the University of Melbourne, and Greg Dvorak at Hitotsubashi University (now at Waseda University) hosted me as a visiting researcher. Beatrice Trefalt at Monash University facilitated my becoming a research affiliate, which enabled me to obtain many online sources readily.

The International Research Center for Japanese Studies (Nichibunken), Kyoto, Japan, awarded me a one-year fellowship from April 2019 to March 2020. The well-resourced library, the mountain trails behind the institute and stimulating discussions with scholars gave me much needed time and space for writing. I appreciate the welcoming gestures by John Breen, Inaga Shigemi, Kusunoki Ayako and Tsuboi Hideto. The staff at the library never failed to impress me with their diligence and the extra mile they went to obtain resources from inside and outside Japan. Nichibunken's director, Inoue Shōichi, magnanimously extended my stay when the Covid-19 pandemic halted my return to Fiji. Moving to the Graduate School of Law at Nagoya University in 2021 gave me a change of scenery. Never before has the teaching of academic writing at Nagoya driven a point home that writing and what goes into it are part of lifelong skills one must always refine.

Chapter 6 is a revised version of my previously published work in *Japan Review* by Nichibunken. Chapter 7 derives from sections of my earlier articles that appeared in *Asia-Pacific Journal: Japan Focus* by the Asia-Pacific Journal, *Pacific Historical Review* by the Pacific Coast Branch, American Historical Association and the University of California Press and *History and Memory* by Indiana University Press. I thank the publishers for allowing me to revise them for this book. These are referenced in the bibliography. CartoGIS Services, Scholarly Information Services at the Australian National University, Mizuki

Production and Nichibunken gave me kind permission to reproduce some of their maps and images.

My family, colleagues and friends near and far kept my spirit high when the going got tough on many occasions. My thanks go to Andrew Connelly, Matthew Kelly, Iwamoto Hiromitsu, Arnel Joven, Jonathan Ritchie, Yasuko Hassall Kobayashi, Takahashi Shinnosuke, Toyoda Yukio, Rowena Ward and Christine Winter. I feel fortunate to have worked with Justin Aukema, Daniel Milne and Mahon Murphy to co-edit a special issue of *Asia-Pacific Journal: Japan Focus*, entitled 'Re-examining Asia-Pacific War Memories: Grief, Narratives, and Memorials'. The special issue and this book went into press almost simultaneously. The special issue is available on https://apjjf.org/2022/10/ToC.html. I owe a debt of gratitude to Matthew Allen (of Broken Nose Vanilla Farm in Australia), Caroline Norma and Peter Williams who have read and commented on parts of my drafts. Invaluable too are the comments by anonymous peer reviewers. Encouragement and support from Bloomsbury's editorial team, Laura Reeves, Emma Tranter, Saranya Manohar and Rhodri Mogford, have been unfailingly superb ever since I submitted my first book proposal. The individuals and institutions named above are beyond reproach for errors and omissions in this work.

This book features only a small portion of all the stories of veterans and citizens involved in the Asia-Pacific War and the New Guinea campaign. It is but a small contribution to rich historical scholarship that came before and will come after. Many more stories remain untold and await to be heard and read. It is to their memories, told and untold, that I wish to dedicate this book.

1

Introduction

For many of us today, Papua New Guinea (PNG) and Japan do not strike us as a pair of nations with close relations like those between the UK and the United States or between Japan and its East Asian neighbours. Though shadowed by the economy of scale of the Global North, Japan and the Pacific Island region, of which PNG is part, have formed well-established diplomatic and commercial ties. Still, many Japanese today know PNG as little more than a place of abundant wildlife or a land filled with stereotypical images of 'exotic tribes'. However, even a cursory look at PNG's history tells us that it was the site of a major military conflict during the Asia-Pacific War between the Japanese and the Allies – Australians and Americans. The campaign embroiled the local residents. In July 2014, the New Guinea campaign received media attention in Japan. The then Japanese prime minister Abe Shinzō (in office, 2006–7 and 2012–20) went on a tour of New Zealand, Australia and PNG. In his address to the Australian parliament, Abe acknowledged that Japan and Australia once were adversaries during wartime and vowed not to repeat the horrors of war, conveying his 'most sincere condolences towards the many souls who lost their lives'.[1] In PNG, Abe paid his respect to Japanese soldiers at a memorial in Wewak, in northern New Guinea Island. Abe told the press, 'We must not repeat the horror of war. I pledged in front of the spirits of the war dead that I want Japan to be a country that thinks about world peace with friends in Asia and the world'.[2] The references to the war remained modest in number and extent, without generating heated responses to other war-related remarks and commemorative gestures. What dominated the coverage of these visits were the economic and strategic partnerships Abe sought to strengthen with the three nations as China's presence in the Asia-Pacific region grew by the day.[3] While the media's pursuit of contemporary issues is understandable, this framing raises the question of whether the memories of the New Guinea campaign or the Asia-Pacific War have paled in significance to more modern concerns.

The question has a familiar resonance in Japan. For decades, critics, scholars and members of the public have raised concerns about the decline of public recognition of the Asia-Pacific War. A few have even singled out the New Guinea campaign. For instance, in 1977, literary critic Noro Kuninobu urged his readers not to forget the New Guinea campaign. His survey of writings by rank-and-file soldiers concludes that the New Guinean campaign had the worst of 'all tragic hardships the Imperial [Japanese] Army experienced'. He asserts, 'If we leave out the New Guinea campaign when we talk about the Asia-Pacific War, it means that we have not said anything.'[4] In a 2009 monograph, military historian Tanaka Hiromi laments the scant attention that the Japanese public and scholars pay to the New Guinea campaign. While Tanaka understands the Japanese victory was unrealistic, he credits the New Guinea campaign as having held crucial significance for Japan. From a strategic perspective, he thinks the Japanese presence in New Guinea managed to delay the Allies' eventual incursion further north to the Philippines and beyond.[5] Noro and Tanaka agree that the Japanese should remember the New Guinea campaign as being a vital part of Japan's recent history. However, treating their concerns as a sign of the Japanese having forgotten or neglected the New Guinea campaign remains a contestable claim.

The overarching question of this book is what perceptions of the New Guinea campaign and PNG emerge out of the stories the Japanese have told over the years. Under the spotlight are selected historical representations of the New Guinea campaign: memoirs, fictionalized films, documentaries and travelogues. The choice draws on Astrid Erll's concept of 'travelling memory' which holds that historical memory travels with time and across space and media. The analyses demonstrate how the Japanese people tell, retell, imagine, reimagine, construct and reconstruct history over the years. This book ultimately argues that far from being forgotten or even erased from popular consciousness, memories of the New Guinea campaign in Japan comprise a highly contested field upon which competing narratives of the past, present and future collide. The examples illuminate multiple modes of circulations of historical memory and interpretations that continue travelling over time and space as well as across various media. Questions about how we remember the past is one of the perennial preoccupations of scholars across multiple disciplines. In recent decades scholars have revisited this age-old question which has been explored in what we now call the field of memory studies. Technological sophistication has not only made it easy and affordable for us to store a mass of data but has also aroused associated anxiety about forgetting. Memories of wars, in particular the

Asia-Pacific War and the Holocaust, have driven the theoretical and practical concerns in memory studies and its close sibling: history. This book contributes to a new wave of memory studies, which Erll terms 'travelling memory', through an exploration of print and audiovisual representations of Japanese war memories from the New Guinea campaign of the Asia-Pacific War.[6] This introduction offers an outline of the New Guinea campaign and its legacies. Then, it will discuss the theoretical underpinning of the book, namely, travelling memory and the implicated subject, and the narratives and interpretations of the Asia-Pacific War in Japan. These form the basis for the analyses in subsequent chapters. The introduction ends with synopses of the chapters that follow.

An outline of the New Guinea campaign and varying legacies

The approach this book pursues lies in the stories and interpretations the Japanese have told and offered after the war. Chronological accounts of the strategies and an evaluation of the operations fall outside the remit of this work; military historians in Japan and elsewhere have provided ample details. Nonetheless, an outline of the campaign and the legacies it left in Australia and PNG should offer the necessary background for this work. Military historians understand that the Japanese strategic interest in New Guinea stemmed from its location. Japanese strategists believed that taking New Guinea was vital to cut off the supply lines between Australia and the United States. The Japanese then conceived of Operation FS. Its goal was to occupy Rabaul on New Britain Island, the capital of the Australian-administered Territory of New Guinea at the time, and then expand to New Caledonia, Fiji and Samoa. On 23 January 1942, the Japanese occupied Rabaul and established a base for their south-western Pacific operations. Following losses in sea battles, the Japanese Army launched an overland attack from Buna to Port Moresby in July 1942. The ensuing battles between the Japanese and the Australians became known as the Kokoda campaign. The Japanese retreated without reaching Port Moresby. Meanwhile, the Japanese defeat by the Americans in Guadalcanal, to the east of PNG, in February 1943 prompted the Japanese to deploy reinforcements to defend New Guinea. The Allies, led by General Douglas MacArthur, launched Operation Cartwheel in June 1943 to push the Japanese westwards and cut off Japanese supplies from Rabaul. In September 1943, the Japanese headquarters shrank the Japanese sphere to the absolute zone of national defence (*zettai kokubōken*) to defend the territories closer to the mainland. Eastern New Guinea and the Island New Guinea lay outside the zone. The Japanese soldiers in New Guinea were practically abandoned. The continuing Allied raids that sank Japanese supply vessels exacerbated the soldiers' shortage of food and supplies (Map 3).

Across many theatres of the war, Japanese soldiers were subjected to excruciating physical and mental ordeals. Demands by officers and superiors had to be obeyed without question however unreasonable they were. Surrendering, becoming prisoners of war and withdrawing from the war zone were unpardonable acts but death in combat was considered a patriotic virtue of sacrifice for the nation. Many soldiers committed suicide to avert the potential

Map 3 Areas under Japanese occupation, 1942. Map reproduced with the permission of CartoGIS Services, ANU College of Asia and the Pacific, The Australian National University.

ignominy that their survival might bring to them and their families. Constant hunger, illness and attacks by the Allies wore down their bodies and minds. Day and night, hot and cold, they carried backpacks whose weight exceeded the recommended limit of half one's body weight.[7] Soldiers deployed to the Pacific Islands contended with an inhospitable climate and unfamiliar terrain; the tropical jungle provoked fear of 'swallowing' the soldiers.[8]

This outline makes it clear that the protracted duration, shortage of supplies and harsh conditions made the New Guinea campaign even more exacting than other campaigns such as Guadalcanal, Imphal and the Philippines. Historian Fujiwara Akira estimated that of some 150,000 soldiers deployed to New Guinea, 127,000 died. Of these, over 90 per cent (114,840) died of illness and starvation, not of direct confrontation with the Allied troops. This rate is 30 per cent higher than the national total of 1.4 million out of 2.3 million (60 per cent).[9] In Island New Guinea, an additional 44,000 died in Bougainville and 30,500 died on New Britain, New Ireland and the Admiralty Islands.[10] What adds more to the chagrin of veterans and the families of the deceased is that the majority of the dead have not been identified or repatriated. Official statistics released in December 2020 note that of the 127,600 total deaths from the eastern New Guinea campaign, an estimated 76,180 remains are yet to be identified and repatriated (59.7 per cent).[11] In comparison, the Allies' casualties were light. The Americans and the Australians committed around 340,000 and 400,000 soldiers, respectively, with 7,000 dead for each side.[12]

The ways in which Papua New Guineans and Australians remember the New Guinea campaign provides a background for the Japanese perceptions. The experience the Papuans and the New Guineans had during the war varies greatly from one locality to another. Post-war and post-independence PNG faced the challenges of forging a single national narrative.[13] For one thing, arriving at the figures of population and casualties across PNG remains impossible for most and can be thought of as estimates at best. By 1940, around 200,000 Papuans and 500,000 New Guineans were registered as residents in areas within the reach of the Australian authorities. Hank Nelson thinks that these figures made up less than half of the entire population.[14] Generally speaking, the extent of casualties varied. The impact was negligible in remote areas such as the highlands with limited or no foreign presence. In communities with sustained exposure to war, people died of direct and indirect causes such as deprivation, exposure to foreign diseases, bombardment and targeted or random assaults. Populations in those areas decreased between a quarter and a half.[15] Moreover, the sudden influx of foreigners had profound social and economic ramifications. The Japanese and the Allies introduced the Papuans and the New Guineans to new goods and cash through barter and trade. The recruitment of the local men as indentured labourers, often by coercion, took the vital workforce away from the communities and exacerbated food supplies and infant mortality. Some communities found themselves in intractable positions of having to take sides between the Japanese and the Australians or suffer retributions. Their complications should not mean a dearth of endeavours. Seminal monographs and oral history projects have chronicled and recorded the wartime experiences in many parts of PNG, with more likely to follow in future.[16]

In Australia, the New Guinea campaign occupies a prominent spot in the popular consciousness to this day. In particular, the Kokoda campaign garnered a reputation as being a crucible of the war. Many Australians credit the Australians' success in Kokoda for halting the advancing Japanese and in keeping mainland Australia free of the adversary. A vital pillar to the Australian narrative is 'mateship', a kind of camaraderie formed among the Australian soldiers and between the Australians, the Papuans and the New Guineans united amidst adverse conditions. Central to the latter mateship is the figure of the Fuzzy Wuzzy Angels, the Papuans and the New Guineans who aided the Allied troops. The Fuzzy Wuzzy Angels have come to embody cross-cultural friendship between men and became a symbol of the loyalty, kindness and compassion that the New Guineans extended to the Australians. The Fuzzy Wuzzy Angels trope helped rectify the racist assumption of the pre-war colonial era, but the trope turned the Papuans and the New Guineans into 'good natives' who still remained subordinate to the Australians.[17] Between Australia's mateship narrative and PNG's fraught positions, Japanese narratives of the New Guinea campaign trod distinct paths. The sketch above shows the multiplicity of the footprint the New Guinea campaign left in the nations involved.

Scholarly communities in Japan, PNG and Australia have conducted and published research on the New Guinea campaign. Two notable initiatives took place from the 1990s to the early 2000s. The Australia-Japan Research Project, launched in 1996, was run by the Australian War Memorial, funded by the Japanese government. The Project maintains an extensive bilingual website and places its publications online (http://ajrp.awm.gov.au). Of which, a fully-bilingual anthology edited by Steven Bullard and Keiko Tamura faetures essays by Australian and Japanese scholars. In Japan, anthropologist Yukio Toyoda and historian Hiromitsu Iwamoto co-ordinated a series of symposia from 1998 to 2003, which resulted in an anthology written in English.[18] Both projects gathered archival sources available in Australia and Japan and filled the gaps with oral histories from various parts of PNG. Some contributors gave fine-grain treatment of individual battles and locations. While the two projects tend towards military history, the primary concern of this volume is cultural history through the analyses of historical works about the New Guinean campaign in Japan. This volume brings the Japanese works into the English-language readership and paves the way for a more ambitious future work of a tri-nation comparison with Australian and Papua New Guinean memories.

Invisible chains of history

Legacies of the past have significant ramifications for the world we have inherited and continue to inhabit. In this understanding of the ongoing impact of history, the past is not a safe haven where people indulge in nostalgia or seek refuge from a troublesome present but is a dynamic and living entity. Tessa Morris-Suzuki calls this 'being implicated in history'; we may not have direct responsibility for violent acts of the past, but we continue to live in the slipstream of the exploitative hierarchy and structure from which we benefit or suffer.[19] Similarly, Michael Rothberg approaches these issues through what he calls 'the implicated subjects' who

> contribute to, inhabit, inherit, or benefit from regimes of domination but do not originate or control such regimes. An implicated subject is neither a victim nor a perpetrator, but rather a participant in histories and social formations that generate the positions of victim and perpetrator, and yet in which most people do not occupy such clear-cut roles. Less 'actively' involved than perpetrators, implicated subjects do not fit the mold of the 'passive' bystander, either. Although indirect or belated, their actions and inactions help produce and reproduce the positions of victims and perpetrators. In other words, implicated subjects help propagate the legacies of historical violence and prop up the structures of inequality that mar the present.[20]

Rothberg advocates that we need to conceive of the implicated subject beyond the familiar categories of the victim, the perpetrator and the bystander, and to think of the web of power and privilege as historically conditioned projects. Whereas complicity connotes the legalistic framework of bearing direct responsibility for the acts committed, the term implicated allows us to think of the lasting consequences. He further distinguishes between diachronic (historical) and synchronic (contemporary) implication.[21] Certainly, not all of us are beneficiaries of past events but some have benefited from the diachronic and synchronic implications. The diachronic implication draws our attention to past violence and exploitation that shaped the contemporary conditions. The privileged lifestyle the people of the Global North enjoy rests on the synchronic implication of the transnational flow of goods, labour, materials and information underpinning today's capitalism. Several contemporary events illuminate this point. Recent global movements such as Rhodes Must Fall and Black Lives Matter seek redress of the institutional racism that pervades the post-slavery, postcolonial, post-racial, decolonized and democratic or putatively democratizing twenty-first-century world. Events like these dramatize the invisible chains of the past that continue to bind us.

The worldviews and identities we form rest with our interaction with history even when we may not recognize directly the role the past plays in their formation. The Japanese born after the war do not bear direct responsibility for the exploitation and violence that occurred during the colonial era and the Asia-Pacific War. Yet, people draw meanings and moral lessons from history and shape or build our identities anchored in the past. Morris-Suzuki says:

> The prejudices which sustained past acts of aggressions also live on into the present, and lodge themselves in the minds of the present generation unless we take active steps to remove them. Though we may not be responsible for such acts of aggression in the sense of having caused them, we are 'implicated' in them, in the sense that *they* cause *us*.[22]

Morris-Suzuki and Rothberg share a common concern of how history lives in the present. Attentiveness to the contemporary world goes in tandem with greater awareness of being implicated in the history. Such visions of history then influence how we perceive ourselves and the world, and how we project our desired future and act.

Another way to see how we are implicated in history is to recognize history as a culturally enmeshed, socially relevant, politically potent discipline that is constantly in the making. History moves with relative ease between the everyday and the academic, the personal and the public. Postmodern scepticism about definitive truth has made us mindful that professional historians cannot assume a monopoly over the narratives of the past and historical truth. However novel it seems, concerns about connections between history and story as well as facts and truth are long-standing matters.[23] Seldom do we acquire historical knowledge and perspectives from a single source. What surrounds us are multiple fragments and representations proliferating the landscape of our historical memories. We have fiction, non-fiction, films, documentaries, theatre plays, TV drama, photographs, pictures, visual and performing arts, heritage sites, statues, computer games, commemorative acts and museum exhibits. Nevertheless, academic history matters: it teases out a chain of cause-and-effects, critiques evidence to draw interpretations and arrives at a particular understanding of truth about historical events and figures. This is what Morris-Suzuki calls history-as-interpretation. She contrasts this with history-as-identification whereby history evokes emotional reactions that drive individuals to identify with past actors, events and communities and calls for us not to underestimate the role of emotion in popular media. This view does not mean 'anything goes' in the name of entertainment or sales. Morris-Suzuki says historical works test the producers' commitment to historical truthfulness, a kind of scrupulousness to history. She is responding to what she perceives as a crisis of history where popular platforms become the megaphones for 'fetishized truth' to the detriment of the ethos and the practice of historical enquiry and scholarship.[24] Controversies surrounding truth claims and historical representations can often be reduced to futile fact-checking procedures. Instead, she suggests we 'trace, as far as possible, the series of mediations through which narratives and images of the past reach us, and why we respond to them as we do'.[25] The intellectual and creative processes that inform historical works influence the complex web of our existence and the historical media that inform and feed off each other.

This expanded conception of history has galvanized the rise of public history as an academic discipline. Jerome de Groot uses the term 'the historicals' for the nodes and modes of representational practices and media which democratized history and challenged the hegemonic position of professional historians. In no way does de Groot suggest that the historicals serve as platforms for 'fetishized truth' at the expense of academic history. Like Morris-Suzuki, he urges us to pay close attention to the ways we assemble, repackage, market and consume these historicals as cultural hybrids that influence how we shape our sense of the past.[26] The pervasive reach of war and its cultural legacy from the battlefield to many corners of civilian life attests to the indelible marks wars leave on collective and individual consciousness. As is the case with many of the historicals inspired by wars around the world, the Asia-Pacific War in Japan has spawned a plethora of historicals that enter our daily lives and generate many controversies. Numerous examples include the treatment of Japan's imperial era and wartime history in school textbooks, manga, television programmes, films, museums, shrines and many more forms of representation. The growing acknowledgement of the multiplicity of historical representation and the fluidity of the ways we acquire historical knowledge and form perspectives reflects transitions in historical scholarship and the advent of memory studies.

Travelling memory: Towards the third wave of the memory boom

The profusion of historicals in Japan and internationally may reflect growing anxiety about forgetting and of reorganizing our understanding of the world when global changes shook the foundations of extant paradigms. The flowering of historicals paralleled the memory boom of the 1990s that preoccupied public and academic discourse after the dissolution of the Cold War order and the fiftieth anniversary of the end of the Second World War. The growth of memory studies into an increasingly encompassing academic field underlines the compelling appeal the memory boom has had for us. At its baseline, memory studies hold that individuals and groups select memories to reconstruct the past and reinvent their identities to meet the needs of the present. Limitations of space here allow for only a brief acknowledgement of the vast and evolving field of cultural and media memory studies.[27] Maurice Halbwachs's *Collective Memory* (1923) is the seminal work of the first phase. Halbwachs presumed that memory is essential to the creation and maintenance of the identity of mnemonic communities. These are groups of individuals bound by common interests and a belief in a shared destiny such as the nation and civic groups. The emphasis of collective memory resides in the homogeneity and the closed nature of mnemonic communities. Understanding of these communities can be enhanced by reference to the work of Pierre Nora, one of the seminal figures in the second phase of memory studies. His *lieux de mémoire* (1984–92) proposed that the centrality of memory lies in 'memory sites' where individuals and communities commemorate, maintain and negotiate their memories and identities. At the same time, as Geoffrey Cubitt points out, whose past we remember and commemorate is always contested and contestable.[28]

The current and the third phase of memory studies seizes on the fluidity of memory across sites, mnemonic communities, time, media and academic disciplines. Particularly useful are the conceptualizations by Mieke Bal and Erll. Bal treats memory as a concept that travels across those categories or boundaries and notes the meaning can change over time and in different contexts. Such movements warrant assessing the shifts and fluctuations 'before, during and after each "trip" '.[29] Taking this further, Erll names travelling memory as 'a metaphorical shorthand' that posits that 'the production of cultural memory, people, media, mnemonic forms, contents, and practices are in constant, unceasing motion'.[30] Individuals move, travel and migrate in their lives and accumulate memories. We create, transmit and receive stories in a multitude of memory media ranging from books, photographs, and videos to social networking sites. Anniversaries, memorials and social and family gatherings constitute some of the occasions to maintain and renew our memories. These acts of remembering and the media reflect or mediate intellectual and institutional climates and can stimulate the empathetic imagination of the audience and motivate solidarity. Erll cautions, however, that misuse and distortion are also possible, as are memory products which make little impact on the audience.[31] More recently, Erll and her colleagues say that travel and 'locatedness' are not mutually exclusive, but rather form dynamics that illuminate the mediated nature of memory.[32] The concept offers an intellectually productive and accommodating foundation to treat multiple historicals in three respects: (1) how to rethink the notions of travel and travellers, (2) how time affects the creation and reception of memory and (3) how memory travels across various media. These three aspects underline the complexity of the historicals as their creators make, imagine and consume history.

First, travelling memory broadens the notion of travel to incorporate temporary spatial movement or even dislocation for a range of purposes such as work, leisure and war. War demands the movement of people and resources and transforms ordinary people into soldiers. They leave their communities for foreign lands and return home with a changed outlook on life, death and violence. They may spend the bulk of time with compatriots and with little exposure to foreign adversaries or civilians and they will have travelled from home to war zone and from peacetime to wartime. Reintegration in the post-war society demands that the veterans adapt to the changed home environment. Soldiers and veterans are a kind of travellers with stories to tell others. Those without direct combat experience and those who did not live during wartime learn about the war from multiple sources and historical representations. The changing modes of transmission of historical memory parallel Marianne Hirsch's term 'postmemory' and Alison Landsberg's 'prosthetic memory'. Originally referring to the memories of the Holocaust, postmemory has come to cover the often unconscious and indirect passing-down of cultural legacies of traumatic experiences from victims to their children and grandchildren. They grow up in the shadows of the trauma that the victims find so painful and difficult to communicate fully and to be understood. It is the said and unsaid that form the backdrop of the familial relationships that influence the moral and intellectual stances of the postmemory generations.[33] Prosthetic memory pertains to film and other technologically aided means of communicating historical memory. It holds that individuals glean the images and perceptions of the past from mediated and often commodified mass culture available in the public sphere. These fragments become prosthetics for us to walk into a past beyond our lifetime and to foster personal and political identity.[34] These theoretical insights draw on North American and European examples but promise to recast travel as an immersive experience into the past whereby travellers mobilize their empathetic faculties to engage in virtual travel.

Secondly, the temporal aspect of travelling memory enables us to chart intergenerational transmission and reception of memories as evolving phenomena, rather than a zero-sum game between maintenance and extinction. Historian Narita Ryūichi devised seminal phases the transmissions of war stories under each phase and generation born before and after the war. The phases and patterns overlap but they indicate not only a shift in patterns but also a shift in demographics. During Phase 0, the duration of the war, the main form of telling was reportage, which was transmitted from war zones as a real-time situation. Some were bare bone summaries of the battles and conditions of the war zones; some injected the writers' subjectivities – to meet state ideological control.[35] In Phase 0, both sender and receiver of information were contemporaries living during wartime (Generation A). Phase 1 goes from the defeat to 1965. Generation A recalls their wartime as experience, as something to look back on in the wake of defeat and without the strictures of the wartime state. In Phase 1, Generation A shared assumptions and lived memories of the wartime. Freed from wartime control, the senders could be frank about the misery and cruelty of the war as well as compare the differences in their experiences.

With time, a new cohort without the first-hand memory of the wartime, Generation B, grows in number and ushers in Phase 2, which stretches from 1965 to 1990. Generation B forms ideas about the war by osmosis of the societal atmosphere of the adults and stories from Generation A passed down as testimony. A war veteran talking about his war experience to his contemporary can assume commonly shared knowledge. He cannot take much for granted when he talks to his children's generation or his grandchildren's generation. Parents telling their children about the war fits into this pattern. Conversely, a rupture between two generations can occur since they have different experiences and values. By 1990, Phase 3 began to form. As the portion of those in Generation A continued to decline, Generation B began sharing their knowledge with their contemporaries and the second generation without living memories of the war (Generation C). By Phase 3, the war has become more abstract and less personal as memories, but more varied sources of information are available to learn about the war. Debates between Generations B and C then represent a clash between conflicting memories. Narita thinks that as the number of individuals in Generations A and B declines, Generation C assumes control and creates more memories of the war. Narita anticipates that from 2015 war memories will gradually gain characteristics of history as living memories and become part of an array of evidence and historical representation.[36] Though Hirsch, Landsberg and Narita conceive various phrases and models, they agree on approaching the various modes of transferring memory as dynamic trans-war phenomena. While predicting future trajectories with certitude is impossible, the matrix of phases, generations and modes of narration should help to demonstrate how time changes the contours of memory (Table 1.1).

The third aspect of travelling memory relates to the notion of memory travelling across media. The proliferation of these historicals, that de Groot observes, suggests the multiple platforms and their cross-fertilization that memory-makers have at their disposal. This trend underlines a crucial feedback loop. Each medium or historical draws on the imaginative powers of their creator to frame their stories, while also being influenced by and influencing other media. Paying close attention to this circuit helps to demonstrate how 'the popular' engenders and participates in the scholarly discussions that many perceive as the exclusive domain of the select few. The work of Philip Seaton is instructive in this respect. Seaton scrutinizes a wide range of popular media discourses on the Asia-Pacific War in Japan in relation to narrative motifs and historical interpretations. Clashes between conflicting ideological standpoints about Japan's wartime history prompt headlines at international and domestic levels. Based on all the agreement, disagreement and emotional intensity that these debates frequently stir, media reports employ labels such as the history problem or history war. Seaton argues that these media mirror the competing ideological and political positions that circulate in Japan and no single narrative or interpretation enjoys hegemonic status. The media reports, particularly the Western media coverage of Japan, render a misleading picture of Japan as unable or unwilling to come to terms with its wartime and imperial past. Instead, he characterizes the landscape of Japanese war memories as 'memory rifts' with deep ideological and political fault lines running underneath.[37] The very contemporary resonance indicates how the debate continues to influence how we see the past, the present and the future.

Table 1.1 Wartime and Post-war Generations and Phases of Transmission of War Stories

Generation A: People with wartime experience (Sensō keikensha), with memories of the wartime as lived experience.

Generation B: First Post-war Generation (Sengo dai-ichi sedai) born between 1940 and the 1960s. They received stories about the war from Generation A and from communities, as well as other mediated sources.

Generation C: Second Post-war Generation (Sengo dai-ni sedai) born after the 1970s. May hear wartime stories directly from Generation A, as grandparents. But greater preponderance for receiving war stories from Generation B as second-hand stories and mediated sources.

Phase and Form of War Stories	Oral		Written	
	Speakers	Listeners	Writers	Readers
Phase 0 1931–45 wartime as real-time situation	Spoken and heard between military personnel		Generation A	Generation A
Phase 1 1945–65 talking about war experience	Generation A	Generation A Generation B	Generation A	Generation A
Phase 2 1965–90 testifying about the war	Generation A	Generation A Generation B	Generation A	Generation A Generation B
Phase 3 1990–2014 turning the war into memory	Generation A Generation B Generation C	Generation B Generation C	Generation A Generation B	Generation B Generation C
Phase 4 2015–to date turning the war into history	Generation A Generation B Generation C	Generation B Generation C	Generation A Generation B Generation C	Generation B Generation C

Source: Adapted and modified from Narita, *Zōho 'sensō keiken'*, Chapter 1; Narita, *Sengoshi nyūmon*, 43.

In these ways, travelling memory underscores the evolving nature of history in the making in both the public and the private spheres, and offers this book an overarching framework to explore the cultural history of Japanese historical representations of the New Guinea campaign. This book differs from extant works that have chronicled military operations, collected veterans' recollections and examined Japanese war crimes.[38] Instead, this volume builds on the works of Morris-Suzuki and Seaton in particular. The former analyses Japanese representations of the Asia-Pacific War and the way these construct historical narratives along with many international counterparts.[39] Seaton analyses how contestations over the meanings and interpretations of the war permeate the Japanese media and lives.[40] While the two scholars address the circulation of memories of the Asia-Pacific War across multiple media of historical representation, this work concentrates on the Japanese historical representations of the New Guinea campaign. The narrow approach can capture cross sections of the historical representations of a single campaign. The analyses of changing and constant perceptions of a single campaign should demonstrate how the authors and creators have contributed to the wider public contestation over the narratives and interpretations of the war. Looking into these individual endeavours can indicate the kinds of history told so far and how they have contributed to the making of collective history. To facilitate the analyses of these historical media, the following sections outline the contours of narratives and historical interpretations of the Asia-Pacific War in Japan.

Three narrative categories

Nations involved in the Asia-Pacific War constructed multiple narratives to explain the meaning of the war, the victory and the defeat, and these stories are found in many historical representations. These narrative plots and their underlying moral stance illustrate Hayden White's influential view of historians' work as organizing empirical facts in culturally recognizable plots. He insists that the facts speak not for themselves but do so when integrated into the narrative schemes.[41] Sociologist Akiko Hashimoto points out that the different narratives reflect various conditions such as history, time and cultural-and-political traditions. The dominant narrative in the English-speaking Allied nations maintains that the Second World War and the Asia-Pacific War were fundamentally a 'good war' between the good democratic states and the evil Axis powers. This narrative reflects both the vantage point of the victorious and the Christian-influenced theory of a just war that legitimizes use of violence against the unjust aggressor.[42] From the opposite perspective, defeated nations develop narratives to turn the grief of the dead and the stigma of aggression into alternative and untainted moral positions. The wartime government framed the Asia-Pacific War as 'a sacred war' to defend Japan's imperial project of a Greater East Asian Co-Prosperity Sphere from the Western powers. Following the defeat, the Japanese reframed the war as a morally wrong war and promoted three major categories of narratives: heroic, victim and perpetrator.[43] None of these three has gained universal acceptance among the Japanese. However, each category informs the underlying morality that the historicals communicate in the reconstruction of the war, death and defeat and the visions for the future and commemoration.

There are archetypal patterns in each category. In the heroic narratives, the soldiers are depicted as making a noble sacrifice for the nation and their actions are justified by way of a retrospective logic which evidences the peace and prosperity of post-war Japan. The dead soldiers are accorded special respect as *eirei*, which literally means 'noble spirits' but translates to 'fallen heroes'. Of these the *kamikaze* pilots receive mythical reverence. The heroic narratives find expression in official statements and garner support from conservatives and nationalists. They claim that post-war Japanese live in debt to the fallen soldiers and demonstrating loyalty to the nation is a way to repay this debt. A case in point is the Yasukuni shrine in Tokyo. It enshrines the spirits of all 2.46 million soldiers who fought for the emperor since the foundation of Meiji Japan, including colonial subjects from Korea and Taiwan and fourteen Class A war criminals of the Asia-Pacific War. Yasukuni is the focal point for nationalists who regard the soldiers as making a martyr-like sacrifice for the nation. Yasukuni regularly comes under the spotlight when politicians visit the shrine to pay their respects even if they maintain that they visit in personal capacities. Supporters believe these visits to be appropriate patriotic gestures while they also invariably draw rebuke from critics in Japan and in East Asia who oppose the visits as they represent an endorsement of Japan's imperial and militarist legacy.[44] The adherents of the hero narrative seem oblivious to the fact that the original purpose of the war was to bring peace and prosperity by winning the war, not by losing it.[45] The admiration for the soldiers obfuscates questions about collective and individual responsibility for the war, and acts of aggression committed.

The victim narratives constitute the most common category. The narratives present the war as evil and Japanese citizens as innocent victims of the political system and the military who initiated the war. These narratives convey that many Japanese were 'duped into' and even 'betrayed' for offering support for the war efforts under the influence of state indoctrination and heavy-handed suppression of dissent. During the war, citizens suffered from poverty, hunger and constant fear of bombardment. Soldiers, especially the rank-and-file, identified themselves as victims of hardship and violent treatment by their superiors. Many soldiers saw themselves as powerless as they had few options but to obey orders and believed that they were exempt from strategic oversight and blunders. The victim narratives helped apportion the blame away from the Japanese people to the amorphous war and institutions. This framing was politically expedient for the US-led Occupation Force and the Japanese establishment to implement post-war democratic reform and to curtail the leftist influence in Japan.[46]

By contrast, the perpetrator narrative brings the Japanese people's responsibility to the fore. It identifies the Japanese as the invaders of territories in Asia and the Pacific and the perpetrators of violent acts meted out on the foreign civilians and combatants. The narrative extends its purview beyond the wartime to Japan's imperial project that sowed the seed for the war. Beneath the perpetrator narrative are regret and remorse for past wrongdoings and the resolve to make amends across national and ethnic boundaries for a pacifist future. To this end, the adherents of the perpetrator narratives tend to pay attention to the organizational structure that gave rise to the acts of violence.[47]

The differences in the underlying moralities do not mean that these three categories are mutually exclusive. Soldiers identify themselves as victims of physical and psychological distress but some of them bullied their compatriots and inflicted serious harm and even killed foreign troops and civilians. Ordinary citizens participated in economic and political activities that aided the wartime mobilization. The victim and perpetrator narratives are imbricated with each other. Nevertheless, as Seaton points out, the victim narratives on the home front permeate many Japanese accounts. By the time of the defeat, the population of Japan stood at seventy-five million. Of these, around three million civilians lived abroad. About 5.47 million were in active service, including 2.94 million in Japanese territories. The extent of the casualties was unprecedented. Of the 3.1 million deaths, 2.3 million were soldiers; the rest were civilians abroad and in Japan (300,000 and 500,000, respectively). Conversely, the Japanese inflicted between 19 and 20 million deaths of whom around 10 million were in China and Southeast Asia. Even though the number of casualties inflicted by the Japanese far exceed that of the Japanese themselves, the proportion of combatants who committed acts of violence was a minority as the vast majority of the Japanese stayed on the home front. Experiences such as hunger, poverty, enemy bombardments and state repression, elevated the victim narratives above any others.[48] From the Allies' perspectives, the Japanese perpetrator narratives are most convenient for the 'good war' narrative as they justify the Allies' actions. Other Japanese narratives, however, pose difficult questions about these good war narratives. The Japanese victim narratives discuss Allies' aerial raids on Japanese cities and atom bombs in Hiroshima and Nagasaki to portray the horrors of the war and the Allies' aggression. These heroic narratives pose uneasy questions about Western imperialism that the Japanese sought to end on behalf of the people of Asia.[49]

One crucial underlying motivation behind these narratives is the question of whose deaths and deeds to commemorate. Hiro Saito distinguishes between nationalist and cosmopolitan intentions of commemoration. The former upholds the centrality of the nation state and endorses the heroic view that consecrates a nation's soldiers as heroes while overlooking what they inflicted on others. The latter commemorates the deaths of the victims across nationalities and aims for critical reflection on nationalistic biases of commemoration to foster transnational imagination towards realizing universal humanity.[50] This is a useful point of view in the light of heroic and victim narratives, but one could make a further distinction between nationalist commemoration and national commemoration. By nationalistic commemoration, mourning the deaths of compatriots as making a heroic sacrifice for the state either develops or reinforces the nationalistic sentiments of the mourners. National commemoration does not articulate nationalistic ideology. Commemorating the deaths of compatriots as untimely, tragic and an unnecessary waste of life due to the militarists' errors can prompt questions about the state-centric rhetoric of commemoration; nonetheless in national commemoration compatriots are still depicted as the primary, if not exclusive, object. Commemoration rituals have private and public purposes and can foster personal sensibilities towards the past, the war and the dead and also provide sustenance for history-as-identification, by which history becomes the vehicle for present- and future-oriented political expression.

The three categories of the narratives, complemented by the modes of commemoration, offer a foundation for more textured ways of understanding how various carriers of memory have inscribed, reinscribed and reiterated historical memory in a range of formats and in different media. Paying attention to the shifting contours and to the stable features illuminates what has prevailed across the media over time and helps to salvage what has been left behind. The seventy-fifth anniversary is an appropriate moment for a dispassionate stocktaking of the categories of narratives employed by the various media to communicate historical interpretations.

Five historical interpretations

According to Seaton, Japanese media have offered five broad historical interpretations of the Asia-Pacific War on a spectrum. He qualifies that the five positions do not fully account for the complexity or the fluidity of the opinions.

Still, he finds that the contestation between the interpretations has shaped the 'memory rifts' of Japanese war memories and driven ongoing debates. As well as the three narrative categories, the five interpretations form the bases for analyses and warrant reiterating at length:

1) Progressives take a categorical stance on violence by the Japanese. They believe that the Japanese pursued imperial projects and committed acts of aggression in Asia and the Pacific in the name of war. Although the progressives acknowledge that the Allies inflicted violence on the Japanese, the progressives squarely place the responsibility for aggressive acts on the Japanese themselves. The progressives reject the claims that the war was inevitable and maintain that the Japanese government must apologize and compensate the victims fully and that acts of commemoration without due recognition of foreign victims are inadequate.
2) The progressive-leaning group accepts that the war was an inevitable result of geopolitical tension and that the Japanese committed cruelty during the war. This group considers the Japanese as victim-and-perpetrator and argues that the West bears some responsibility in incidents such as the firebombing of cities and the use of the atom bomb. This group believes that the Japanese government should apologize to and compensate the victims.
3) Conservatives defend the cause of the war as justifiable if not just. They concede that the Japanese committed violence but regard these acts as individual or unit actions instead of imputing them to the higher echelon. More than the progressive-leaning group, victim consciousness is more prominent in the conservatives' view. The conservatives emphasize stronger moral equivalence between the aggression committed by the Japanese and the Allies. To make this point, the conservatives cite the Allies' raids of Japanese cities and atom bombs. The conservatives believe that Japan has made sufficient gestures to fulfil responsibility by paying compensation and issuing repeated apologies to foreign states and victims.
4) Nationalists comprise a small minority and argue that the war was a just one of national defence. They cast the Allies as the aggressors and deny the cruelty and aggression the Japanese committed, as seen in their denial of the Nanjing Massacre and the military comfort women. Instead, they project affirmative images of Japanese bravery and sacrifice for the nation. Nationalists believe apologies and compensation are unnecessary consequences of defeat. The most extreme nationalists, *uyoku*, worship the emperor and criticize individuals and groups in the progressive camps as masochistic. The

resurgence of neo-nationalists in the 1990s is, to an extent, a pushback against the preceding short-lived political shift. Despite their limited support the nationalists make their presence seem greater than the others.

5) 'Don't-know-don't-care' are mostly young people born after the war. They see that history and memory of war have little relevance to their identity and values. While not completely ignorant, they know some things about the war. Some may form their opinions later in their lives as they gain more information about the war from various sources.[51]

Seaton finds that except for the small support for nationalists, opinion polls reveal a roughly even distribution of four positions and reflect the highly contested nature of Japan's wartime memory. However, the even spread can feed into the common perception in English-speaking former Allied nations that the Japanese have not reached a consensus on how to face up to the past and have failed to atone for wartime aggression.[52]

Further complicating the interpretations come from the issue of responsibility. The Japanese intelligentsia distinguish between war responsibility and post-war responsibility. Where the former connotes actions during wartime, the latter extends beyond wartime to account for the imperial era and even for contemporary ramifications. Historian Ienaga Saburō was the most ardent proponent of Japan's war responsibility. He insisted the younger generation needed to face up to war responsibility by virtue of their birth in Japan. Ienaga's claim drew criticism for imposing a quasi-ethno-nationalist view of inborn guilt, although his intention resembles diachronic implication. The logic of post-war responsibility approximates to both diachronic and synchronic implication. Its proponent philosopher Takahashi Tetsuya avers that the contemporary Japanese need to respond to the voices of the Asian victims and the legacy the Japanese left in order to earn their forgiveness. Takahashi's stance risks consecrating the concerns of the Asian peoples and nations even when they pursue a nationalist agenda.[53] These opposing views resonate with the idiom of the implicated subject and remind us that the Japanese have home-grown discursive sensibilities to position themselves in relation to the others.

Part and chapter outline

This book is comprised of three parts with two chapters each. The first part consists of Chapters 2 and 3 which deal with the memoirs of soldiers and medical personnel. The second part, Chapters 4 and 5, explores feature films and documentaries. The third and final part, Chapters 6 and 7, examines travelogues. In no way does this book claim to cover the vast array of historicals available dealing with the PNG campaign. Limitation of space led me to concentrate on a relatively small number of genres and omit fictional works such as novels, allegorical films, museums and works of performing and visual art.[54] The vast majority of materials are commercially published or released. Commercial availability is a vital and common criterion for selection; it signals the creators' willingness to have their works enter the circulation of historical knowledge and to have their views known to members of public who 'consume' these works to gain an understanding of historical events. The process of making, consuming and remaking the history of the New Guinea campaign should offer a window into the Japanese image of the war in PNG and even the Pacific Islands. These narratives and insights can easily be overlooked while many news reports, publications and productions in Japan concentrate on domestic issues and diplomatic disputes with east and Southeast Asian states and the former Allied nations. Table 1.2 lays out the media each chapter analyses and the nature of journeys the authors and creators took in producing their outputs.

Part 1: Memoirs of soldiers and army doctors

The war memoir is a first-person narrative about the war by which veterans make sense of their experience in hindsight. Win or lose, the veterans legitimize, laud, even condemn war as well as negotiate their personal demons. The Second World War veteran-turned-historian Samuel Hynes finds that the war memoir shares elements of autobiography, travelogue and history, but still remains a genre of its own. The autobiography discusses the whole lifespan of the author; the war memoir relates small-scale accounts of the war. In contrast, history synthetizes multiple sources to make an argument about a past phenomenon and uses the memoir as a source.[55] Hynes makes a perceptive connection between the war memoir and the travelogue. The purposes of travel are different, but both genres relate the experience somewhere far away. Survival and return home mark a rite of passage. It is the claims of personal growth and discovery of something about themselves and the world that comprise the substance of *Bildungsroman*.[56] Studies of war memoirs is a known field in Japan. Memoirs on the New Guinea campaign do feature in

Table 1.2 Travelling Memories and Media

Medium	Travellers	Types of Journeys	Nature of Medium	Process of Creation
Memoirs	Combatants – soldiers and army doctors (Generation A)	First-hand experience and impressions. Imaginative journeys back to wartime New Guinea while writing	Personal experience turned into written words	Based on personal experience; supplemented with others' experience and hearsay and historical accounts
Films *Minami-no-shima ni yuki ga furu* 1961	Katō Daisuke (Generation A)	First-hand experience and impressions. Imaginative journeys back to wartime New Guinea while writing and acting	Personal experience into written words and performance on a feature film	First as a memoir: Based on personal experience; supplemented with others' experience. Then as a film: Katō re-imagining and re-enacting his wartime self.
Minami-no-shima ni yuki ga furu 1995	Mizushima Satoru (Generation B) and the cast (Generations A and B)	Imaginative journeys back to wartime New Guinea during conceiving the film, acting, shooting and editing.	A fictionalized film based on a memoir and the 1961 film version	Consumption and reimagining of memoir and a previously released film; with significant alterations
Documentaries	directors/producers (Generation B) War veterans (Generation A)	Imaginative journeys back to wartime	Directors/producers: physical trips to PNG and in Japan. War veterans and local residents, sharing their recollections as testimony	Consume, imagine, reimagine and present memories as documentary films. Film-makers interpreting and reinterpreting and packaging war history with multiple audiovisual sources and the cast's words
Travelogues Mizuki Shigeru's travel writing as prose and manga	Mizuki Shigeru (Generation A)	First as a veteran; later as a friend of villagers	Prose essays and manga based on personal experience	Reinterpreting experience with revisions
Japanese travel writing about PNG battle sites	travellers (Generation B)	Vicarious consumer travel	Travel writing	Consuming and imagining history at the sites; reimagining history while writing.

them, but dedicated attention to soldiers and military doctors remains a less charted territory.[57]

Many veterans believe in the exercise of personal agency through the writing of war memoir. Yuval Noah Harari distinguishes between eyewitnessing and 'flesh witnessing'. Whereas the former connotes observation, the latter encompasses subjective experience such as privation, illness, hunger and pain. These forms of witnessing form the basis for the 'experiential authority' that elevate the status of the veterans' accounts.[58] However, we cannot always expect the veterans to be reliable narrators or witnesses.[59] Many veterans make claims such as 'you'll never know until you go to war yourself' and 'I can never describe the war fully'. These may be honest admissions to the difficulty in rendering and communicating the war truthfully. Others, especially those of the post-war generations, may take such remarks as a kind of barrier between them and the witness.[60] Notwithstanding these limitations, Chapters 2 and 3 treat the war memoir as one of many historicals that shapes travelling memories of the New Guinea campaign.

Japanese memoirs of the New Guinea campaign are limited in number and in their range of topics. Hiromitsu Iwamoto identified that the Japanese National Diet Library held a total of 1,143 memoirs published between 1942 and 1998, of which 471 were books and 672 magazine articles. This represents a mere 0.4 per cent of the 130,000 returned soldiers.[61] Iwamoto found that most of the accounts stressed soldiers' suffering and struggles during the wartime, overshadowing controversial subjects such as Japanese interactions with the Papua New Guineans. The veteran authors' dominant motivation was to mourn the deaths of their comrades and console their spirits.[62]

Chapter 2 takes up the oft-made allusion of war as journeys to hell and back, and zeroes in on Japanese veterans' accounts of cannibalism during the New Guinea campaign. Of several acts of atrocities, cannibalism was the harrowing consequence of extreme privation the veterans witnessed and even participated in. This chapter asks how the veterans' opposition to and rationalization of cannibalism shaped their visions of the war. Through reconstructions of scenes and dialogues, the veterans draw upon Buddhist-inspired notions of life, suffering and hell. These issues serve as the backdrop to formulate veterans' resistance to or justification of cannibalism. What emerges from the inner turmoil is that whichever decision the soldiers made, their imaginary as creatures in hell complicates the binary between the victim and the perpetrators and speaks of the damage to their ethical compass.

Chapter 3 turns to the memoirs of military doctors and applies Michel Foucault's notion of the medical gaze – specific ways for doctors to see and diagnose patients. The observations of these army doctors convey the desperate and hopeless wartime conditions and show solidarity with the soldiers as victims. The medical gaze galvanized the doctors' resolve to instil discipline in themselves and others to counter the sense of helplessness. Yet, the inherent focus on the self conceals as much as it reveals the aspects of work that privilege the doctors' status within the military hierarchy.

Part 2: Films and documentaries

The second part continues the cross-media ethos of historicals through exploration of feature films and documentaries about the New Guinea campaign. The second part serves as a bridge in the transition of the Japanese historicals of the New Guinea campaign from 'warscapes' to 'memoryscapes'. The former connotes the landscape bearing the scars of war. The latter pertains to the sites connected with intangible and even invisible memories of the past.[63] Chapters 4 and 5 develop the emerging consensus among film historians to position film-makers as historians who make historical arguments in public spotlight. A main advocate to this approach, Robert Rosenstone, emphasizes the film-makers' craft of story making and storytelling. Film-makers research historical events, use various cinematic techniques to recreate scenes of the past with 'dramatic' relishes, and build a relationship with the audience.[64] Similarly, Robert Burgoyne thinks that film-makers frequently infuse their beliefs and anxieties into the allegorical bases of the films. The film-makers' optics of the present can influence the content and message as well as the ways of engaging the audience with the cast and the past.[65] Their approaches do not diminish the significance of historical or factual accuracy in films. Rather, checking the faithfulness of the cinematic representation to the original sources is important but can lead to the frequent complaint that 'the book is better than the film'.

Film-makers are mindful of multiple considerations shaping their works. They face many artistic, technical, financial, commercial and political considerations. Compared with fictionalized films, documentary film-makers generally have less latitude for creative or fictional licence but more liberty to pursue subjects and perspectives as the documentary is cheaper to make and has less commercial pressure.[66] For Japanese film-makers of the Asia-Pacific War, the defeat makes the inevitable and necessary backdrop for how the films treat the defeat and participate in and even generate contemporary discourses of the war. In his survey of Japanese war films produced between 1945 and 1995, film scholar Kasuga Taichi identifies two polarizing receptions. If a film emphasizes the sorrow of war, nationalists will deplore it as pacifist propaganda. A film portraying soldiers as heroes triggers criticisms of endorsing militarism. Kasuga qualifies this characterization as creating ultimately unhelpful stereotypes, but acknowledges that it illustrates the power of the film to become a subject of contestation over interpretation and ideology.[67] Kasuga's summation reinforces the point that the film-makers are historians and agents in travelling memory who make their personal views on history known in public. Put differently, historical films, in the words of Greg Dening and Hokari Minoru, 'perform', 'practise' and 'do' history.[68] Many fictionalized feature films and documentaries deal with the Pacific campaign. The New Guinea campaign provided the setting for several of them. Chapters 4 and 5 concentrate on a small number of films, which in turn allows for an unpacking of the scenes that best represent the film-makers' methods in conditioning our empathetic engagement and historical consciousness.[69]

Chapter 4 offers a cross-reading of two feature films adapted from a veteran's memoir by actor Katō Daisuke (1911–1975). Katō served as a medic stationed in Manokwari, Dutch New Guinea, and in the post-war years became a distinguished stage and film actor. His memoir *Minami-no-shima ni yuki ga furu* (Snow Falling in a Southern Island, 1961) relates his experience of leading a theatre group and performing *samurai* plays to lift the spirits of Japanese soldiers in Manokwari. The scenes that brought the audience to tears featured a snowscape of rural Japan. The emotional responses led Katō to identify acting as his *ikigai* – a popular concept denoting the thing that makes life worth living. Not only of interest for its unusual theme, the two adaptations released in 1961 and 1995 make fine examples of Katō's war memories travelling from his memoir to two film adaptations remade three decades apart. The analysis of the two adaptations illuminates more contrasting elements than commonalities in the ways each film represents the notions of *ikigai*, and honourable and miserable death. Furthermore, these adaptations reflect the aspirations and concerns of the film-makers at the time of production, shedding light on the anxieties of the historical periods in which each film was made.

Chapter 5 approaches four documentary films as co-performance spaces between the film-makers and the subjects. The chapter explores how four documentaries elicit viewers' emotions through representations of painful memories of people who have experienced traumatic events. The documentaries are *Yukiyukite Shingun* (dir. Hara Kazuo, 1987), *Senjō no onnatachi* (dir. Sekiguchi Noriko, 1989) and its English version *Sensō Daughters* (1990), and *Nyūginia ni chitta 16-man no seishun* (dir. Ushiyama Jun'ichi, 1991). All four documentaries were made and released at a critical period when many veterans were in their advancing years, and the nascent resurgence of the idea of the Japanese as perpetrators challenged the binary of the heroic and victim interpretations. In sum, this chapter demonstrates a wide variation of examples in which film-makers present testimonies to communicate their understanding of history.

Part 3: Travelogues

The third part turns to Japanese travelogues about war sites in PNG. Chapters 6 and 7 provide insights into the dynamics of travelling memory in which the traveller bridges spatial and temporal binaries between home and away and between the wartime and the present. The part welds two interrelated fields of dark tourism and travel writing studies and elevates the status of the travelogue as a historical. Chapters 6 and 7 ask how journeys to former battle sites inform perspectives on the relationships between the traveller, the past and the people and the destinations. The progenitors of dark tourism, John Lennon and Martin Foley, conceive of it as travelling to sites associated with disturbing memories of suffering, violence, deaths, disasters and destruction.[70] While dark tourism scholars continue to refine the definition and its parameter, suffice to say that sites related to war constitute one vital category.[71] Meanwhile, a caveat from postcolonial scholars indicates the potential for further maturation of the field. They find that dark tourism has tended towards the supply side, that is, the creation and management of the sites, and calls for examining travellers' experiences and reflections. The travelogue is one suitable medium that can tilt dark tourism towards the travellers' perceptions and experience.[72]

Preceding the surge in studies of dark tourism are studies of travelogues. Travel writing scholars agree that the travelogue is a first-person prose narrative in which the main subject is the author's travel. The authors adopt and adapt multiple conventions from fiction and non-fiction such as literature, diary, journalism, history and ethnography. The diversity in the conventions lends itself to the variation between the content that can range from personal introspection to observational accounts of the peoples and customs.[73] One abiding question in travel writing studies is the relations of power between travellers and those whom Mary Louise Pratt calls travellees – the people whom travellers meet and describe. As the travel writer holds the power of the pen, the travelogue often favours the travel writers' representations of the travellers at the expense of the travellees. This is not to assume the relationship is stable. The interactions the travellers describe and reflect upon are tempered with *zeitgeist* surrounding the travellers and travellees, as well as the anxieties, tensions and resistance to the travellees by the travellers.[74] Anthony Carrigan forecasts a convergence between dark tourism and travel writing studies whereby the travelogue draws more attention to 'points of tension and reinforcement between capitalist industry demands, competing nationalist ideologies and the reassertion of marginalized or suppressed histories – all of which hold strong resonances for postcolonial research'.[75] The dual lenses of dark tourism and the traveller–travellee relationships can recast Japanese travelogues as historical products of a nation afflicted with ambivalent attitudes towards its imperial and wartime past in Asia-Pacific regions.

Chapter 6 examines the accounts of the journeys to New Britain Island, eastern PNG, by Mizuki Shigeru (1922–2015). In the post-war years Mizuki became a manga artist and rose to critical and commercial success. Less known, however, are Mizuki's travelogues about post-war New Britain, which offer a window into his shifting perceptions, first as a soldier and later as a traveller. While Chapter 2 discusses the centrality of hell in veterans' images of the war zone, Chapter 6 shows how Mizuki created his own paradise amidst wartime hell and sought to relive it in *in situ* and in his imagination. What makes his travel accounts unique are his multiple retellings and redrawings over the decades and his long-standing friendships with the villagers on New Britain Island which were initially formed during the war. Chapter 6 argues that Mizuki's accounts expose the inherent paradoxes of his yearning for the South Seas paradise that rested on the dynamics of the relationship between Japan and PNG from the wartime to the post-war era.

Chapter 7 takes an alternative route and analyses seven travelogues by six authors about war-related sites across PNG. Unlike Mizuki, none of these authors had first-hand war experience as combatants or were adults during the wartime. Nor are they family members of deceased soldiers who fought or died in the New Guinea campaign. The temporal and relational distance to the war may afford the six travel writers less subjective stances to the war. Still, the travel writers find travel stimulated them to engage with the memories of the campaign and draw conclusions about it and the whole war. The travelogues examined in the two chapters are not exhaustive or definitive samples but should offer insights into how travel from one place to another informs the dynamics of history-as-interpretation and history-as-identification. The processes make the travelogues a fertile ground for what I name vicarious consumer travel. In a nutshell, it is a mode of travel through which the travellers engage with history by empathizing with particular groups of people. This chapter argues that travellers with domestically oriented sensitivities tend to view the Japanese as victims and heroes. Those with cosmopolitan leanings regard the Japanese as perpetrators. Analysis indicates that regardless of the travellers' views of war history, the travelogue projects the writers' intellectual and emotional growth as a result of vicarious consumption of historical memory. Chapter 7 offers ways for reconsidering the travelogue as a medium of reimagining or recreating history after consuming it on site.

The term travel in this study encompasses a variety of spatial and temporal journeys that groups and individuals undertake in which war and its memory form one of, if not the main, purpose. Binding wartime and post-war accounts are the claims of 'being there', including an encounter with unfamiliar people and environments. These meetings influenced the portrayals of PNG and its people and encouraged some authors to reflect on their understandings of the war. Between what is said and what is not said is the potential for reimagining how we, today's citizens, are implicated in the past. This book not only contributes to the cultural media history under the travelling memory flag, but also joins in a transnational and cross-regional dialogue between Japan, the Pacific Islands and the Allied nations that other scholars have created.

Part 1

Memoirs of Soldiers and Army Doctors

2

To hell and back: The question of cannibalism in memoirs of the New Guinea campaign

Majima Mitsuru (1915–1997) was a combat engineer deployed to China and New Guinea. His memoir, entitled *Jigoku no senjō Nyūginia* (New Guinea Battlefield in Hell), chronicles his haunting memories of the New Guinea campaign. Hunger was a constant feature in which he 'struggled in *kiga jigoku*' (hell of starvation).[1] He recalls New Guinea as 'an aimless journey of starvation and death' and 'a journey of death [resulting in] a complete beating of mind and body' in which the sight and stench of corpses assaulted his senses.[2] His allusions to war as a futile journey to hell speaks to many soldiers' experience of the Asia-Pacific War. Even during the wartime, soldiers whispered to one another: 'Java is paradise. Burma is hell. You cannot come back from New Guinea alive.'[3] This macabre humour validated the familiar allusion of war as hell and foretold of the mental and physical anguish soldiers could expect. Japanese servicemen experienced severe privation in various theatres of the war. New Guinea was one area where soldiers resorted to cannibalism for survival.

Several Japanese memoirs relate cannibalism as one of the worst consequences and manifestations of hell. Robert Thomas Tierney's study of colonial Japanese literature finds that Japanese authors began exploring cannibalism in the wake of Japan's defeat. The Asia-Pacific War provided the setting and the actual incidences of Japanese soldiers' eating the flesh of other humans for survival. He understands the proximity between imperialism and the cannibal was more distant in Japanese imaginary than the West. For centuries, the figure of the cannibal developed in lockstep with imperialism that embodied fear and anxiety in the West. Consequently, the cannibal became 'the savage other' that the West justified to conquer. In Japanese imperial discourse, the head hunter was the more dominant figure of 'the savage other' than the cannibal.[4] To illustrate how the trope of the savage survived in the post-war and post-imperial Japanese imagination, Tierney analyses three Japanese novels published in the early post-war years dealing with Japanese wartime cannibalism. He finds the portrayals of the savage shifted with the changing political climate, framing the Japanese defeat from collective guilt to victimhood. He suggests that further investigation should attempt to reveal how Japanese writers struggled to reconcile with the changing circumstances.[5]

This chapter responds to Tierney's call but begins its enquiry from a different point, looking at the soldiers' view of hell as the existential and physical backdrop to the qualms over cannibalistic acts. Whereas Tierney's interest lies in novels, veterans' memoirs are also a significant medium for relaying personal testimonies of their perceptions of the war. Closer scrutiny can remind us of the value of the memoir as raw material for subsequent representations and interpretations, such as novels and films. The central concern of this chapter is the images of hell in veterans' memoirs, looking into how the views of hell paralleled the descriptions of cannibalism and aided the veterans' narratives of victimhood. The memoirs examined provide two opposing attitudes to cannibalism. On the one hand is the refusal to consume human flesh for ethical and moral reasons while on the other hand is the view that resorting to cannibalism was merely a matter of survival. This is what David C. Stahl calls survival egoism, an extreme form of rationalizing one's personal survival even to the detriment of the social cohesion of a group.[6] Underlining these two attitudes is what Nancy Sherman calls moral injury, which denotes the profound inner struggle veterans go through after committing, witnessing and learning about acts that betray one's morality and conscience. They perceive that they have failed to uphold the moral standards of a good soldier and citizen.[7] The focus of this chapter is the worlds the veterans perceive and create through their recollections of cannibalism. Thus, the relationship between cannibalism and war crime trials as well as the military chain of command remain outside the purview.[8] Before delving into the veterans' accounts, this chapter outlines the nature of cannibalism in the New Guinea campaign, followed by a brief sketch of hell in Japanese cultural imaginary.

Questions about cannibalism in the New Guinea campaign raised concerns among the Australians. In June 1943, Judge Sir William Webb of Australia initiated an investigation after receiving eyewitness accounts of mutilated bodies and abandoned Japanese mess kits with human flesh inside. The records point to two phases of Japanese cannibalism in the New Guinea campaign. The first was during the Kokoda–Gona campaign of late 1942 to early 1943, widely known as the Kokoda campaign in Australia, and the second in the Aitape–Wewak area between late 1944 and early 1945.[9] Similarly, Peter Williams establishes that the

Japanese had sufficient supplies until the heavy rains of September 1942. Even when the provisions were exhausted, many soldiers adhered to the Japanese military code and chose to die instead. However, some soldiers resorted to cannibalism for survival. When the news reached Australia, it grew into one of 'the Kokoda myths' of Japanese barbarity that has been embedded into the Australian collective memory.[10]

In post-war Japan, the subject of Japanese soldiers' cannibalism remained a disturbing spectre of the wartime that most Japanese would rather not discuss in public. The reticence does not equate to complete silence. Ōoka Shōhei's autobiographical novel *Nobi* (Fires on the Plain, 1951), set in the Philippines, depicts the protagonists' ethical and theological dilemmas about cannibalism. *Nobi* makes one of the earliest public references to Japanese soldiers' cannibalism in the New Guinea campaign. The troops claim to have survived the New Guinea campaign only by resorting to cannibalism before transferring to the Philippines. Episodes of cannibalism in war memoirs began to feature from the mid-1960s. Some were mere hearsays of other soldiers' eating human flesh but some reported their experiences of it; they often qualified that they were offered monkeys' flesh, only to be told afterwards that the flesh was human.[11]

Later, Yuki Tanaka made use of Australian, American and Japanese sources and established that the Japanese killed, mutilated and consumed the flesh of other Japanese, Allied soldiers and Asian labourers that the Japanese had brought to PNG, as well as members of the local population. The indiscriminate nature differs from other forms of cannibalism that attach cultural significance to the consumption of in- and out-groups. Tanaka concludes that the overwhelming motivation behind Japanese cannibalism was survival.[12] He probes who bore the ultimate responsibility for soldiers' cannibalism. He disputes the previously accepted view that cannibalism arose from the erosion of military discipline and argues that the Japanese soldiers were perpetrators. Tanaka maintains that the option of cannibalism was not simply an individual choice, but that the ultimate responsibility lies in 'a systematic and organized military strategy, committed by whole squads or by specific soldiers working within the context of a larger squad'.[13] The case in point is an Australian interrogation report that referred to an order by Major General Aozu in November 1944. Aozu reiterated that cannibalism was a crime punishable by death but exempted the consumption of enemy flesh. Tanaka interprets this exemption as an admission of the army strategists' inability to stop the soldiers consuming human flesh, irrespective of nationalities, in violation of previously issued orders of prohibition.[14]

While these accounts offer the minutiae of wartime cannibalism, how rank-and-file soldiers recalled severe hardship remains relatively overlooked. The widespread whisper of New Guinea provides a fertile context to explore their perceptions of cannibalistic experience in New Guinea under the generalized epithet of hell. Although we cannot know how well versed each veteran was, the frequency suggests how thoroughly the concepts of hell permeated Japanese intellectual, spiritual and sociocultural spheres and shaped the Japanese worldview. Picture scrolls of hell drawn throughout centuries kept images of hell within the bounds of the possible and in people's daily consciousness.[15] Philosopher Umehara Takeshi insists that the ideas of hell became a strong force in Japanese culture that wielded enduring influence on Japanese literature for centuries up to the modern era.[16] The references to hell in war memoir merit consideration as examples of the influence filtering down to ordinary soldiers (Figure 2.1).

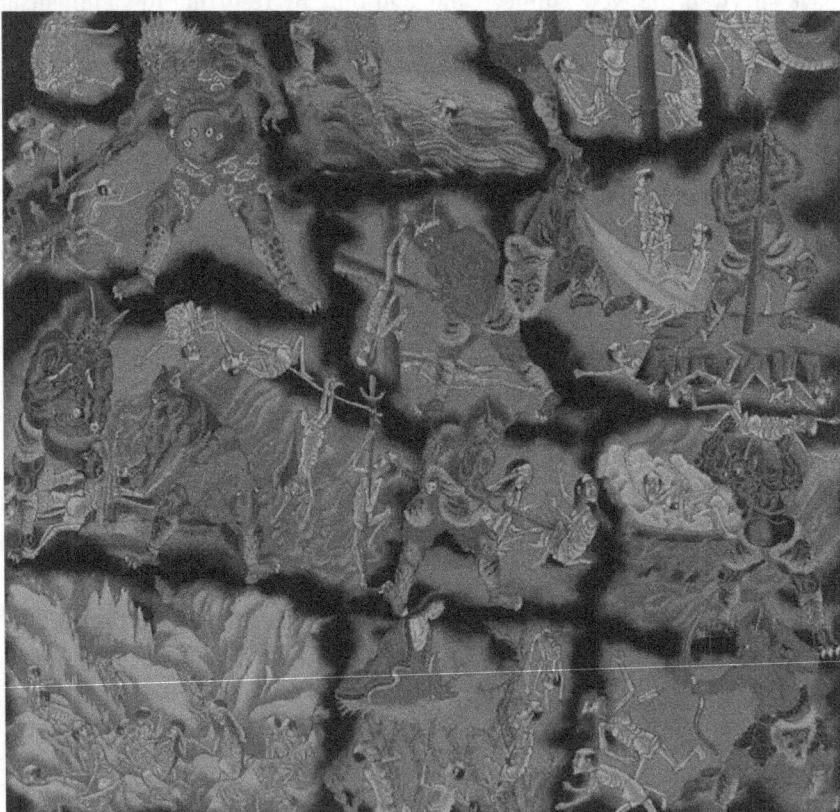

Figure 2.1 A pictorial scroll of hell. This is one of many images of hell painted and told over centuries in Japan.
Source: *Naraku no shiraba jigoku ezu* (painter unknown, n.d.). Courtesy of the International Research Center for Japanese Studies.

The main source for the Japanese conception of hell was Buddhism, which was introduced in the sixth century CE from China via Korea. It regards human life and hell as two of the *Rokudō* or Six Realms of Existence. The world in which we live is the realm of humans. Upon death, it is believed that the deceased will end up in one of the five other realms depending on their accumulated karma – good and bad. The realm of hell is the worst of the six, where the dead cannot escape the fate of receiving punishment that fits the offence they committed. Yet, each of the Six Realms is a temporary phase. Lives can and will reincarnate into other realms upon completion of another karmic cycle. In comparison, in Christian tradition, human life is finite, and hell is an external and eternal realm for the dead. These temporal dimensions make Buddhist hell akin to Christian purgatory. Moreover, in traditional Christianity, humans go to hell for the offence they cause to God and for sins committed against the Ten Commandments which govern human lives. In Buddhism, people receive punishment not for any offence caused to Buddha, but as a consequence of their own actions.[17] What have received little attention from scholars, including Umehara, are the roles hell played in veterans' ethical dilemmas to resist, rationalize, or to formulate the veterans' positionality in relation to the military and the war.

Soldiers' opposition to cannibalism

Veterans' memoirs show that despite the extreme conditions, soldiers resisted cannibalism. The aforementioned Majima and Private Ogawa Masatsugu (1917–2009) fall into this category. The images of hell aided exploration into how soldiers could and should maintain human civilization amidst hell. Ogawa thinks of cannibalism as the lowest point of ethical and moral degradation of the Japanese soldiers.[18] Following their defeat in the Battle of Finschhafen, he and his company went on a three-month westward retreat from December 1943 to March 1944 through the Finisterre Range in northern New Guinea. A passage translated by Tanaka is the first of Ogawa's many encounters with mutilated bodies and cannibalistic practice:

> Here I saw something genuinely horrible. There was the body of a soldier lying on the track, and a large part of his thigh had been hacked off. [In Captain Cook's diary were accounts of cannibals. I took a look at the flesh, wondering if there still were people who did such things. But it was not by the natives [*sic*].] ... Later I was walking along a track with [soldier] Y when we were called by a

> group of four or five soldiers who were not in our troop. They had just finished a meal, and there were mess-tins [scattered] nearby. They said ['We have a large cut of snake meat, do you want to join us and eat it?']. But we didn't like the way they were [smirking at us] as they said it. We [instinctively] felt that they were not telling us something. It was as if they wanted us to be 'partners in crime'. There was something unusual about the ways they were staring at us, as if they were waiting to see our reaction. Y felt the same way about the situation and said, 'No thanks, maybe some other time'. The situation was very tense. We left hurriedly, but cautiously, scared that they might try to shoot us. After we had walked a while, Y said to me, 'It's very strange. What do you think they were doing? If that had been snake meat, they would never have given any to us. Don't you think they were trying to drag us into the crime they had committed?' ... In fact, we saw many bodies which had their thighs hacked off.[19]

Struck by disbelief at what he saw, he tries to work out what happened. He rules out the possibility that the mutilation of the corpse was the act of the New Guineans and suspects that it was the Japanese who did it. By this stage, Ogawa had seen enough to know that soldiers could become taciturn and uncharitable towards one another when food supplies were short or exhausted. Hunger among the Japanese grew so acute that sources of animal protein were highly coveted, and those who managed to obtain meat would not readily or willingly offer it to others, especially those outside their immediate group.[20] This is the backdrop that raises Ogawa's suspicion towards the group's offer of snake meat. Ogawa and Y sense that the smirks accentuated the malevolent attitude that had taken hold of the minds of those soldiers. Even after his regiment left the mountain range and walked along the shoreline, the rumours of ravenous Japanese soldiers persisted:

> We heard stories that seemed like ghost stories of the medieval era. 'Several strongmen left the company and hid at Cape M. They became *oni* [ogres] and attacked passers-by' – stories like this. We were warned, 'Be careful when walking near Cape M. *Gaki* will come and get you'. We decided to walk during daylight because the illusions scared us and the stories seemed true. We could not forget that someone was watching us from somewhere.[21]

The encounter and the rumours prompt Ogawa to imagine that he was no longer in New Guinea in the 1940s. His allusions to *oni* and *gaki* speak to his altered perception of New Guinea as hell in a time earlier than the 1940s. Who or what are *oni* and *gaki*? *Oni* (鬼), usually translated into English as 'ogres' or 'demons', are permanent fixtures in many ghost stories and pictorial representations of hell. Folklorist Noriko T. Reider summarizes these supernatural creatures as follows: '*Oni* are mostly known for their fierce and evil nature manifested in their propensity for murder and cannibalism' and 'hideous creatures emerging from hell's abyss to terrify wicked mortals'.[22] The evocation of *oni* and *gaki* as the personification of cannibalism suggests the Japanese once possessed such savage characteristics. While the acquisition of civilization put the savage qualities at abeyance, if not into obsolescence, *oni* and *gaki* could still be brought back to contemporary consciousness. As John W. Dower points out, it was no coincidence that the wartime regime tapped into the centuries-old cultural arsenal of *oni* to vilify the Allies and portray them as fearful foes.[23] For Ogawa, shocking encounters and hearing reports from other soldiers nullify the Japanese state-sanctioned belief of Allies-as-*oni*. Nor was it tenable to hold onto the stereotype of the New Guineans as the archetype of 'the primitive' or 'the savage' Pacific Islander cannibals.[24] Ogawa implies that even if the Japanese had attained civilization to become an imperial power, circumstances dictate that the Japanese could still assume *oni*-like characteristics. The enemies were not the Allies or New Guineans, but fellow Japanese who turned into *oni* and *gaki* who ogled at him as potential food.

Ogawa's evocation of *gaki* accentuated his fear of the other Japanese soldiers who resorted to cannibalism. The *kanji* for *gaki* (餓鬼) literally meaning 'starvation' and *oni* denote hungry demons or ghosts typically associated with *gaki jigoku*, a hell destined for those obsessed with jealousy and greed. In many pictorial representations of *gaki jigoku*, *oni* catch the deceased and, forcing their mouths open, pour in molten iron which causes their innards to burn up immediately.[25] Having witnessed soldiers possessing *gaki*-like qualities, Ogawa and his comrades are beset with frightening illusions that harked back to Japanese Buddhist notions of hell and death. Ogawa comments on how Japanese soldiers' ethical standards changed as the war continued:

> Towards the end of the war, we began calling white people white pigs and black people black pigs. It seemed futile to be human and to live within the bounds of good and evil. One could say humanity was in danger. We heard harrowing rumours. The 'human' screamed to resist the pressure to metamorphosise into beasts. The response given by around 80 to 90 percent of survivors was, 'I didn't want to do it myself, but if someone served it in a mess-tin I would eat it'. Will the day come when we get pushed beyond the limit? This is the scream of 'animals' on the brink of starvation.[26]

Ogawa's comment is pivotal in his shift of thinking. He graduates from the portrayal of ogres and beasts in hell and brings his consciousness back down to the earth. Indeed, terms such as white and black pigs confirm Tanaka's summation of the prevailing attitude among soldiers. Moreover, in elaborating Sherman's notion of moral injury, the former US General-turned-philosopher James K. Dubnik considers an ultimate infraction of moral injury occurs when soldiers cease to see themselves and others as people and begin to view them as objects.[27] This is the world that Ogawa saw but his refusal to eat the flesh of the other humans turned into a crucible against moral injury.

Ogawa's allusion of the *oni* and, by extension, of hell projects the Japanese as descending the ladder of civilization, which refers more to the temporal spectrum of the Japanese people than the hierarchy of civilization between the Japanese and the others. His revulsion finds a common resonance with responses other people have made about Japanese cannibalism in New Guinea. Tierney cites interviews conducted in the 1990s with the Takasago *giyūtai*, indigenous Taiwanese volunteers, who accompanied Japanese troops in New Guinea as subjects of the Japanese empire. The Takasago volunteers were astounded to witness the Japanese descending into savagery under the desperate conditions. Tierney finds that the recollections by the Takasago *giyūtai* invert the colonial relationship whereby the Taiwanese were the putative 'savages' and the Japanese were civilized.[28] A similar reaction came from anthropologist Donald Tuzin's work on the Arapesh of the East Sepik, in New Guinea. The Arapesh and the Japanese had formed cordial relations to the extent that the Arapesh regarded the Japanese as their kin and benign protectors. As hunger grew more acute in 1945 when the Australian forces were gaining ascendancy, the Japanese killed their own comrades and attacked the Arapesh to eat their flesh out of desperation for survival. The Arapesh knew the fear of starvation and the encroaching Australian attacks had gripped the minds of the Japanese. However, the Arapesh ruled out the reasoning of physical survival. Instead, they believed that the Japanese had become insane to the extent of abandoning their humanity and deculturating into cannibals. What the Arapesh saw in the Japanese predation was the phantom of 'the cannibal-parent' in the Arapesh nightmare.[29] The logic afforded Arapesh to manage the unthinkable; it created 'defensive distancing' from the emotional hurt of what could have otherwise been a treacherous act on the friendship they had thus far built.[30] Ogawa's evocation of *gaki* not only communicates his imaginary of himself and the Japanese in hell, but also bears witness to his compatriots descending into barbarity. His imagination winds the clock back to the times when the images of *gaki* and *oni* were closer to the popular consciousness. In this, his reaction concurs with the disbelief by the Takasago *giyūtai* and the reasoning by the Arapesh. Ogawa's evocation of *gaki* depicts the moral injury Japanese soldiers inflict upon themselves and their senses of 'good and evil'.

Ogawa's imagination of hell and *gaki* then takes on a political dimension. He develops an objection to cannibalism that turns into a veiled criticism of the militarists who put him and fellow combatants under such extremity. He finds that the choice between eating human flesh at the most pressing occasion or abstaining from it poses a serious test of humanity. He remains convinced that he is a human and has the duty to remain so. Meanwhile, he does not hold the soldiers responsible for eating human flesh for survival. Rather, he draws a sympathetic portrait of the soldiers turning into *gaki* in hell who were unwilling to eat human flesh but did so out of sheer desperation. It is, as he implies, a minority who took an active part in cannibalism. Ogawa's rendition of hell and the minds of the soldiers falls short of direct criticism of the militarists and the strategies that put the soldiers through hell. This absence may reflect the purpose of the war memoir which was conveying the personal experience, observations and mourning the loss of Ogawa's comrades.

Similar to Ogawa, Majima develops his opposition to cannibalism through his depictions of hell. Majima fuses a bird's-eye view of the New Guinea campaign with his personal recollections. A chapter entitled 'Jigoku no itchōme' (Square One of Hell) narrates his passage from Cape Bushing on western New Britain Island to Lae on the New Guinea mainland. The memoir evokes a sense that Majima and his comrades are only at the entry of hell which is to unfold. The chapter opens with a description of a dark and humid tropical jungle where his unit subsisted by catching wild game and fishing to supplement their meagre supplies. Majima recalls that it was at that time he had heard a rumour from Guadalcanal: 'Black pigs (black people) tasted good, but white pigs (white people) tasted bad.'[31] Majima does not pass any judgement on this rumour, but the mention of it adds more to the ominous chapter title.

On the New Guinea Island, Majima relates how the rumour from another island was becoming a reality. While he is walking in a dense and dim jungle, he encounters the corpse of a middle-aged New Guinean man. Majima speculates shrapnel from a recent American raid has hit and crushed the man's head. More than ten other soldiers gather by the corpse:

> The sight of dead natives [sic] was not rare. But what I found eerie was the atmosphere. ... I saw the body had an arm severed. A soldier held a sword in

one hand and the severed arm in the other. To me, the glitter of that soldiers' eyes looked stranger than the others'. The fingers of the severed black arm were clenched and seemed to express anguish. The severed section reminded one of red beef, but the strangeness of it did not whet one's appetite.

There is a proverb, 'Well fed, well bred'. It was in New Guinea where I really understood its meaning. Possibly, the decline of morale after losing battles and starvation following the shortage of food had to do with it. No one paid respect to officers. No officer disciplined us. But this incident of insanity was something an officer could not ignore.[32]

Majima's report creates an image of hell similar to but different from Ogawa's. Both recognize that the dire physical hardship posed soldiers with the moral dilemma between survival egoism and human civilization. Whereas Ogawa says little about the roles of officers, Majima introduces the officer as a moral figure. By this stage, the officer's moral authority has waned to a level where the officer has failed to restrain his subordinates. The seriousness of the incident has demanded the officer recover his authority.

Majima continues to elaborate on the scene. The officer warns the soldiers against eating human flesh even if they were hungry and curious, because such an act would make them 'the same as the Papuan cannibals'; he insists that they take pride as human beings.[33] He also warns the soldiers that they would 'shoulder a lasting burden of guilt and live with it for the rest of their lives if they returned home alive'.[34] Majima finds the officer's persuasion appealed to the soldiers' conscience. The soldiers' resistance to the temptation to 'eat the forbidden fruit' exemplifies their disciplined commitment to 'noble humanity despite dying in anguish'.[35] Underpinning the officer's worldview is the Buddhist concepts of reincarnation and discouragement of eating meat, let alone, human flesh.[36] Even if the soldiers returned to Japan alive, their guilty conscience could confine them in continual purgatory while awaiting the other soldiers. Majima overlooks the officer's racist assumption that the New Guineans are cannibals, and the Japanese should never emulate them. Still, Majima creates a narrative of triumph of civilization over raw, biological desire that wartime hell exposed.

Another incident validated Majima's belief that the soldiers had to maintain humanity even when hunger and frustration wore down their morale. In July 1943, in Lae, in the northern New Guinea Island, the Japanese captured an American pilot. The Japanese Major decided to leave him unharmed and transferred him to another unit as a prisoner of war. The decision left ordinary

Japanese troops disappointed. Majima suspects that the soldiers expected to watch the pilot to be beaten or executed to vent out their frustration over continuing hunger and Allies' raids. This reaction jogged Majima's memory of how starvation and combat fatigue strips humans bare of layers of civilization and expose deep-seated characteristics. He elaborates how they manifest and what they could do:

> Calling white people white pigs, black people black pigs – thinking of human flesh as edible meat is a response to starvation and the encroaching fear of death. It comes from desperation as the war deteriorates.
>
> The longer the adverse conditions persist, the less resistance people have against tasting human flesh. Even in civilized societies, people still maintain the potential to adapt to a primitive lifestyle. In a nutshell, we may look like gentlemen on the surface, but we can revert to beasts if we flip ourselves over.[37]

Majima's reflection endorses the view that the decline of individual discipline caused cannibalism. He recognizes the physical and mental toll on the soldiers and that the greater the severity of the circumstances, the less resistant the integrity to maintain civilization against external influences; this much he is sympathetic to the soldiers. The officer's intervention has presented an example where, if given the corrective logic, the soldiers could restore their human civilization. Yet instead of questioning the officers' roles in perpetuating a dilemma with such hell-like conditions, Majima ultimately remains convinced that the soldiers' responses to 'desperation' decided who was civilized and who was not.

As with Ogawa, Majima's motif of hell frames his objection to cannibalism and instigates further defence of human civilization over cannibalistic impulses. In this sense, both Ogawa and Majima follow the observations by the Takasago *giyūtai* and the Arapesh. Both veterans witness the incidents in horror at the Japanese soldiers' regression to putative savagery, as the Takasago *giyūtai* saw in their Japanese superiors, and employ the rhetoric of hell in similar manners to the 'defence distancing' by the Arapesh. Although Ogawa and Majima have much in common, one crucial distinction is the influence of others on their thinking. Ogawa's memoir says little about the roles fellow soldiers played on him. Rather, he projects his steely determination to defend his principles. Majima's objection to cannibalism crystallizes with his growing belief in individual responsibility to managing the response to the hell of the war zone.

Pragmatic adoption of survival egoism in cannibalistic hell

Very few Japanese war veterans have admitted to committing acts of cannibalism during the New Guinea campaign and explained their rationale for it. Speaking about it in public makes an even rarer occurrence. Corporal Nishimura Kōkichi (1919–2015), who fought in the Kokoda campaign, was the only survivor in his platoon. In one interview, Nishimura says:

> At first, we shot enemy soldiers and crawled out to drag in the bodies and check their pockets for food. We'd eat that and it kept us going. But after a while they didn't seem to be carrying any food on them so there was no other way to survive but to eat them. We'd cut slices off and cook it. Anyone who was in the front line at Buna and is still alive today and says they did not eat human flesh is telling a lie. What I'm telling you about cannibalism at Buna is quite true, but I don't like talking about it. I'd rather tell you about the time we knocked out the Australian tanks.[38]

His subsequent interviews repeat how pragmatism won over his aversion to consume human flesh. Nishimura told journalist Charles Happell: 'Nobody wanted to do it, but that was their last resort. It was eat or die'.[39] Nishimura further stated on the Japanese TV that he and his comrades never ate the Japanese because they had little flesh on their bones. Instead, they ate the Australians and the Americans who had more to offer the starving soldiers.[40] His imperative of survival makes a sobering admission of the reality of the Kokoda campaign. Yet, his reluctance to discuss cannibalism, as seen in his preference to boast about his military feats, leaves a lacuna of how he imagined the war zone and arrived at his decision. Filling the gaps are memoirs by other veterans. The memoirs evoke the imagery of wartime hell to situate the authors' personal battle with cannibalism. Logics the veterans used to justify and oppose cannibalistic acts provide important elements in the ways they perceive themselves as the victims of the circumstances of the New Guinea campaign.

Nukuda Ichisuke (1907–1973) was a conscript who fought in China, Manchuria and New Guinea, who took pride in his adoption of survival egoism and presented it as his personal victory against the odds. His candour may have to do with the time during which he wrote and his publication history. Nukuda began writing shortly after his return to Japan in February 1946 and completed it on 15 August 1946 – the first anniversary of Japan's surrender. Following his death, his son decided to have it published, with the understanding that it is no masterpiece. However, he believes that the memoir reflects his father's urgent desire to reflect on the war and his lost comrades 'as if possessed by something'.[41]

A crucial aspect of Nukuda's memoir is that he superimposes Japanese wartime cannibalism to the Six Realms of Existence and recounts his experience through the lens of Buddhist hell. He acknowledges that hunger dampened the morale of soldiers and, subsequently, the law of the jungle dictated that the weak and the sick would perish and the strong would find and eat anything to survive.[42] Nukuda observes further changes in the soldiers' character and behaviour: 'Theft is only the beginning. We even risk our lives to find food. And in the end, we kill people to eat their flesh. This is where starvation leads. It has been said that eating humans is akin to *chikushōdō* or the realm of beasts'.[43] *Chikushōdō* is one of the Six Realms of Existence, positioned one below the human realm and regarded as the beginning of the three realms for sinners. According to orthodox Buddhist doctrine, those reborn in this realm become beasts and live in constant fear of the strong preying on the weak.[44] The conditions in New Guinea led Nukuda to invoke *chikushōdō* as more than an analogy. It sets the historical precedence for scenes of humans-eating-humans and embodies the physical, mental and even spiritual desperation the soldiers find themselves in.

Nukuda's worldview laced with the netherworld strikes one as a cold-hearted endorsement of survival egoism. The physiological need for survival entailed abandoning human ethics, which transported them to *chikushōdō* where soldiers ceased to see humans as anything other than food. In this account, Nukuda suggests the fragility and mutability of the notion of civilization. If humans see no hope of relief from suffering in sight, then, he argues, they will adopt the requisite mentality to ensure survival, whereas Ogawa and Majima reject eating human flesh as tantamount to the debasement or abandonment of human civilization. Although Nukuda's memoir preceded theirs, his defence dismisses the basis to compare the Japanese soldiers' acts of cannibalism with the Papua New Guineans. He then exposes the bias towards civilization by drawing on his observations of the Papua New Guineans:

> People say that New Guinea is an unexplored or a mysterious territory because its peoples are cannibals. But this practice derives from their belief systems and is different from eating [human flesh] out of hunger. It is us who claim to be civilized and call the natives [sic] black pigs and white people white pigs. Can we kill people and eat them? No. But if faced with death, we humans will do anything. We even have tools to kill people. Hunger numbs our conscience and drives us into desperation. We don't realize what we really end up doing and lose sight of what is and is not food to the extent that we eat other people.[45]

Nukuda defends survival egoism as the overarching motive for Japanese soldiers' cannibalistic acts. In supporting survival egoism, he jettisons the hierarchy of civilization and the assumption of who is more civilized than the others. He even explains that the New Guineans' practice of cannibalism is grounded in their values and civilization and not a product of savagery. For Nukuda, civilization offers no effective objection to the Japanese soldiers' cannibalistic acts. Nukuda explains that the racist labelling of 'black' and 'white' human flesh was a consequence of extreme starvation. Nukuda's defence mirrors Tanaka's summation of Japanese wartime cannibalism and Sherman's and Dubnik's concept of moral injury. Moreover, Nukuda has created a parallel universe for the Japanese and the New Guineans. For Nukuda, the war zone the Japanese occupied was closer to and even equivalent to a Buddhist cosmology of hell:

> In the past it was said that human flesh tasted sour. Even then, once we ate human flesh, we could not stop. As we descended into *gakidō* [the realm of hungry ghosts], we kept on eating human flesh. The Buddhist precepts viewed cannibalism as the worst possible offence because cannibalism had taken place in the past. But one could also say that waiting for death by starvation without doing anything shows a lack of common sense.[46]

Nukuda accepts that the consumption of human flesh is a grave sin in Buddhism. Yet, he subverts the severity of cannibalism and embraces it. His welcoming of the sin of cannibalism comes through in a new realm of hell to where he perceives that he and his comrade have descended. In Buddhism, the realm that *gakidō* denotes is different from *chikushōdō*. *Gakidō* is the realm of hungry ghosts, a place that denotes a more severe existence than *chikushōdō*, the animal realm. In *Gakidō* sinners receive punishments related to food such as food turning into flames that burn the body from the inside, insatiable hunger, and only being able to eat filth and one's own brain.[47] His realization, however, renounces the Six Realms of Existence and associated Buddhist concepts of hell. However, the gravity of punishments in *gakidō* did not deter Nukuda from consuming human flesh. He defied the concept of *gakidō* and the committing of sins that would doom him to rebirth there. He decided that 'waiting for death by starvation' was an unwise and passive choice. He actively became a beast in *chikushōdo* to ensure his survival.

Nukuda's decision galvanizes his defiance against his fate in hell and his will to come out alive. He relates an instance of sampling human flesh for preparation when the genuine need arose. One day, he and a comrade were walking on the beach. They rested for a while in an empty hut, and his comrade went out to search for food. He returned with a lump of flesh wrapped in leaves, which he then boiled in sea water several times to remove the odour:

> I half-jokingly asked 'What is this meat?'
>
> 'Hmm', he looked like he grasped my point. We were not starving, nor were we desperate. The portion [we consumed] only amounted to sampling it. Since this is something everyone does. I thought that keeping quiet about it was more dangerous.[48]

Both Nukuda and his comrade knew they were violating the moral censure against cannibalism in 'the civilized world'. The sampling session marks a rite-of-passage that inducts them into *chikushōdō*, in preparation for eventual starvation. Evident here is that neither soldier believed that the conditions would improve soon: adaptation to the wartime hell was more important. Stating 'everyone ate' may have exaggerated the extent of cannibalism but allows him to feel little regret, shame, or guilt, and even elevates himself into 'an anti-hero hero' who finds heroism by adopting contrary qualities.[49] The Japanese military ethos upheld sacrifice to the empire and dying for its war as the ultimate forms of heroism; defeat and surviving were dishonourable. Nukuda embraced and defied the taboos of the Japanese Army and the Buddhist worldview. Surviving till the very end of the war, even if it meant consuming human flesh, was the path he pursued to become a hero on his own terms.

Nukuda's attitude becomes most conspicuous after Japan's surrender. The Australians rounded up Japanese soldiers and began disarming them. Nukuda found the sight humiliating. He was appalled at the sight of thin, gaunt and dejected Japanese acting obsequiously to the well-dressed, muscular and proud Australians. The last paragraph in his memoir says:

> I am tall. I had managed to maintain my stamina. So, I put my chest up and took long strides. I wanted to show my pride as a Japanese to the [Australians]. Even though we have fallen so far, weren't we the best of the Japanese Army? ... We did not necessarily lose. We fought to the end, and by order of the Army, we are now having Australians disarm us.[50]

Even in defeat Nukuda carries his survival ethos and maintains his dignity as a survivor even as he was facing the humiliation of the former adversaries disarming him and his comrades. He acknowledges that Japan did lose the war but what he refuses to admit is that he and his unit had lost a war against the fate of death in hell. Instead, he believes that staying alive until the end is his hard-earned victory and a way out of hell. With this renewed confidence, being held captive by the Australians or the foreign *oni*, as in the wartime propaganda, are no grounds for losing pride in being a Japanese soldier.

Nukuda's ability to reinvent his personal victory needs to be considered against the *zeitgeist* of his memoir. Shortly after the war ended, Prime Minister Higashikuni Naruhiko appealed to the nation to share the burden of defeat in order to take the vital first step towards reconstruction. His words morphed into the popular catch phrase *ichioku sōzange* (repentance of the hundred million). However, critics viewed Higashikuni's plea as shifting the responsibility of defeat to the people and playing down the role of the elites, especially the emperor.[51] To returning soldiers, *ichioku sōzange* added yet another layer of shame, sorrow and guilt. Within the confine of the private memoir, Nukuda protested against *ichioku sōzange* and asserted his position as a proud veteran. Hell provided him with the vital framework for his narrative arc of his becoming not a victim but a proud anti-hero.

Ruminating before and after enacting survival egoism

Toyotani Hidemitsu (b. 1921) was another veteran who broke the silence about wartime cannibalism. His narrative elaborates on his shifting attitudes with additional political and spiritual dimensions. He imagined himself first as a victim of circumstances in realms of hell and nature and adopted survival egoism. The consumption of human flesh brought him to admit that his conscience always finds him. No matter how hard he tried to imagine himself as a non-human creature, he was nonetheless a human and had to live with the guilt that his cannibalistic acts brought upon him afterwards. Compared with other memoirs examined, Toyotani's understanding of Buddhist notions of hell is sophisticated and detailed. He became an ordained Buddhist priest before conscription. He published two editions of his memoir in 1979 and in 1996. Although most of the text is identical, the discussion below pays attention to significant points of difference between them.

Toyotani's decision to write and publish his memoir underscores his desire to place his private recollection in public circulation. What motivated him to write his memoir was an epiphany he experienced during his return journey to PNG in 1977. He saw '[a] small ray of "the light of contrition" beamed into [his] mind'. It dawned on him that during the wartime he had 'personified extreme evil, extreme vulgarity and extreme insanity'.[52] He sensed that the time was right for him to disclose his experience. He believed that the passage of time would protect him from potential persecution under the wartime law that made the consumption of corpses a criminal offence. Toyotani had learnt that one of the two comrades with whom he ate human flesh was dead. Toyotani could not re-establish contact with the other.[53]

Following his conscription as a reservist, Toyotani arrived in Hansa, New Guinea, as a private. In January 1944, his unit embarked on a march from their base in Kiari, on the northern shoreline of New Guinea to Madang. It was a long march of attrition. Supplies ran out and could not be replenished. Toyotani and his remaining comrades walked without food for several days. Many soldiers got sick and died. These conditions triggered images of hell and influenced his decision to commit cannibalism:

> This [cannibalism] is an unimaginable emergency measure that we cannot conceive of as a human act. It involves committing a grave sin that can make every hair on my body stand on its ends, to replenish animal protein. If we are willing to sell our souls to evil demons (*akki*) and take the deviant or heretical path (*gedō*), then we could find ways to live – most of my comrades already reached this silent consensus.[54]

Toyotani's self-portrayal as a creature in hell frames himself as a victim of the war and conveys elements of protest against the Japanese state. He and his comrades were 'evil demons' who departed from their principles of the material world to 'the deviant or heretical path'. These self-effacing words register Toyotani's veiled criticism of State Shinto. Early in the Meiji era reforms, the state made Shinto the national religion to bolster the legitimacy of the emperor and the state. In 1868, the state decreed the separation of centuries-long syncretism between Shinto and Buddhism – including the priests and deities. This triggered persecution of Buddhists, known as *haibutsu-kishaku*, which escalated into widespread destruction of Buddhist temples and artefacts. The Buddhists survived, albeit with a much-reduced profile.[55] This background may not be obvious to many readers but it nevertheless forms vital layers to Toyotani's victimhood. He shared the common victimhood of being thrown into the war zone with other soldiers. Moreover, he carried this legacy as a member of the persecuted and of a marginalized faith.

Adopting the notions of demons in hell lets Toyotani continue to map his journey through hell in the Buddhist paradigm of *karma* (transmigration). As with other memoirs, he pictures himself and his comrades as the dead in *gakidō* teering on the edge of becoming *gaki*. He goes further than other veterans by quoting an excerpt from the Buddhist scripture, *Daichidoron*:

> Even after a hundred years we cannot eat or drink. Nor are we *gaki* allowed to see food or liquid refreshment. Our necks are thin like vines; only our stomachs are bulging. We are nothing but darkened skin and bones. We cannot distinguish ourselves from faeces and bodily discharge. The dead suck bloody pus. We are about to engage in an act that plunges us into *gakidō*.[56]

Toyotani's citing of *Daichidoron* demonstrates his knowledge of Buddhism and fuses the war zone and Buddhist hell together. He conveys his deep unease more strongly than Majima's reporting of the rumour from Guadalcanal. Toyotani teeters on the precipice of hell but steels his determination to face any consequence as he walks into the realm of the hungry ghosts. Once the soldiers began marching into dense bush, he and his two comrades lagged behind the others. They suddenly discovered a dead body on the narrow path with its head blown off; blood and gore were splattered across the chest. Toyotani had seen corpses similar to this one and judged that the soldier had committed suicide by detonating a hand grenade. Toyotani and his comrades discussed what they should do with the body. Toyotani recalls he was wrestling with his own conscience while persuading the other two to eat the flesh.[57]

Toyotani gives three reasons, all underpinned by utilitarian ethics. First, eating the corpse was justifiable because none of the soldiers were responsible for the death. They were mere passersby who stumbled upon the corpse. Second, Toyotani speculates that the dead soldier would have wished for his body to be useful to other soldiers rather than letting maggots eat it up. He emphasizes that if he had decided to commit suicide, he would have wished for the same and would have even left a note encouraging surviving comrades to eat his flesh.[58] The effect and the extent of moral injury on Toyotani's mind are apparent. He justifies the corpse as an object: 'Once the spirit departed the body, it ceases to be a living organism. It becomes an ex-human. A thing. A container. Can it be such a grave sin to receive a tiny bit of it?'[59] Applying the dualist logic of separating the body and the mind enabled him to pre-empt the guilt he would have felt had he not adopted survivor egoism. Third, Toyotani convinces himself that he was a maggot. He regards the maggot as a low form of living organism without any faculty for thoughts or consciousness like humans.[60] By this stage, he thinks of himself both as a *gaki* in hell and a maggot in nature, with the underlying imperative to eat the dead to survive. Toyotani defends his decision on the grounds of moral relativism. He understands that the moral and legal sanctions against cannibalism rest on human knowledge gained over time. He further believes these are just to punish those who mutilate a corpse and eat it. However, he thinks the war zone in New Guinea has transported him to another realm:

> Before humans were ruled by the facts of ethics and law, humans could only sustain life by faithfully following the truth and the rules of biology and physiology. Unfortunately, our individual biological needs are far higher and holier than the fealty of the Imperial Japanese Army [in the lines of] 'Accept the commands by officers as issued in the name of the Emperor'. Of course, those truths and rules do not necessarily come with ethical justice. But can we not say that for the living to live and to do something to live are the truth, justice and rules in pure biological and physiological terms?[61]

Toyotani's defence echoes the other veterans' views. The war zone enveloped them in a world where survival is the sole objective. Toyotani agrees with Nukuda on biological imperatives but resents those who fail to appreciate his situations. Toyotani asserts that those refusing to take animal protein to stay alive are 'full of deception and lies' and 'traitors of living organisms'.[62] He then reiterate that he 'would rather quit being a human today, right now. A solider in the Imperial Japanese Army? I practically quit it long time ago. I'm going to quit being human and join the group of maggots'.[63] His renunciation of humanity and martial identity strengthens his determination to embark on his journey and abandons his pride as a human.[64] Toyotani's thought process have similarities to the Arapesh understanding of Japanese cannibalism. As the Arapesh used the esoteric mysticism to shield themselves from the horror of the event, Toyotani evoked his Buddhist worldview to protect himself from the potential moral injury his action could cause. Both Toyotani and Nukuda invert the prized values of civilization to those of survival. However, their goals rest on different motivations. Whereas Nukuda draws strength from his pride as a Japanese in order to survive, Toyotani is driven by his aversion to human ethics and civilization to justify his transformation into a *gaki* and a maggot.

So far, Toyotani's account in two editions of his memoirs remain identical. Where the two editions differ the most are in his descriptions of the preparation for and the consumption of human flesh and the feelings afterwards. The first edition presents the extent of Toyotani bearing the brunt of moral injury. The torment he underwent presses the point that he is a victim of circumstances in becoming a wilful agent of cannibalistic acts. The emotional cycle from anxiety, pleasure, relief and then to remorse makes up the sum of his moral injury. The second edition omits these details and replaces them with a simplified narrative of his victimhood, flattening the depth of his torment which stemmed from having to turn to cannibalism against his will.

The first difference is the descriptions of his tumultuous emotions in the lead-up. In the first edition Toyotani recounts his central role in persuading the other two to co-operate and shows how the other two assisted in the work. Once the preparations were under way, Toyotani suddenly grows so nervous that he suggests the group offer a prayer to the dead soldier. Toyotani puts on his Buddhist robe and prayer beads which he had carried with him all along. He then chants *Hannya shingyō* (the Heart Sutra), a popular sutra in Japan, 'to pray for the dead to go to the Buddhist paradise (*gokuraku*)'. The first edition prints the entire 262-character sutra.[65] However much he emphasizes his transformation into a *gaki* and a maggot, his pangs of anxiety show the depth of his Buddhist sensibilities. Toyotani claims that the rite helped the three make up their mind and let them go about their business without a painful conscience. They found a deserted hut, cooked the flesh and ate it.[66]

Toyotani's chanting of *Hannya shingyō* marks a decisive moment in his moral injury. Amidst the myriad of interpretations, the essence of the sutra lies in the enlightenment that comes from understanding the emptiness in all phenomena. It further holds that such enlightenment will result in deliverance from suffering.[67] In this sense, his chanting of the sutra sends the dead soldier to paradise and validated the group's decision to think of the dead soldier merely as a body. The sutra fulfils an additional purpose of relieving Toyotani's party from feelings of anxiety towards cannibalism. However, the subsequent passages show that the sutra does not guarantee erasing ambivalence in Toyotani's mind. The second edition omits references to his persuading his comrades to eat the human flesh and the comrades' complicity in cannibalism. The deleted text amounts to four whole pages of text describing his decision to become a *gaki* and a maggot to the scene at the hut where the group ate the flesh.

The second major difference is the cycle of relief and remorse Toyotani experienced when he tasted the human flesh. The first edition declares Toyotani could never forget how well it tasted. He even remembers that the flavour reminded him of wild chicken or pheasant. The corpse had more body fat than initially anticipated and fibres gave it a more delicate texture. Toyotani even admitted, 'I was eating the flesh to survive so desperately that I felt so moved that I could die'.[68] However, soon afterwards, Toyotani feels an overwhelming burden of guilt that puts him into the cycle of recrimination. He explains that various kinds of hell in *Rokudō* are where the dead go, and the *gaki* belong in these realms. In the first edition, Toyotani asserts 'I cannot be a *gaki* as long as I am alive'.[69] However, he soon reiterates his determination to live even if other people deride him as a *gaki*, especially since he is not guaranteed that he would ever return to his family alive.[70] These statements reveal his ambivalence and difficulty in reconciling his multiple identities as a soldier, human, *gaki* and a maggot. Beneath his conflicted sentiments is his willingness to accept whatever consequence his actions bring forth.

In contrast, the second edition reduces all of these recollections into a brief statement – 'I have omitted the eerie scenes and incomparable descriptions of taste out of various considerations'.[71] While Toyotani does not explain these considerations, the preface of the second edition says the first edition generated heated and abusive responses from readers. Some readers complained that Toyotani besmirched the dignity of the veterans. He took these responses as 'attempting to kill off and suppress the truth'.[72] Deleting the text was a compromise and has impeded the reader from engaging with Toyotani's decades-long moral ambiguities.

Besides these differences, Toyotani's two editions offer the identical rumination that consolidated his victim narrative. At night, when he regains his human-senses, he regrets how his actions brought his dignity down to the barbarism of the New Guineans.[73] The realization that he wilfully 'downgraded' himself to the New Guineans leads him to another realization he finds hard to accept. More than at any other time he saw the strategy of the Japanese army was to use him as an expendable body. His mission was to continually kill the enemy to ensure his own life. Toyotani grows convinced that the Japanese leadership caused harm to his moral compass and resulted in many violent and unnecessary deaths:

Aren't these calculated orders for mass murder? Aren't the few strategists in safe places the real cannibals who eat away the lives of hundreds of thousands?

Yes, this is it. The government agencies, military headquarters and general staff office are replete with cannibals. These cannibals outnumber the maggots that feast on dead bodies in jungles and have taken over the core of the Japanese state. They are killing and eating the Japanese people – cannibals with a lot of medals dangling around their necks. I will not hesitate to curse at them. Our biggest enemy is not the devilish Anglo-Americans, it's the Japanese! You hear me? You, cannibals with medals![74]

Toyotani's angry outburst makes clear to whom he holds responsible for his physical, spiritual, emotional and intellectual damages. Up to this point, Toyotani sees himself as the victim of the war and its historical legacy. Then, he adapts himself into a perpetrator of cannibalism. The imagery of hell and the figure of the *gaki* assists with this change. He realizes that he is the victim of 'real cannibals' in the upper echelon of the Japanese government and the military. His new awareness resonates with Stahl's work, which applies the theories of psychiatrist Robert Jay Lifton to analyse Ōoka's works that deal with his war trauma. Lifton believes that coming to terms with traumatic events demands transcending self-recrimination and striking a balance between 'appropriate blaming' and 'scapegoating'. The former apportions the responsibility to relevant parties while the latter concentrates anger on a single target to the extent of impeding the assimilation of traumatic memories.[75] For Toyotani, blaming the army strategists opens the way to extricate himself from a self-recriminating vision of *gakidō*. Similar to Ōoka's outward expression, Toyotani's imagery proved vital in expressing trauma and post-traumatic stress at a time when such concepts were not available in ordinary parlance. The concepts took root in Japan through the recognition of citizens affected in the Great Hanshin-Awaji earthquake of January 1995.[76]

Towards the end of his memoirs, Toyotani develops hindsight as a survivor of hell who returns to the human realm, and from a *gaki* and maggot back to a human. Still, Toyotani remains unable to unshackle his guilty conscience. He worries about how the family of the dead soldier would have felt and dreaded what his own family would have thought had they been at the scene to bear witness to his cannibalistic acts. He relates how he copes with his haunting memories:

> I want to be a maggot. I will become a maggot. I want to quit being human. I cannot help but to eat even if I had become a vulture. These are the words I used to persuade and console myself. While I kept showering myself with these words, I saw the torment of *mugen jigoku* [hell of interminable suffering].
>
> However much I wished to be a maggot, I was a human being that could not be a maggot. I wonder if this awareness brings my guilt and affirmation to light. ... I felt like screaming 'Help!'. It doesn't matter who, but just help me. I cannot sort this out myself.[77]

Toyotani accepts the grave remorse as immutable and inevitable, recognizing that he must live with this never-ending torment. The despair he feels about *mugen-jigoku* is so strong that he repeats these words in both editions of his memoirs.⁷⁸ The passage shows, however, that the more severe the remorse, the greater his desire to escape it. On this score, his 'maggot fantasy' pays homage to a popular television series and its cinematic adaptation, *Watashi wa kai ni naritai* (I Want To Be a Shellfish, 1958 and 1959, respectively). The protagonist is a veteran who was sentenced to death for a war crime he had not committed. It ends with a scene where the veteran reads out his will stating that he wished he had been born not as a human but as a shellfish leading a quiet life at the bottom of the ocean. Yoshikuni Igarashi interprets the shellfish as speaking to the veteran's desire to isolate himself from the world, in other words, societal aversion to confronting the tragic legacy of the war.⁷⁹ Toyotani shares the same desire but chose to confront his past demons. Notwithstanding the changes to the second edition, Toyotani's allusions to hell serve as no mere storeroom of metaphors but a taproot of introspection into the trans-war and transnational nature of his victimhood and moral injury.

Conclusion

Cannibalism is an awkward episode in the memoryscape of the Asia-Pacific War. This chapter has argued that the evocative power of hell propelled the veterans' rationale for and against cannibalism and influenced their narratives of war. Though a small number, the Japanese veterans' memoirs show how the veterans juxtaposed questions about cannibalism against the Buddhist-influenced notions of life, suffering and hell. Majima and Ogawa see themselves as being placed at the junction of various realms of existence or hell and exercised their powers of observation to create distance from the incidents. However, they refuse to internalize the landscape and its horrific features. To do so would not only undermine their ethical standards as human beings but also transform them into creatures below human civilization.

The memoirs by Nukuda and Toyotani accept survivor egoism and justify the consumption of human flesh as indispensable for their personal survival. Nukuda and Toyotani internalize the images of hell to mark their departure from human ethics, law and civilization and embraced the laws of hell and the jungle. Both Nukuda and Toyotani prioritize physical survival over the principles of civilized conduct. Nukuda shows little sign of moral injury or victimhood. He is content with recasting his herodom as he sets survival as his new objective. Toyotani's elaborate and conflicted cycle of his identification with a *gaki* and a maggot informs the gravity of moral injury and a generalized sense of his victimhood. His anger at 'the real cannibals' signals his victimhood evolving beyond his self-recrimination. Their images of hell and thoughts of cannibalism make for the most ethically demanding moments in their journeys to hell. These recollections provide ample raw material for the subsequent generations to grasp, negotiate, amplify or even filter out in the making of new historical representations.

3

Army doctors' struggle with medical crises and self-discipline

Yanagisawa Genichirō was an army doctor in the 15th Independent Engineer Regiment. The Regiment accompanied the Nankai Shitai (the South Seas Detachment) whose mission was to invade Port Moresby along the Owen Stanley Range. The ensuing battles against the Australians made up the Kokoda campaign. In the epilogue to his memoir, Yanagisawa relates that writing the memoir had been an emotionally difficult experience. He recalls crying alone quietly in his office many times during the writing process. Yanagisawa then looks back at his work:

> [Serving as an army] doctor is a demanding job. Army doctors constantly exposed their lives to the futile circumstances and saved the lives of servicemen, whose duty was to dedicate themselves to the nation. I am constantly troubled by the question of whether I accomplished my role. I had to keep all my sad memories inside my heart. In retrospect, it was a difficult position.[1]

Yanagisawa articulates an inherent paradox of military medicine. He has known all through his career that army doctors are like any other doctor whose fundamental duty is to prevent illness as well as treat the sick and injured. The specific contexts of the army and the war added a crucial layer. The army doctors have to restore the soldiers' health as soon as possible and bring them back to the frontline or active duty. However, the Japanese soldiers would injure and even kill the enemies.[2] The paradox intensifies in the case of how Japan as a nation-state insisted on soldiers dying for the country and prohibited surrender. Yanagisawa's wartime experience has grown into one of deep sorrow, doubt and trauma that lasted for years. His candid admission raises questions about the nature of the dilemma the doctors countenanced and the personae their writing presented. As with soldiers' memoirs, the doctors' memories, impressions and interpretations form a historical that can inform broader discourse of the Asia-Pacific War. This chapter scrutinizes eight accounts by Japanese army doctors who report, in real time and with hindsight, the New Guinea campaign as a zone of medical crises. Under the purview of this chapter are the difficulties the doctors experienced in practising medicine to undernourished and disease- and illness-prone soldiers, the doctors' own impressions of their physical and mental health and their efforts to discipline themselves to face up to the tasks at hand. This chapter argues that the doctors exercised discipline and resisted becoming helpless victims of the circumstances but could not ultimately reconcile with various constraints and qualms.

Army doctors' roles, status and discipline through writing

The role of army doctors is gaining recognition as a branch of social history. Joanna Bourke positions doctors serving in the military as 'a buffer between servicemen and the harsher forms of military justice' that necessitated managing troops' health and behaviour.[3] Her conceptualization echoes Michel Foucault's positioning of doctors as the beholder of discipline and relative power within given bureaucratic strictures. For Foucault, a central pillar of modern medicine and its profession is the medical gaze, the trained eye used to observe and diagnose patients. The medical gaze embodies scientific knowledge, power, discipline and autonomy: the ethos of modernity. The doctor–patient relationship rests on the medical gaze through which the doctors assume the power to regulate, control and discipline the individual.[4] If the work of the doctor in a nation-state during peacetime offers an insight into bureaucracy under 'normal' circumstances, clashes between nation-states can offer alternative insights into the operation of the bureaucracy in wartime. Bourke reminds us that army doctors worked within the bounds of the military institution and hierarchy and ultimately served the needs of the military to mitigate 'the consequences of indiscipline' among soldiers that could affect their health and overall morale.[5] The insights Japanese doctors derived from the New Guinea campaign not only complement those of the soldiers as the last chapter has shown but also form a small but important piece in the jigsaw puzzle of Japan's pursuit of modernity and its imperial ambitions. In addition to soldiers, army doctors also wrote their impressions of wartime. Despite none of the eight doctors' writings presented in this chapter rising to critical acclaim or gaining wide public recognition, these memoirs nonetheless form a historical genre that illuminate the extent of the medical gaze in the context of the New Guinea campaign.

Private writing by army doctors and the medical gaze seem like odd bedfellows but a nuanced look at the two reveals numerous parallels. As with the medical gaze, the underlying assumption of discipline matters to private writing. Aaron William Moore's builds on Foucault's notion of discipline to read American, Chinese and Japanese soldiers' war diaries kept during the Asia-Pacific War. Moore positions the soldiers' diary as 'both a site for discipline and the evidence of the disciplinary process; it was a battlefield where the inarticulate desires of the individual struggled and the well-spoken demands of authority conducted a daily struggle'.[6] In the light of Moore's study, this chapter expands the writings to published diaries as well as memoirs. While diaries and memoirs show different time lags between the events and the time of writing, both exhibit the subjectivity of the writer. This chapter asks how the army doctors created worlds and personae. These came from the words they wrote on the issues of self-discipline, authority and autonomy that comes with the privilege of their status and the constraints they faced within the military. While the soldiers' memoirs test the assumption of the heroic images of the soldiers, the doctors' memoirs reinvestigate the limits of the medical gaze and add new layers to the Japanese perception of the New Guinea campaign and PNG as a whole.

Examining the memoirs enables a reassessment of the stereotyped images of the Japanese army doctors in the post-war imagination of Japan and the West. On the one hand are images of army doctors maintaining composure while performing intricate operations amidst battles. Well-known epithet holds that they aided the putative fanaticism of Japanese soldiers and the cruelty of the Japanese military. Lee K. Pennington says influential in the formulation of this view were works by Ruth Benedict and Ienaga Saburō. Benedict's famous work, *The Chrysanthemum and the Sword* (1946), attributes this apparent cruelty to inadequate supplies, the non-existent medical system and the untrained medical personnel who killed sick and wounded soldiers who could not be evacuated. Benedict's portrayal drew on accounts of US soldiers who had served in Guadalcanal, but began speaking for most of, if not all, the Japanese medical corps in the Asia-Pacific War. Similarly, Ienaga reported that the Japanese military gave priority to suicide and execution by commanding officers over the provision of medical care to wounded Japanese soldiers in conformity with the ideology of sacrifice for the nation. Pennington finds Benedict and Ienaga generalized the situations in the 1940s when Allied attacks severely disrupted the Japanese supplies to overstretched battle zones and disregarded the sophisticated and effective chains of triage and treatment practised in the 1930s.[7]

As a context for analysing the doctors' reflections, the following outline summarizes the roles and responsibilities of the military engaged in military campaigns, including that in New Guinea. In the first instance, when a soldier sustained an injury, medics (*eiseihei*), who received only rudimentary training in wound management, treated them at dressing stations and sent them back to the front. If the injury was too severe, then the soldier was sent to a field hospital. Military doctors (*gun'i*), comprised of volunteers and recruits, typically worked in field hospitals located some distance from the frontline. They were the first to determine the extent of an injury and the course of treatment. If the field hospital could not provide adequate treatment, the soldier would be treated at a military hospital in Japan.[8] The doctors garnered much respect from soldiers. Soldiers typically addressed them as *gun'i dono*, which loosely translates into 'Honourable Military Doctor'.[9] The army doctors' relative distance from the frontline action and their comparatively privileged position within the military provide a helpful backdrop to the medical gaze in these writings.

Doctors' views of New Guinea as a zone of medical crisis

The doctors' narratives, like those of the soldiers, indicate how the extreme physical conditions shape much of their thoughts and behaviours. The shortage of food, poor hygiene and the climate made soldiers susceptible to illness with multiple tropical diseases claiming their lives. Malaria was the biggest killer. Steven Bullard and Iijima Wataru agree that preventing malaria was crucial to determining the outcome of the campaigns in areas with malaria. In short, the Japanese fared worse than the Allies in developing anti-malarial medication and robust medical infrastructure and treatment regimes to prevent and treat malaria. The Japanese occupation of Java in Dutch East India in March 1942 gave the Japanese ready access to the world's largest supply of quinine, a vital ingredient of anti-malarial drugs. The Japanese delayed increasing production while the Allies sped up their manufacturing of an alternative synthetic anti-malarial drug, Atabrine. The Japanese were inconsistent in providing supplies of medication, mosquito nets and repellents to the field, and equally insufficient in ensuring that soldiers took the recommended doses of anti-malarial tablets.[10]

The failure to implement preventative measures against malaria exemplifies how powerless individual doctors had become through no fault of their own. A memoir by army doctor Watanabe Susumu relates an episode that provides a nuanced understanding of the larger issues of the war. Watanabe arrived in Hansa in northeast New Guinea in May 1943 and worked at a base for the rearguard 44th Company. The prevention of malaria posed a major difficulty to Watanabe and his colleagues. Part of the difficulty arose from the oversight of the tropical climate in the design of the anti-malarial quinine tablets and jars containing them. He reports that after opening a jar, moisture got inside and soon melted the sugar-coating. The tablets then stuck together and turned into a single lump. Few had expected this aftereffect to occur with the tablets. Although seemingly trivial, this made it well-nigh impossible to monitor if each soldier was following the correct dosage of one tablet a day. Watanabe and his colleagues wished that the army had supplied moisture-resistant quinine tablets made with hydrochloric acid.[11] The doctors' regret sheds light on the disconnect between the Japanese military headquarters and the concerns of the doctors in implementing anti-malarial regimes. The circumstances set a critical context for exploring how doctors responded to situations far removed from home where they could not assume exercising the medical gaze as they had been trained to back home.

In addition to widespread tropical diseases, malnutrition was another recurring issue adding to the medical crises. Soldiers and doctors constantly and, often bitterly, complained about insatiable hunger for animal protein and salt. Eating grass to fill their stomachs was only a temporary measure. They resorted to catching and eating wild game and even insects. Moreover, deficiency in salt as well as other minerals caused cognitive impairment. An army doctor stationed in Rabaul, Hatano Katsumi recalls how severe malnutrition impeded soldiers' recovery. In November 1944, he treated a patient who had sustained burns in his lower limbs. He injected the patient with glucose and Ringer's solutions. By the next morning, his conditions rapidly deteriorated and he then died. Hatano concludes that malnutrition weakened his immunity so much so that his body failed to absorb the nutrients to achieve recovery. To improve the conditions for the soldiers, Hatano encouraged them to fish and make coconut oil to provide soldiers with sufficient protein and fat.[12] Along with the vignettes by Yanagisawa and Watanabe, Hatano's sympathetic view of soldiers builds up the victim narratives of army doctors while bolstering the victim narratives of the soldiers' plight. The accounts level criticism at the military strategists for altering the nature of the doctors' work to the extent of making them feel disempowered.

The doctors' feelings of helplessness increased as conditions on the frontline deteriorated. They became discouraged and doubted whether they could provide any meaningful treatment to save soldiers' lives. While Yanagisawa registered his disappointment, Peter Williams paints a different picture. The Japanese were generally well equipped and in better health than the Australians in the early phase of the Kokoda campaign. However, the decline began in September 1942 when heavy rain and flooding severely disrupted transport of Japanese supplies and was exacerbated further after the Battle of Buna-Gona in December 1942 and January 1943.[13] By mid-November 1942, the Japanese were on a retreat to Giruwa. Yanagisawa observes:

> Malnutrition by famine grew even more severe. [The soldiers] became extremely thin. Their cheeks caved in, and hair and beard grew unkempt. Eyeballs protruded and shone with a bizarre glow. The eyes looked sunken, jaws stuck out. Necks, arms and legs were so thin that when you took hold of them with your hand, your thumb reached the index finger. Their skin became sallow and their bodies exuded an odour like corpses. This was the appearance of the labourers who were working under atrocious conditions. Furthermore, the combination of malarial fever and amoebic dysentery made soldiers very thirsty. There were dead soldiers who had their faces stuck in muddy water; presumably, they had gone out of trenches at night [to get water]. … Everyone in Giruwa feared death as their destiny. What mounted every day were danger, deprivation and filth creating extreme hardships for humans to endure.[14]

Yanagisawa sees no muscular men and renders a grim yet sympathetic picture of the soldiers' physical conditions. His medical gaze gives finer details of the changed bodies of the soldiers without resorting to the dehumanizing association of soldiers as creatures in hell (Chapter 2). Without food and medicine, all Yanagisawa could do was to accept the desperate sight.[15] The report resonates with what Yoshikuni Igarashi says about the wartime Japanese state's rhetoric of the Japanese body. The state envisioned the physical and metaphysical transitions of the men into patriotic and obedient bodies in its war effort. The reality of the emasculated bodies on battlegrounds exposed the fallacy of the imperial project.[16] Yanagisawa's medical gaze at the desperate conditions propelled inner reflections.

Yanagisawa questions the war and his role in it. Following an Allies' attack on 5 January 1943, Yanagisawa saw twenty-four dead soldiers and thirty-odd injured in a camp in south Giruwa. By then, he had experienced and witnessed the effects of famine on himself and the soldiers for nearly six months. He found the sight of dead soldiers and those still alive but screaming in pain appalling. His recollection departs from the outward medical gaze at soldiers to an inward one at his profession:

At this instant, I just stopped and stood. I was not afraid of the harsh realities of war. Nor did I wish to walk away from my responsibility as an army doctor. I felt the pain of being a doctor. I did not have gauze or bandages. I did not have disinfectant or antiseptics. I did not have medication for soldiers to take or for me to inject. Syringes and medical equipment were now [rusted and] beyond use. What could I do as a doctor? All I could do was to staunch the blood by tying pieces of string and try to keep the soldiers alive as long as possible. An army doctor has to face soldiers teetering on the brink of death on atrocious battlegrounds, and then give treatment to those soldiers. Only at this scene did I feel confused about being a doctor. 'Am I really a doctor? Yes, I am a doctor. I am an army doctor.' Excruciating and heavy feelings mounted in my mind.[17]

For the first time in his career and in New Guinea, Yanagisawa admits that his identity as an army doctor came under serious existential threat. The damage to his medical equipment and the shortage of medical supplies robbed him of the necessary tools with which to perform the bare minimum responsibilities as a doctor. After exhausting his efforts in improvisation, his job changed to one of emotional labour, which was all he could do to care for the untreatable patients. The crises brought the focus of his medical gaze to his own self-discipline. He adjusted his goal to continue to do his work without succumbing to the futility of his circumstances and to preserve his identity as a doctor.

Yanagisawa's inner resourcefulness to take his hardship in strides reached its limits. On 3 September 1943, in the jungle near the Markham River, the Australians fired at the Japanese, which resulted in some Japanese soldiers losing their lives. While Yanagisawa feels the sight of the dead soldiers was cruel, he notices another sensation: his lack of empathy, 'Before my eyes are bodies of my comrades, but I do not feel sadness or sorrow. No feeling wells up. Why?' This incident led him to wonder whether witnessing death could rob him of emotions and intellect.[18] Blocking emotions might well have aided in the discharge of his professional duties and physical survival. However, as we saw in the breakdowns after the war, the exercise of individual discipline came with an emotional toll that were masked behind the brave and steely face he put on at the time.

Doctors' views of combatants' fits of insanity

The army doctors' perception of the war zone enveloped in a medical crisis comes from their observations of the soldiers' psychological states. Though lacking in knowledge of psychiatric theories, these accounts provide a vital counterbalance to the prevailing assumption about the absence of combatants' war neurosis. As historian Nakamura Eri reminds us, wartime propaganda reinforced a military culture that equated mental and physical prowess as a touchstone of masculinity and propelled the soldiers towards sacrificial deaths.[19] During wartime, psychiatrists routinely attributed combatants' psychological disturbances to personal inefficiencies such as a lack of manliness or courage, and registered far fewer cases than observed.[20] In July 1943, by request of the navy, psychiatrist Uchimura Yūshi conducted a survey of pilots and aircrew in Rabaul. While he found that only a few soldiers exhibited clear symptoms of war neurosis, he warned that many had stress-related health issues that could escalate into serious problems.[21]

Uchimura's report implies that the military headquarters neglected war neurosis even though they were aware of the adverse effects of stress and exhaustion on soldiers. Still, Uchimura's warnings went unheeded. Soldiers deployed to the South Pacific with mental disturbances made up a very small proportion of those repatriated and admitted to psychiatric hospitals in Japan. Nakamura establishes that of the available records of 8,002 patients admitted to Kōnodai Psychiatric Hospital, the leading institution in Japan at that time, seventy-two (0.9 per cent) and fifty-two (0.7 per cent) soldiers came from New Guinea and the adjacent Bismarck Islands, respectively. Nearly 87 per cent of the soldiers developed psychiatric disturbances in China, followed by Japan and Manchuria.[22] The disproportion is staggering even if one considers that the soldiers deployed to the latter areas outnumbered those sent to the South Pacific and the difficulties of transporting the soldiers back to Japan. Army doctors' private accounts help us uncover unreported and under-reported cases of physical and mental strain that the soldiers suffered as well as the doctors' own responses to the zone of medical crisis.

Yanagisawa was a perceptive and empathetic doctor who noticed the soldiers' mental conditions as early as December 1942. Nankai Shitai were then defending South Giruwa. Yanagisawa writes what he observed in the frontline troops:

> As the soldiers grew pessimistic, they suddenly went crazy. Paranoia, auditory hallucination, sensory illusion, perceptual and auditory illusion, dulled alertness, inability to focus, incoherence, acute fearfulness, extreme anxiety, illusions, melancholy, excessive talking, excessive eating, refusal to eat, self-harm, singing loudly, dancing around, refusing anything and everything, and so on. Impairment to intellect, emotions and decision-making manifested. In

short, these conditions represent the image of a man on the verge of breaking down, suffering from acute dementia because of extreme malnutrition.[23]

Many memoirs by soldiers and doctors use the term *hakkyō*, which translates into bursting into fits of insanity, as a broad category to describe the specific behaviour. Yanagisawa's description goes far beyond this. He finds that the soldiers became unusually excited, irritable and then eventually morose as the conditions grew progressively trying and tense. Yanagisawa concludes that the soldiers lost their mental faculties which regulated their thoughts and behaviour after suffering from 'extreme malnutrition' and going past the breaking point. We do not know whether Yanagisawa received any psychiatric training as a medical student or if he had only acquired such knowledge after the war. Still, his description reflects his perceptive medical gaze and sensitivity towards the soldiers.

Yanagisawa relates further incidents, as if to substantiate his claim. On one occasion, his unit received bags of rice from another unit. When a frontline soldier saw the bags, he 'screamed and broke into a sudden fit of insanity. The sight went beyond calling it tragic'.[24] The soldier's maniacal reaction was a clear sign of the stress and famine undermining his mental faculties. Later, on 5 January 1943, Yanagisawa came across one soldier in South Giruwa who shouted, 'Long live the Emperor' and lay down on the ground. Yanagisawa found his actions odd as it did not fit in with what he had witnessed before. By then he had seen enough soldiers dying and nearly all of them had expressed a desire to see their family, not make a pledge of loyalty to the emperor. Yanagisawa then walked over to the soldier, took his pulse and ascertained he was still alive. Suddenly the soldier sprang up, saluted Yanagisawa and shouted, 'Everything is fine'. In the end, Yanagisawa judged that the man had gone 'completely insane'.[25] While Yanagisawa does not explain further, the description conveys the overbearing pressure of patriotism placed upon soldiers. The soldier's effort to maintain his identity as a patriotic soldier created the contrary impression of abnormality. What was a dutiful and exemplary statement for fit and healthy soldiers would not hold true to the unfit and ill soldiers. This is the fallacy Yanagisawa has identified not through the medical gaze representing the interest of the military, but the one based on his prior observation of the soldiers' mental conditions.

Other doctors' accounts contain similar observations and, at times, offer interesting cases for analyses. By January 1944, Watanabe in northern New Guinea found soldiers' morale had sunken further as recurrent malaria and war-related malnutrition had sapped their energy. Along with the physical symptoms of malaria, he found soldiers suffering from the high-fever phase in the malarial cycle caused them to show insubordination to their superiors and even leading some to commit suicide.[26] While Yanagisawa simply lists the conditions, Watanabe writes about what the soldiers did under those conditions:

> The only time we could give treatment was when we were on the base in Hansa. In May 1944, we left Hansa and went into retreat. After that, we gave antimalarial tablets to soldiers and had them take them. Or we had medics administer the medicine they had with great care. That's all we could do.
>
> Some patients developed brain symptoms during high fever [in a malarial cycle]. They jumped up and down naked and sometimes became completely crazy. They took swords out and went on a rampage. Inevitably everyone held them down, fastened them to stretchers and put them into bunkers. In some cases, we gave injections and waited for the delirium to subside. In addition, some became melancholic after the fever dissipated. They gradually descended into a state of dementia and their faces became blue. They sat in one corner of the mosquito net, did not eat, defecated and kneaded their own faeces. There were other instances of gradual debilitation.[27]

The drastic measures described above reflect the attitude of the military who regarded these soldiers not as victims but as deviants who needed to be restrained and even excluded from the sight. Watanabe reveals that he was rendered helpless in quelling the scourge of malaria, which escalated soldiers' outbursts of insanity. The antifebrile injections he gave succeeded in calming soldiers down for a time. He reasserts his agency as an army doctor who manages not only to contain the behaviour of the troops but also to restore order among them. His medical gaze bolsters his position as the army doctor who prioritized his duty to contain the consequences of ill-discipline of the soldiers.

These frequent outbursts of insanity could certainly have put further pressure on officers who had to control their subordinates. Hirao Masaharu, a navy doctor, served stints in the Solomon Islands and the New Guinea campaigns. His memoir describes his witnessing an officer disciplining a lieutenant commander. Hirao grows disturbed as the officer's admonishment escalated into sadistic outrage. While Hirao qualifies that he was not a psychiatrist, he notes that several minutes of observation were enough to convince him that the officer was suffering from war neurosis. Hirao conjectures, 'What causes this is the schism between the desire to flee a dangerous environment like a warzone and the sense of duty not to flee, creating a mental dilemma and triggering neurosis'.[28] Be they army or navy doctors, the general picture that emerges is that psychological disturbance can strike any soldier irrespective of rank as the war continues to exert pressure on the soldiers.

One such instance is found in the memoir by Mitsukawa Motoyuki, a doctor who served in a rearguard 44th Company. He writes about his superior, Lieutenant Keiyama, reportedly a competent and well-respected officer. By January 1945, Mitsukawa's unit, which had been subsisting in a village, began relying on the villagers' largesse for survival. On one occasion, Mitsukawa saw over a hundred bananas hanging off the beams of Keiyama's hut. These were the bananas the villagers had entrusted Keiyama to distribute to soldiers. Keiyama kept them out of the sight of the others and never distributed them. On another occasion, Mitsukawa saw Keiyama stepping out of a villager's hut. The moment the two men's eyes met, Keiyama smirked at Mitsukawa. Mitsukawa suspected that Keiyama's reaction tried to disguise his embarrassment at eating a full meal while everyone else was starving. Mitsukawa knew Keiyama was a principled man with a calm temperament and his recent strange behaviour was out of character. Mitsukawa concludes that a long period of excessive stress drove Keiyama to act in this way.[29] His medical gaze on Keiyama is a sympathetic one that delivers implicit criticism of Keiyama's superiors, either in Japan or in New Guinea, for placing him under inordinate mental strain.

The medical gaze and self-discipline: Observing the self

These adverse situations with little hope of improvement would readily erode the morale of the doctors. Army doctors made efforts to instil personal and professional discipline in themselves so that they could set the standards for others. For instance, in his memoir, Hatano claims that it was his duty to preserve the lives of the soldiers during an early phase of his time in Rabaul in December 1943.[30] In late July 1944, he saw patients with malnutrition while he was suffering from another bout of serious diarrhoea himself. Unable to concentrate as his diarrhoea had persisted for four days, he resorted to injecting himself with vitamin B to raise his energy levels to perform his duties. He then confides in his diary, 'When I see patients, I become anxious, but I say "Damn it!" and encourage myself.'[31] This brief remark is reminiscent of a kind of 'pep talk' directed at himself and underscores Moore's point about the diary being the site of self-discipline. Moreover, Hatano's remark highlights the gap between his own thoughts and how others perceived him. In the epilogue, a Japanese veteran Imai Kazuo writes in praise of Hatano. Imai thinks that Hatano personifies 'the image of a calm doctor when administering treatment to the wounded'.[32] Even considering the function of the epilogue, Imai's words tells us that Hatano's exercise of self-discipline inspired confidence in other army doctors.

In contrast to Hatano, the responses by career army doctor Suzuki Masami sound more nuanced. He had served in Manchuria, Mongolia and China before arriving in Rabaul in late November 1942. He was then deployed to New Guinea in March 1943. Following the Australian landing at Arndt Point, north of Finschhafen, on 22 September 1943, he received an order to accompany a 120-man unit. The party of soldiers was to leave coastal Madang on small boats and travel down along the coast. The unit would then march inland to Mount Sattelberg, the site of the headquarters of the 20th Division. Along the way, Suzuki observed field hospitals and gave soldiers words of encouragement. By then, he had grown accustomed to the sight of emaciated soldiers lying on beds, almost abandoned in field hospitals without nurses or medication. His unambiguously sympathetic response may indicate the sustained period he served in war zones, away from the upper echelons of the military establishment and was, therefore, less identified with its ideology. One day, he visited a remote and ill-equipped field hospital in the mountains. It was full of sick and injured soldiers and the sight of maggots covering their bodies and eating the pus on every possible wound made them look even more wretched. He then sensed: 'From invisible darkness came a strange odour. As I detected the feelings of the innocent wounded soldiers in the odour, I felt my heart tightening. I was yelling as I walked from one shed to the next.'[33] This episode brings the paradox of the medical gaze into sharp relief. We learn that Suzuki felt sympathetic towards the 'innocent' soldiers on their deathbeds but had no medicine or equipment. At the same time, out of desperation, he found himself yelling at the soldiers – even though he had meant to encourage them as he had at other field hospitals. His previous deployments had exposed him to considerable death-saturated landscapes. Yet, the desolate and morbid sceneries in New Guinea overwhelmed and broke even the battle-hardened Suzuki like nowhere else had before.

Other doctors, however, hardened their resolve to do their best as the conditions grew adverse. The published diary by Asō Tetsuo exemplifies the dilemma many army doctors faced. He recorded his fluctuating moods that coloured his perception of his work, fellow soldiers and the Japanese military institution. He aired his irritation in his diary and instilled discipline in himself. In a succession of entries, Asō encouraged himself to recover the morale he had lost. He arrived in Rabaul, New Britain Island, in December 1942 after serving as an army gynaecologist in China between November 1937 and April 1941. His main duty in China was to inspect the health of comfort women who served the sexual needs of Japanese soldiers. Soon after arriving in Rabaul, he found the provision of food far worse than in China. He saw the effects of malnutrition on the soldiers and his conditions. Barely a month after arriving in Rabaul, he contracted dengue fever, a mosquito-borne disease and had a temperature running up to 38°C. He writes, 'By next month I will have sunken gloriously into the Solomon Seas. How pathetic that I become sick now in this filthy part of the world. I am a doctor! Luck is in heaven. I can only wait for nature to heal me.'[34] Albeit brief, Asō's annoyance shaped a victim narrative with a sarcastic and fatalistic undertone.

The targets of Asō's irritation were himself and the Japanese military strategists. As a doctor, Asō found it unbecoming to succumb to dengue fever within a month after arrival. He resented becoming another ineffectual body unable to fulfil his responsibilities to his fellow soldiers. Rather, he became a risk to other soldiers as mosquitoes can bite those infected and transmit the virus to others. He castigated himself and condemned the ideology of patriotic sacrifice and death. He satirized the prospect of an inglorious death from dengue in 'this filthy part of the world'. The despondency and fatalism embedded in Asō's medical gaze epitomize the paradoxical nature of practising medicine in the war zone.

Recovering from dengue did not guarantee the improvement of his morale. His diary entries of ensuing days repeated descriptions of seeing endless streams of patients during the day. In the evening he wrote medical records, official reports and his private diary. The fear of the Allied raids striking at any time was of constant concern. His placement at a barrack away from Rabaul exacerbated his loneliness and isolation. Three consecutive entries in June 1943 show signs of burnout and his effort to bring himself out of it. On 6 June 1943, he complained that conscripted civilian doctors like him were disposable and wondered if military-trained career doctors held easier administrative positions. He then tried to restrain himself from wallowing in self-pity:

> I am not complaining about my coming to Rabaul. Rather, [unlike other doctors] I am free from any restrictions and can do as I wish. Fuck promotion; fuck medals! Every day I am seeing gaunt soldiers who look like angels destined for hell. I don't even know when I'm joining their fate. Fortunately, I am healthy, and I am putting up with punishing tasks day in, day out. I see the sick coming to my tent like [a bunch of] Draculas sucking away my blood. Such a thought tarnishes the medical profession. Fingers crossed; I won't sink that low.[35]

Asō suffered under the weight of adverse circumstances as manifested in his vacillating emotions. His sentiments validate Bourke's point about the awkward position of army doctors caught between the necessities of their military role and humanitarian concerns for patients. While he appreciated the benefits of isolation, he bore grudges against the career-minded doctors whom he perceived as beneficiaries of favouritism, as opposed to a conscripted doctor like himself. He immediately consoled himself with his relative autonomy. Asō lashed out at soldiers, too. After describing them in angelic terms, he compared them to blood-sucking Draculas. He soon chided himself and revolved the high ideals of his calling. These examples epitomize Moore's view of the military diary as a private sphere to train and regulate self-discipline. After releasing his tension and anger, he cautions himself that he could not afford to descend so 'low' as to become like one of the career doctors whom he despised. Conflicted as he was in his outlook towards his work and patients, his diary becomes a personal war zone within the war zone outside.

The next day Asō channelled his emotional energy towards another aim – himself. The anti-malarial medication afflicted Asō with the side effect of ringing in his ears. His awareness of his situation did not deter him from a foul mood. He complained that his work was now merely responding to malaria-infected soldiers:

> What's more – every patient has malaria. Malaria is everywhere. The patients are ready to rob my health as soon as they see a tiny window of opportunity. Under such circumstances, if I do not get into a battle first, I do not know when malaria will get me. … How come we ended up like this? Whose fault is it? Have I reached my limit as a doctor? I'm trying so hard.[36]

In addition to the private diary, Asō kept an official daily report of duties submitted to his superiors. The published diary features some of his official reports alongside his private diary. The official report mixes complaints and resentment:

> From seven in the morning till three in the afternoon, I have the stethoscope stuck in my ears. Reserve army doctors must do better. Bodies are treated like consumables. But remember they are the subjects of the Japanese Empire. My superiors, listen well, the minds of the soldiers sacrificing for the nation is one. You take nothing; your body is nothing but useless dolls. You must treat the soldiers.[37]

Frustration, side effects and exhaustion continue to colour Asō's private dairy and official report. Asō's report directs his ire at reservist doctors stationed at large bases in Rabaul and paints an image of his lone battle against a thankless war against malaria. For him, the reservist doctors were indolent, ineffective and unpatriotic bodies who neglect the welfare of the soldiers' patriotic bodies. Asō's praise for the soldiers carries the rhetoric of the Japanese empire and the war and places him on the moral high ground from where he lambast the reservist doctors. His diary vented frustration at the soldiers. He saw them like mosquitos swarming around ready to 'get him'. He then turned to himself and doubted his calibre as a doctor. However fleeting, his questioning anticipates Asō's self-discipline through writing. In the following entry on 8 June, he wrote at night, a time of freedom, to restore his hope and to dream about meeting his family. He felt that 'no matter how busy his day was, a good night's sleep helped restore his vitality and motivation to face another day' and even led him to say that his work was 'worth dying for'.[38] Asō's mood swings are no mere temper tantrums. This is precisely the point about the diary serving as a disciplinary space and device. Still, his upbeat words might be mere words to psych himself up. His oscillating moods that emerge between the lines convey the depth of his resentment at the war and his work.

The medical gaze and self-discipline: Sexual desire and appetite

Asō's medical gaze extends to the issues of sexual desire and masturbation that few army doctors have written or spoken about in public. He associated sexual matters with the discipline he deemed necessary for himself and other soldiers. The views expressed in his diary remain consistent with the Christian morality he adopted in his youth and maintained throughout his life as well as the scientific and medical discourse of sex at the time. Asō's writing makes a self-effacing admission to his moral shortcomings. This admission foregrounds his observations of the soldiers' conduct and elevates Asō above them. The juxtaposition sets the standard for what he deemed appropriate discipline.

Asō's stance on sexual matters comes with an admission of his failure to keep sexual fantasies out of his mind. On 15 June 1943, he performed examinations on comfort women and soldiers with sexually transmitted infections at a comfort station near a field hospital. He told himself not to get aroused during and after the examinations, but to no avail. Sexual fantasies kept him awake into the night, and when he fell asleep, he experienced a nocturnal emission. He believed that the examinations had stimulated a yearning for the opposite sex.[39] Asō attributes his pent-up desire to excessive workload and distance from

Rabaul town that prevented him from recreational activities. In his previous posting in China, he served as the Army gynaecologist and examined women in the comfort stations. Outside his duty hours, he frequented dance halls and socialized with women but refused to go to comfort stations or officers' clubs where soldiers engaged in sexual intercourse.[40] Asō's lament is consistent with a report entitled 'Positive Methods for the Prevention of Venereal Diseases' that he submitted to the Army in July 1939. The report was in response to frequent occurrences of venereal diseases in China among Japanese soldiers and comfort women. Sabine Frühstück stresses that the wartime regime, including the military, regarded soldiers as a vital constituent in raising Japan's stature as a modern nation-state, claiming that their health, which included their sexual health, was not only a matter for individual soldiers' concern, but also that of the nation's body politic.[41] That Asō authored the report indicates the military and the state took soldiers' private sexual lives as matters of concern for the state.

One of Asō's recommendations was proper sexual education and thorough supervision of military prostitutes and soldiers to counter the debilitating effects of venereal diseases. What Asō favoured, above all, was for soldiers 'to achieve a more hygienic lifestyle' through sexual abstinence. To this end, he recommended the army 'find suitable methods of recreation to eliminate the idleness that gives rise to sexual desires'.[42] Asō's report endorsed the sexual morality of the time known as the hydraulic model, which held that blockage of men's sexual energy undermined physical and mental well-being. Japanese sexologists and intellectuals held that non-marital sex, homosexuality and masturbation could cause physical and mental harm. Such a mentality warranted the socialization of soldiers to a stance in which regular entertainment was deemed necessary and the female bodies were instruments for this aim.[43] Asō's endorsement of the hydraulic model did not stop there. Later, he advocated, 'if we were to launch a 100-year plan for East Asia, a one- or two-year period of sexual abstinence could not be considered excessive'.[44] Taken together, Asō's report largely mirrored the dominant concerns within the Japanese military and health authorities. What is noteworthy is the army's failure to provide Asō and the other soldiers with opportunities to divert their sexual desires in favour of a 'hygienic lifestyle'.

Asō's attitude towards sexual desire extended to soldiers' practice of masturbation. Two short comments in his personal diary make rare references. On 26 August 1944, he proposed a novel design for the latrine to his captain, featuring only a roof. Asō deemed doors and walls were unnecessary because these would provide privacy that could give soldiers the opportunity to 'sneak in photographs of beautiful actresses'. His open design would 'prevent soldiers from expending energy by masturbation'. The battalion commander rejected Asō's proposal. Without explaining the captain's reasoning, Asō finished the day's entry by speculating that the frequency of masturbation had strong correspondence to the recurrence of malaria.[45] Later in January 1945, the sight of so many sick soldiers convinced Asō that he stayed healthy and fit because he led a healthy lifestyle. Along with hard work and abstinence from smoking and drinking, he credited abstinence from masturbation prevented him from becoming sick.[46] Asō's comments come without overt moralistic tones and evident attempts to present masturbation as a matter of prurient interest. Instead, he applies his medical gaze to identify causation and correlation between masturbation and health.

Asō's opinion agrees with the dominant view of sexual educators, state medical administrators and the military of the early 1900s. They viewed masturbation as a cause of physical and mental degradation that would undermine the discipline and combat capacity of the soldiers and eventually Japan's social cohesion. In the 1920s, studies by young experts challenged this view and argued that masturbation was part of normal sexual practice.[47] Asō's medical gaze on sexual desire spoke the language of anti-masturbation and let him present himself as more disciplined than others. His open admission to his heterosexual urges makes him appear more human rather than as a paragon of virtue. His imperfection allowed him to criticize the army's apparent failure to ensure hygienic lifestyles for him and the soldiers.

In contrast, the means of self-discipline adopted by Mitsukawa involved both the conscious and subconscious. One day in May 1944, Mitsukawa noted that he was depressed; unable to sleep, he became exhausted and was losing his appetite. He tried force-feeding himself only to find that his dry mouth would not secrete saliva and pushing the food further into his throat only made him feel like vomiting. The sight of soldiers devouring their meals made him want to stop eating. He decided 'if I am going to die, I might as well keep a detailed diary in my pocket memo book'.[48] He had been keeping a personal diary and medical records, but his resolve at breakfast on that day was a crucial turning point in his medical gaze and crystallized his commitment to his work. In addition to his diary, he kept records of illness and famine in his unit in the hopes that future generations would find them useful in learning about the futility of war.[49] To conserve pencil and paper, he wrote in small characters; he wrapped the diary in a plastic cover to protect it from rain and kept it in his backpack. This measure saved his notebooks from the tropical climate until surrender. Upon surrender,

Japanese officers ordered troops to burn all of their writings. Mitsukawa hid some of his writings and other essential information in his backpack.[50] Keeping the physical copies safe was an act of self-preservation as a soldier, a doctor and a human being. It allowed him to monitor his medical gaze in real time and later to complete his memoir and research papers.[51]

While his resolve to keep writing was evident, the less conscious and involuntary manifestation of his discipline was the toll the war took on his body and his mind. After noticing the waning of his appetite, for the next five days of the march he noted that he managed to consume only 500 calories a day. He pondered how he could possibly survive.[52] The standard daily ration for domestically stationed soldiers was 3,400 calories until September 1944, when it was lowered to 2,900 following the decline of food supplies across Japan.[53] Present-day nutritional science recommends an intake of 2,800 to 3,000 calories a day for a moderately active young male. A soldier in training on hilly terrain expends 3,429 calories a day, increasing to 4,238 and 4,738 calories for those training in cold conditions and the jungle, respectively.[54] Without means of verifying Mitsukawa's self-declared calorie count, we have to take his calculation at face value. Even then, his intake reached only a little over 10 per cent of what was needed for a soldier active in the tropics. He spent yet another day feeling starved, but without any appetite. He even gave the rice in his mess tin to a comrade to make his pack lighter, which left him staring at the full moon and wishing for a healthy appetite. He felt 'beaten by hunger, lack of appetite, fatigue and despair' and mused, 'This cold reality was a lesson from the moonlight'.[55] The consequences of his loss of appetite would have been more severe than others. Elsewhere in his memoir, Mitsukawa relates that when conscripted his height was 160 cm and he weighed 46–47 kilograms. Moreover, he had been a sickly child and only when he was in medical school did he discover he had a congenital heart condition.[56] In the safe confines of his diary, his statement makes a personal protest to the war over which he had little control.

Mitsukawa conveys much sorrow as he evokes an image of the moonlight shining on his gaunt face and emaciated body in the dead of the night. However, his description falls short of analyzing how and why he lost his appetite – joining the dots between the psychosomatic and the physical – and articulating the consequences it had for him. This oversight in his medical gaze speaks of the limit of medical sciences at that time. An interview conducted by psychiatrist Noda Masaaki in the post-war era can shed light on this gap. Ogawa Takemitsu, a former army doctor posted to Beijing, found that many soldiers had developed physical symptoms of malnutrition, even though they had enough to eat. The disparity confused him. He later discovered that the soldiers had refused to eat or vomited the food they had consumed. Noda concluded that these soldiers had eating disorders resulting from their rejection of the war and the sociocultural expectations to build and maintain patriotic combat-ready bodies with a hyper-masculine ethos.[57]

Further clues about malnutrition come from another army doctor, Aoki Tōru, who served in China, Nomonhan and Iturup Island (Etorofu-tō, in Japanese). He investigated the causes, symptoms and consequences of war-related malnutrition, questioning the theory held by most army doctors that amoebic dysentery caused those symptoms as opposed to malnutrition itself. Furthermore, he posited that the symptoms developed in two stages. In the first stage, soldiers were on the receiving end of unreasonable demands that caused them tremendous physical and mental strain. When the strain exceeded their limits, the second stage set in. The body would begin to consume itself to the extent of disrupting homeostasis in the brain, especially, the feeding centre that regulated appetite. The impaired feeding centre then sent signals that contradicted biological needs, such as drinking water to quench thirst, but refusing to eat to satisfy hunger.[58] Given the commonality in the circumstances and behaviour between Mitsukawa and Ogawa's patients, Mitsukawa's loss of appetite may have been related to the change in his mood, but also had roots in the disturbance of his homeostasis. It was the work of his subconscious self-enacting discipline to engage in a hunger strike against the war and what it demanded of him.

Mercy killing

The doctors' observations of the patients and themselves paint grim pictures of life on the battlefield. Asō's writing on sexual matters exposed a blind spot in the medical gaze. Another issue few doctors publicly discuss is mercy killing that was referred to under the euphemistic term of *shochi*. It can translate into medical treatment or even disposal. Historian Yoshida Yutaka argues that the objection to *shochi* ebbed away as more Japanese troops became sick and sustained injuries. The Battle of Guadalcanal (7 August 1942–9 February 1943) was the harbinger of more *shochi* as the Japanese had lost their strategic advantage to the Allies. Following the Battle of Guadalcanal, doctors and medics abandoned or even killed soldiers who could not retreat to safety. At times, the medical corps encouraged the weakened soldiers to commit suicide. Their deaths precluded the soldiers from violating the Field Service Code of 1941 (*Senjinkun*). Its injunctions prohibited soldiers from being caught alive and becoming prisoners of war. Dying during military operations accorded them the status of the honourable dead for a cause greater than their survival. *Shochi* then became a useful measure to save the face of the soldiers and their families, and to attenuate the unit leaders' responsibility for the deaths. Japanese veterans testify to *shochi* recurring, as did resistance to it, in the ensuing campaigns including New Guinea.[59]

None of the doctors' writings considered in this chapter described the doctors' conducting *shochi* or their witnessing of it conducted by other members of the medical corps. If soldiers witnessed these incidents, it is reasonable to assume that someone carried them out, or at least, authorized such acts. Miyoshi Masayuki (b. 1917) of the 224th Infantry Regiment deployed to Dutch New Guinea was one doctor who broke the silence with his privately published memoir. The memoir is a short booklet shy of forty pages. It charts a young doctor's hardship abroad and his return home as a new changed self. Even considering its brevity, Miyoshi's memoir reads like a condensed version of an army doctors' memoir of ordinary quality. In the epilogue, Miyoshi states that his writing tells 'the truth of the extreme conditions as a duty for his dead comrades'.[60] Six years after its publication, in November 2010, Miyoshi participated in an oral history project conducted by Japan's national broadcaster, NHK, called *Sensō shōgen ākaibusu* (Archives of war testimonies). His forty-eight-minute interview, available freely on the Internet, contains a five-minute segment in which he describes his injecting morphine to frail soldiers.

Miyoshi recalls seeing many soldiers suffering from starvation and diseases and losing the will to live. Soldiers in such a mental state begged Miyoshi to put an end to their lives.

Miyoshi: This is a contract between the army doctor and the soldier – to ease him of the pain. Everyone used morphine in the end.
Interviewer: Is it a 'contract'?
Miyoshi: Well, it's not that formal like a 'contract'. But it's a discussion between the soldier and me, really. I wouldn't put it in a complicated word like 'contract'. It's an agreement after a discussion [*hanashiai*], right? [Soldiers pleaded,] 'Please give me morphine at any cost'. So, I gave the injection.[61]

Miyoshi further elaborates that he made case-by-case judgments upon examining the soldiers. Only when he determined that the soldiers did not have much life left, would he then administer the injection like 'euthanasia in today's language'. He insists that he had no regrets about giving the injections because he discussed and obtained the soldiers' consent.[62]

Miyoshi's backpedalling on the word 'contract' underlines his concern about the interviewer and the viewers misinterpreting its meaning and nuances. Mutual agreement by discussion softens the formal and institutional differential in power between Miyoshi and the soldier. 'Agreement' can make the decision seem more like an outcome of a discussion between equals. In the interview, Miyoshi makes sure to distinguish himself from other doctors. He accompanied soldiers at all times, even to the frontline, while other doctors typically remained aloof. He believes that the bond he created with the troops gave him plenty of information with which to make his decision. The point Miyoshi makes is that his exercise of his medical gaze and decisions for *shochi* rested on the trust he built with the soldiers and compassion he felt for them. His claim contrasts with the type of *shochi* out of strategic and ideological necessity to 'cut the losses' as in abandoning the infirm and persuading them to die for the honour of the Japanese empire.

Miyoshi's rationale and process for mercy killing differ from those of the *shochi* others committed. He stresses his empathy for soldiers and subverts the images of dispassionate army doctors. Still, his recollection tempts questions about the relationships army doctors had with others over matters of life and death. The soldiers' witness accounts can give clues to the power of the army doctors in the medical corps. Journalist Hosaka Masayasu, who has dedicated his long career to researching the Asia-Pacific War, spoke with one former army doctor deployed to New Guinea. He recalled that army doctors typically delegated medics, their subordinates, with tasks associated with mercy killing. The medics had to lie to soldiers that they were taking painkillers when the medicine was cyanide. The medics pressed the cheeks to force the mouth open and shoved the tablets in. Some soldiers used the little power that they had left to resist the medics, often ending in a scuffle.[63] Indeed, these accounts validate Bourke's assertion that the doctors' relatively privileged status predisposed them to execute the demands of the military. However, it may be wrong to equate the army doctors' silence or reticence to discuss awkward matters as being simply a reflection of the doctors' lack of humanity. Miyoshi's interview retroactively fills the awkward silences in ways written memoirs, including his own, do not. During the segment on injecting morphine, his expression becomes stern and his pauses grows longer than other segments. These non-verbal cues indicate the gravity of the memory etched in his body and mind over the decades. He does not explain exactly what prompted him to 'tell-all' on camera. Dismissing the interview as a public confession to justify his decision and action is tempting. However, a more pertinent point is that Miyoshi's interview offers the possibility of overcoming the emotional burden of the medical gaze and its underlying self-discipline even decades after the war.

Conclusion

Contrary to the images of the army doctor appearing calm, collected and at times bordering on cruel, army doctors' impressions reveal how they dealt with a multitude of professional and personal challenges in the war zone of medical crisis. Personal writings such as memoirs and diaries comprise a medium in which they sculpted the disciplined self through the exercise of the medical gaze set on others and themselves. Reporting the miserable conditions of the soldiers and the adverse conditions under which they practised medicine could well have overwhelmed and reduced the doctors to a sense of inadequacy. The writings gave a personal space in which the doctors instilled discipline in themselves to resist their becoming helpless victims of the war and other circumstances. Instead, they exercised self-discipline to affect the thoughts and behaviour of the soldiers as they desired to do on themselves. We have seen how Suzuki sympathized with the soldiers, which also elevated him to the upper echelon of the military establishment. Mitsukawa's determination to observe and record the conditions of his fellow servicemen did not extend to applying his medical knowledge to understanding how the wartime conditions drove him towards passive resistance. Asō fused his medical gaze with his morality to project his physical, mental and even spiritual fitness over the other soldiers. In his video interview, Miyoshi attempted to reconcile an area of his experience left unaddressed in his previous writing.

Alienation, frustration and burnout are overarching themes of the writings by army doctors that were introduced in this chapter. The army doctors have identified themselves as victims but exercised the medical gaze so as not to become completely powerless victims. The doctors' observations of the others and themselves laid the foundation for the discipline they held within and expected the others to continue with their soldiering roles. However, the doctors' self-portrayals do not typically extend to more self-reflective questions about their privileged status within the military and in their relationship with the soldiers or the patients. The memories the veterans carried home and put to words turned into the raw materials for others to process and form historical narratives. Part 2 explores how audiovisual media engaged with the memories of the New Guinea campaign and what narratives and interpretations they offered to the public.

Part 2
Films and Documentaries

4

Finding reasons for living and dying in a war zone: Cinematic adaptations of Katō Daisuke's *Minami-no-shima ni yuki ga furu*

Previous chapters have shown how the lives of Japanese soldiers were replete with misery during the New Guinea campaign. Regardless of these circumstances, soldiers still found ways of entertaining themselves. An extraordinary initiative took place in Manokwari, Dutch New Guinea. Katō Daisuke (1910–1975) was a stage actor deployed as a medic. By instruction from his superiors, he led and performed in a theatre group (*engei buntai*) for Japanese comrades for several months during the war and up to the eventual repatriation. In an interview in the *Asahi* newspaper in 1961, he recalled how the theatre group gave him a much-needed creative outlet: 'When I heard about the theatre group, I jumped at it … I never thought the audience would be so happy.'[1] Katō acknowledged that he was an exception while many of his contemporaries had their acting careers curtailed during the war. The tragic circumstances he witnessed led him to rediscover and share the joy of performance with the others.[2] The soldiers in the audience, too, recalled the theatre performance was a welcome tonic for their lowered morale.[3] Entertainment seemed frivolous and even detrimental to the discipline of the soldiers. However, the reactions by Katō and the audience say much about the importance of finding meanings in life when death was on everyone's mind.

After the war, Katō followed his rekindled passion and pursued a career as a film actor. Additional fame came after he published his memoir, *Minami-no-shima ni yuki ga furu* (Snow Falling in a Southern Island, hereafter *Minami-no-shima*). In it, he related his involvement in the theatre group. Upon publication, *Minami-no-shima* was adapted into TV dramas (1961 and 1964), several stage productions (the last commercial and professional performance in 2015) and two films made in 1961 and 1995.[4] In the television and the 1961 film adaptations,

Katō took the leading role and played his wartime self. Although neither of the two cinematic adaptions attained lucrative box-office sales or won awards, these adaptations add to the list of historical films about the New Guinea campaign in Japanese cinema.[5]

This chapter compares the two cinematic adaptations of *Minami-no-shima* along with the conflicting notions of life and death that shaped the discourse of the Asia-Pacific War and its memories of it in Japan. Differences in the interpretations of these concepts outweigh the commonalities. The chapter argues that these differences mirror contemporaneous concerns of the film-maker at the time the films were made. As will be discussed below, the two adaptations have attracted different reviews. For instance, in a recent short review, film historian Kasuga Taichi views the 1961 adaptation as a comedy with nostalgic recollections of the hard times. His review, however, neither offers a critical appraisal nor compares this film with the 1995 adaptation.[6] The comparison not only rectifies the disparity, but also raises the relative significance of *Minami-no-shima* in the rich lineage of what Isolde Standish names war-retro films in Japan – retrospective war films made after the war – that broke from the films made under strict media control by the Allied Occupation (1945–52).[7] The years the two adaptations of *Minami-no-shima* were made, 1961 and 1995, were periods with markedly different concerns about the world, Japan and war memory. The cross-reading demonstrates the capaciousness of the cinematic representations of history and the ways memories travel across media (from memoir to film) and time (thirty-four years between two adaptations).

As touched upon in the introduction, the historical film carries values far greater than entertainment. Popular sentiments and audience reactions towards films reflect and shape national civic discourse and consciousness. Robert Rosenstone and Robert Burgoyne conceive of the film-makers as historians marshalling available techniques and historical sources to present an argument with the historical film as the product of the contemporaneous sociopolitical *zeitgeist* surrounding the film-makers, cast, audience and critics. The historical film, as with other commercial enterprises, is a medium in which the production team and the audience engage in imagining and re-enacting the past as allegories for viewers' collective and individual aspirations and anxieties.[8] Likewise, scholars of Japanese war-retro films agree on their fundamental premises and analyse films against the historical contexts. During the Occupation years, Japanese war films sent pacifist anti-war messages to educate the Japanese and mould them into democratic citizens. After the Occupation, the war-retro films explored themes and issues that had been barred from public discourse and became a field of ideological contestation.[9] Pacifist anti-war films carried the war-as-evil message further and depicted the soldiers and civilians as victim-heroes and victim-heroines who come to tragic ends. 'Revisionist' films portray soldier-protagonists as patriotic heroes with quintessentially masculine qualities. These films evoke nostalgia for the imperial days and remind the viewers that not everything about wartime was to be condemned.[10] Indeed, Japan's prominent film critic Yomota Inuhiko finds that Japanese grieving and comforting the souls of only the Japanese is an idea many Japanese films have used in different forms, and was an appealing narrative to neoconservatives in the 1990s.[11] Alternatively, sociologist Fukuma Yoshiaki pays greater attention to not only how and why gaps between the print and the film occur, but also what these slippages mean. He notices that popular Japanese war-retro films in the twenty-first century such as *Hotaru* (Firefly, 2001) and *Eien no zero* (Eternal Zero, 2013) romanticize *kamikaze* pilots' ethos of sacrifice and obedience, but tone down historical contexts and the soldiers' painful memories. The emphasis and muting create a rupture to the kinds of memories transmitted to younger generations.[12]

Central to this analysis are three concepts concerning life and death running across the two adaptations: *ikigai*, (what makes life worthwhile), *sange* (meaningful death, lit. glorious death) and *nanshi* (meaningless death, lit. difficult death). One prominent post-war intellectual and writer who reflected on these concepts was Oda Makoto (1932–2007). The experience of aerial raids over Osaka city where he grew up prompted him to question the gap between the rhetoric of *sange* by the state apparatus and the grief people felt about deaths in war. He thought that the wartime state had elevated *sange* into a national virtue of 'glorious death' in a holy war in the name of the empire and the emperor. The public, including soldiers deployed abroad and families left behind in Japan, may have agreed with the rhetoric of *sange* in public but demurred in private. The gravity of the grief of losing loved ones, comrades and their own lives seemed futile as Japan experienced repeated defeats in battles. He asked how such deaths could have benefitted the Japanese empire and argued that what was regarded as *sange* was, in fact, meaningless death (*nanshi*). Oda extended his questions about *sange* and *nanshi* to get beyond the characterization of the Japanese troops as victims. While many Japanese soldiers did suffer, soldiers reacted to the pressing prospect of *nanshi* in various ways. Many resorted to inflicting damages to or killing their adversaries, and even comrades and civilians. Oda believed that such behaviour had stemmed from the Japanese state's regard of its people as subjects rather than individual citizens. Portraying soldiers in the clear-cut binary of victims or perpetrators fails to account for the complexity of the war and the military on the combatants' thoughts and behaviour.[13]

Where the intellectual current looked back at the competing meanings of soldiers' deaths, Katō's involvement in the Manokwari theatre group addressed the issue from a different angle. *Minami-no-shima* foreshadowed the ethos of the individual pursuit of fulfilment heralded in post-war Japan. Japan's post-war constitution redefined the Japanese people as citizens with civil liberty as opposed to subjects. *Ikigai* became the new code for avenues for self-actualization. However, Oda cautions that the individual is never entirely free from the constraints of the collective society.[14] Furthermore, Gordon Mathews finds how class and gendered divisions influence the perceptions and modes of *ikigai*. The majority of men and women find *ikigai* in family and leisure rather than the work they do. Finding *ikigai* in a chosen field of work, or vocation, is 'a privileged masculine prerogative whereby he can pursue the freedom to choose the source of *ikigai*'.[15] That Katō turned his wartime deployment to his advantage sets him apart from less fortunate contemporaries and underscores the special status and circumstances he enjoyed. This comparative analysis is limited to scenes that offer pressing examples of *ikigai*, *sange* and *nanshi* in each film.

Katō's memoir and war in Manokwari

Although evaluating the adaptations against the memoir is not the main objective, the memoir informs us of the significance Katō drew from his wartime experience. Katō wrote the memoir only because other people encouraged him to put his unique experience into writing and never anticipated its success. The passage of sixteen years, from repatriation to the time of writing, enabled him to find cheerful aspects in an otherwise miserable wartime. However, he never forgot that he owed his life and career to his comrades, deceased or alive.[16] Though never explicit, his nostalgic recollection acknowledges *ikigai*, *sange* and *nanshi*. The memoir begins with Katō's sudden conscription in October 1943, aged thirty-two, that brought him to Manokwari in December 1943. Soon he met comrades who shared a background in music and theatre, and took the initiative to put on performances of music and dance to entertain the soldiers. When the news reached their superiors, they charged Katō with the task of forming and leading the theatre group in order to lift soldiers' morale and cultivate their sentiments. The formation was possible not only because the superiors were theatre fans, but also because much of the Manokwari campaign was a war of attrition with infrequent movement. After the campaign in East New Guinea, the Allies, led by the Americans, launched an offensive at Hollandia in April

1944 and proceeded westwards until eventually shifting north to the Philippines. Although the Allies spared Manokwari from a full-scale offensive, raids on Japanese supply vessels and Japanese strategic errors caused starvation, disease and death, reducing the army from the initial 20,000 to 7,000 men by the time of Japan's surrender.[17]

A distinctive aspect of Katō's memoir is the contrast between extensive descriptions of the theatre group and the minimal description of the war and his duty as a medic. He wrote at lengths about his efforts to assemble a theatre group which was as professional as possible. He conducted auditions to select actors and craftsmen with the skill and ingenuity to improvise costume, makeup and stage props with whatever materials they could find. Adding to the unique challenge was the absence of females that compelled male soldiers to perform female roles. This contingency mirrors the convention of *onnagata* in *kabuki* theatre, which assigns male actors to female roles.[18] The great care the theatre group took to create an alternative world of home away from home with feminine characters is ironic in an environment where the soldiers were conceptualized as the epitome of hyper-masculinity. Katō concedes that the audience enjoyed seeing the landscape, stage props and *onnagata* more than the plays, as these features reminded them of home and women they were missing.[19] What impressed Katō and the theatre group the most was the audience reaction to a scene of snow created out of unused materials such as parachutes. The scene evoked tears from the homesick soldiers who never expected to return alive to see snow again.[20]

The snowfall scene brings the memoir to its final segment where Katō resolves to pursue acting as his *ikigai*. After his repatriation, a playwright told him to take pride in his leadership of the theatre group because the purpose of acting was to entertain people. His words galvanized Katō's commitment to acting as his vocation and duty to honour his dead comrades.[21] This ending endows his memoir with a future-oriented character. He does not express despair, anger or resentment about the war or the decisions of his superiors. What Katō emphasizes is the strong rapport he developed with the members of the theatre group and the officers who supported it. Only on rare occasions does he complain about ordinary soldiers who thought that Katō and his group had an easy and leisurely time. He insists that the theatre group's work was over and above the normal duties allocated to members in their respective units.[22]

Katō's memoir offers an alternative war story that looks more to the present and the future than the past. While the theatre group found fulfilment in staging theatre performances, the audience also had their yearnings to see snowfall satisfied on the faraway South Sea Islands. *Minami-no-shima* still manages to send an indirect anti-war message. Katō's detailed descriptions of the theatre group captured the absurdity of the war in which the Allies or battles receded to the back of his and his comrades' minds.[23] However, as essayist Hamada Kengo laments, the snowfall episode garnered far more attention, disproportionate to its coverage in the memoir. The episode takes up no more than 10 pages in the total of 260 pages and overshadowed the other episodes and sentiments Katō had wanted the reader to appreciate.[24] Hamada's criticism reminds us why it is important to look beyond the snowfall episode that gave the memoir its title and give the two film adaptations the sustained analysis they deserve.

The 1961 adaptation: Katō finds his *ikigai*

The 1961 adaptation presents a feel-good drama in a straightforward structure. The first third of the film narrates the forming of the theatre group. The remaining sections narrate the rehearsals and the theatrical performances. A chain of amusing episodes, occasional challenges and poignant cameos sustain and build momentum. Reviews at the time of its release recognized it as a humanist drama in which the theatre group's performance consoled homesick comrades, but offered little critical investigation.[25] This analysis shows that the film idealizes Katō's discovery of his *ikigai* as an endorsement of an exemplary work ethic underpinning the conservative turn in national politics. The film glossed over the thorny issues of *nanshi* and *sange* in favour of a comedic narrative in the classic sense of a happy-ending story and not in the mould that boomed between the late 1950s and the 1960s. Michael Baskett notes that Japanese war comedies used irreverent humour, slapstick and bumbling characters to criticize the absurdity of the war, the military and the political system through comic media in ways 'serious' films could not.[26] *Minami-no-shima* fits into this trend and uses comedy to reflect on the atrocities of the war Katō experienced, but a closer inspection reveals how it also overlooks salient issues in the memoir itself. A nostalgic and even comical look back at a horrendous experience such as war can be a sign of individuals and society at large having moved on and into a new frame of mind to reimagine and recreate the past in present.

The 1961 adaptation followed the creative direction of 'forward-looking and healthy films' that Tōhō, the major film studio that produced the film, had recently adopted. At the same time, Tōhō was producing popular comedy series such as *Shachō* (1958–70) and *Ekimae* (1961–5). Each depicted the daily lives of *sarariiman* (office workers) with the buoyant aspirations of the era with comedic flourishes. The films reflected the optimism in Japan's economic growth from the mid-1950s under the conservative rule of the Liberal Democratic Party. Its control grew following the bitter struggle over the US–Japan Security Treaty in 1960. The contestation consolidated Japan's path for capitalist development. In making *Minami-no-shima* Tōhō marshalled the scriptwriter, director and actors, including Katō himself, from these series.[27] Swapping the suit-and-tie with the military uniform seems anachronistic. However, the *sarariiman* became the archetypical male white-collar corporate warrior who powered the Japanese economy during this time of revitalization. The *ikigai* that Katō found in his own military and civilian lives form the common but not wholly identical *esprit de corps* running from the wartime to the 1960s.

Katō's discovery of *ikigai* unfolds through his growth into a leader. He develops bonds with fellow actors in the theatre group. One such actor is Private Tsutayama who turns up at the audition. Tsutayama performs his dance and song routine with confidence. Katō flatly rejects him because his style clashes with what Katō wants. A stunned Tsutayama begs him to reconsider, saying that returning to his unit will bring him shame. He asserts that he will do his best to learn how to perform to meet the theatre group's needs. Tsutayama adds, 'If you cannot take me on, I am committing suicide'. He steps back, sits down, takes out his penknife and puts the blade against his stomach. Then, the camera turns to Katō and Captain Murata, an officer sitting next to him as a co-judge. Murata whispers to Katō, 'Don't you think you should take him on?' Katō grimaces for a moment. He is keen to make the theatre group 'authentic' to ensure the best possible performance for the audience.[28] Katō tells Tsutayama, 'I'll take you on. But if you show no promise, then you're out!' The scene closes with a relieved Tsutayama going down on his knees to thank Katō and Murata. The rapid turn of events fails to explain why Katō changed his mind, but says much about Katō's moment of growth. No one knows for certain whether Tsutayama's plea is genuine or a manipulative ploy. Murata takes Tsutayama's word at face value and persuades Katō to moderate his wish to recruit only the best. What matters here is Murata neither shouts Katō down nor demands his obedience as his superior. Murata's comportment, without militaristic pretensions, makes him an avuncular figure. The condition Katō places onto Tsutayama highlights the former's enthusiasm to form a professional group and his ego as a leader. Katō's compromise in this scene foreshadows his subsequent maturation as a person who believes in the guiding principle of *ikigai* and help other people's pursuit of *ikigai*.

The subsequent scenes develop the rapport between Tsutayama and Katō. In rehearsals, Tsutayama struggles to unlearn his familiar performance styles much to the irritation of Katō and the theatre group. Tsutayama vows to practise hard and improve. Soon, he goes from a reject to a fully fledged member. The inaugural performance in the newly built theatre was a resounding success. Afterwards, the theatre group members exchange their impressions in the dressing room. Katō walks outside and sits on a step. Tsutayama follows, sits beside him and offers him a cigarette. The dialogue affords a rare glimpse into the thoughts of the two men:

Katō: Everyone enjoys taking part in the theatre. When we are performing, we can forget everything.
Tsutayama: When I am on stage, I feel as if I were on a performing tour in Tōhoku.

The men agree that acting boosts their morale. Katō sees his performance as providing him with a purpose in life and giving his comrades a diversion from the unpleasant and mundane realities of war and the constant fear of death. Tsutayama also says acting in Manokwari gives him more than a nostalgic yearning for his home. Then, he moans:

> I really don't like war. We've come all the way to the jungle, and we're told to charge into the enemy. [*Pauses*] But there's one thing I appreciate about the war. I've been able to put in a genuine performance. I understood what I did in the past 30 years was not performance.

Katō: Really? [*Turns to Tsutayama, smiling*]
Tsutayama: Performance has to be authentic. [*Smiles*]
Katō: That's right.
Tsutayama: Leader, there's one thing I want to say. If I really make it back in Japan, I would like to pursue the honour of performing as an actor for the rest of my life.
Katō: Me too. I have come to appreciate how valuable it is to be an actor. Yes, let's stay alive and get back to Japan together.
Tsutayama: It'll be too bad if we die here. But I'll make it back to Japan no matter what. I'll never die. I'll make it back to Japan.

The scene stresses how maintaining hope for the future offers a more meaningful outlook on life than dwelling on the futility of the war. Tsutayama's complaint about the war remains a fleeting acknowledgement of the general sentiments of the soldiers and segues the encouragement Katō and Tsutayama give one another. Evident in the dialogue is Tsutayama's gratitude to Katō for saving him from existential limbo or the fate that awaited many of his comrades. Additional audiovisual elements enhance the optimism growing within Katō and Tsutayama. The dialogue ends with a popular song 'Rabauru kouta' (A Ballad for Rabaul).[29] The lyrics speak of a Japanese soldier on a repatriation ship from Rabaul. As the ship departs, the soldier thanks a woman for coming to see him off and anticipates how he will miss the time he spent there. The scene in the film then switches to a sunset on a tropical island. The combination of the song and the sunset hint at the setting of the Japanese imperial sun and the beginning of a future for both men. The episode affirms Tōhō's 'forward-looking and healthy' policy. Pursuing one's career can help us reap the rewards of *ikigai* instead of harbouring grudges against the past. The dialogue, nonetheless, remains oblivious to the privileged positions of the two men to pursue their *ikigai* on their own terms, something not afforded to many people during and after the war.

Residues of the empire in 'Shūchō no musume' (Chieftain's Daughter)

The endorsement of *ikigai* comes in subtle ways. A brief performance of the popular song 'Shūchō no musume' (Chieftain's Daughter, 1930) is one such scene. This is an additional feature found in both cinematic adaptations but not in Katō's original memoir. In the 1961 film, the performance highlights the overall enjoyment and *ikigai* shared among the actors and the audience. Yet, the film leaves the problematic assumptions of 'Shūchō no musume' and *ikigai* it has inspired unchallenged. In the 1961 adaptation, a dancer appears onstage alone against the background of tropical trees and the sun. The male dancer poses as the eponymous chieftain's daughter, donning a bandana and a bikini top with a sarong, with their face and body painted in brown. The audience and the other actors immediately cheer, sing and clap along to the upbeat musical accompaniment. Such reactions celebrate the effort of the *onnagata* actor to entertain the audience. However, the film fails to challenge the underlying assumptions of the song. The song is sung with slightly modified and truncated lyrics:

Watashi no raba-san, shūchō no musume
Iro wa kuroi ga Nanyō ja bijin
Sekidō-chokka, Māsharu Guntō
Yashi no kokage de teku-teku odoru

Odore, odore, dobroku nonde
Asu wa ureshii kubi no matsuri
Odore, odore, odoranu mono ni
Dare ga oyome ni yuku mono ka

The lyrics translate into English as follows:

My lover is the chieftain's daughter
She's black but in the South Seas she's a beauty
Down by the equator in the Marshall Islands,
in the shade of the palm trees
Dance, dance! Drink up your spirits!
Tomorrow is the happy headhunting feast.
Dance, dance! Who would [the daughter] marry if you don't dance?[30]

The lyrics and the performance reveal masculine heterosexual desire that was enmeshed in the attitudes present in imperial Japan. In his analysis of the song, Greg Dvorak contends that it creates iconic yet ambiguous images of the chieftain's daughter as the prize of imperial conquest. The daughter lures Japanese men into a romantic relationship in the Marshall Islands, which came under Japanese rule in 1914. Men need not worry about her dark skin, as her beauty and social standing compensate. The song warns of the putative laziness and savagery of the islanders. However, it dares Japanese men to drink and dance away their worries about 'going native' and primes them for interracial marriage.[31] As the performance of the song stimulates the sagging morale of the soldiers in the audience, it can also appeal to the viewers' residual nostalgia for 'the good old days' of the Japanese Empire.

Furthermore, the scene highlights the effect the performance makes on the soldiers' heterosexual desires. During the performance, raucous cheering from the audience encourages the dancer to make erotic moves. The dancer removes the bikini top and sarong, while giving a knowing look that warns that the chieftain's daughter is not the ingénue she appears to be. Next the camera shows the dancer from behind, facing the audience. As the song finishes, the dancer strips off the bottom piece of the bikini, revealing underpants covering the genitalia. This reminds the audience and the viewers that the dancer is, after all, a male. A soldier in the front row of the audience suddenly climbs onto the stage and tries to grab the dancer by the thigh. Other soldiers pull him back down and admonish him for getting carried away. When the curtains close, another soldier climbs onstage and puts his head between them to get a glimpse of the dancer. The scene swiftly ends when other soldiers force him off the stage. The two failed attempts signify the soldiers' impaired capacity to distinguish between fantasy and reality – even caricature – when their male desires are involved. The striptease by the *onnagata* and the audience's reaction seem to cause no qualms for the theatre group. Even Katō claps and cheers when the song begins. He then goes backstage to get ready for a play he is performing later. When the song ends, a member of the theatre group reports to Katō, 'Leader, it's a hit! Everyone loved it!' Katō nods and carries on with his preparation. His tacit approval implicates him in the chain of imperial nostalgia. Viewers may regard the scene as a relic of the bygone past. However, writing it off as simply a reflection of outdated views loses sight of the wider questions of imperial nostalgia that continues into the post-war years and the ideal of *ikigai* the film promotes.

A curtailed debate on *sange* and *nanshi*

The film presents the notions of glorious deaths (*sange*) and *nanshi* (meaningless death) but downplays the tension between them. In its place, the film amplifies the harmonious relationships between members of the theatre group. A cameo appearance of Lieutenant Mori is one such instance. Mori takes his troops to the theatre and performs a song between entertainment pieces. The following day, Mori lines up his troops and tells them that the enjoyment from the performance should leave all of them, himself included, with no regrets about leaving the camp and embarking on a march to Babo, south of Manokwari. The camera then shows the troops *en masse* but seldom focuses on their reactions. As the troops depart, Shinozaki mutters, 'I suppose they won't come back'. Katō replies, 'How sad it is to push such good people into the jaws of death'. The cameo ends with his response. The exchange signals the emotional capacity Shinozaki and Katō have to sympathize with the soldiers' impending fate. They see it as *nanshi* and not as *sange*. Although the scene is too brief to let this sentiment develop, it nonetheless functions as a building block in the narrative and serves as a source of *ikigai* for Katō and the theatre group.

The curtailed exploration of *nanshi* and *sange* aids the film's emphasis on the optimism of *ikigai* and Tōhō's 'forward-looking and healthy' ethos. The emphasis towards the post-war present comes with the absence of the context of the march. The march has roots in an actual operation that took place in July 1944. Of the 20,000 troops in Manokwari, the operation had 12,000 relocate to Idore, 170 kilometres south via Babo, and left the remaining 8,000 in Manokwari. The strategists intended to reduce the pressure to feed the troops in Manokwari, while getting the troops in Idore to start cultivating crops to sustain themselves. The march went ahead without gathering intelligence on the route and without enough food or supplies. By January 1946, only 800 of the original 12,000 survived to be repatriated to Japan. The remaining troops in Manokwari began farming under the direction of the new officier, Fukabori Yūki. Tanaka Hiromi credits Fukabori's measure for saving the lives of the soldiers, a directive that the commander of the Second Army Teshima Fusatarō should have adopted much earlier.[32] In his memoir, Katō notes how he envied the departing troops because Idore promised better prospects for survival. Only after the war did Katō learn that the march ended in colossal failure.[33] Katō's awareness highlights the slippage in the transition between Katō's memoir and the film. Reading the cameo against these contexts helps us see how Mori wanted to motivate himself and his subordinates to follow the script of *sange*. Whether Katō and Shinozaki anticipated or approved Mori's use of the theatre remains underexplored in the film adaptations.

The last glimpse of snow

The penultimate sequence in the film builds the momentum for the final scene where Katō states his *ikigai*. The sequence has the theatre group performing a play for troops from the Tōhoku region. The play features a scene of snowfall; Katō decided it would make the troops from the snowy region happy in the unlikely setting of Manokwari. Moreover, the snow signifies multiple layers of *ikigai* both for the audience and the theatre group. Seeing snow before their eyes even in the most hopeless times of war in the South Seas Islands could remind them that life is worth living. The experience could encourage them to be resilient so as to be able to see real snow back home again. In turn, the satisfaction the theatre group gives to the audience confirmed that their efforts were worthwhile.

When the curtains opened, the audience roared at the sight of the snowscape in the *mise-en-scène*. Snowflakes, made from cut pieces of paper, fall onto to the stage from a basket set above it. Behind the actors is a white backdrop made of unused parachutes. The camera closes in and fixates on the stunned faces of the soldiers watching the snowflakes, their eyes welling up with tears. The camera turns to the theatre group waiting in the wings, transfixed by the audience's reaction. Katō comments, 'Everyone must be reminiscing about their homes'.

Tsutayama chimes in, 'Everyone must be glad'. A sick and emaciated soldier named Ōsawa is in the audience for the performance. He begged his comrades to let him walk together to Manokwari from their base in Warpami, a few days' walk away, to 'see Japan just once' and promises his comrades that he will not be a burden. Ōsawa takes a piece of paper with the little energy he has left and puts it against his cheek.

Meanwhile, the play moves to a sword fight between Katō and Shinohara in the falling snow. Ōsawa's severely emaciated appearance arrests both actors' attention but the two soon regain their composure and complete the performance. Immediately after the play ends, Katō and the crew rush to Ōsawa and bring him onto the stage. Katō tells the crew to shake the basket to make snowflakes fall. As the camera focuses on snowflakes falling onto Ōsawa's face, his captain mutters, 'This is a lucky man. He saw snow at his death'. Katō suddenly bursts into tears and turns his back to Ōsawa. Tsutayama moves next to Ōsawa and promises to tell his family about his passing if he returns home alive. The camera zooms out as the theatre group and Ōsawa's comrades weep. Katō's narration brings the film to a close:

> Happy times, sad times. We had many memories and continued to perform plays to the best of our ability. We felt tremendous joy in supporting the soldiers to remember home and their parents. Our performances continued ceaselessly until the day repatriation ships arrived. In June 1946, together with 7,000 soldiers, we, the theatre group, stepped onto the real soil of our homeland.

Katō's concluding remark completes his nostalgic gaze at his discovery of *ikigai* and paints a self-portrait of a man humbled to find his *ikigai* out of his theatrical performance for the memory of the dead. Indeed, he made the best of the hopeless situation, building up the theatre group in unison under the common labour of love and while discovering his own *ikigai* and passing it to the others. The 1961 film marked a symbolic departure from the extant anti-war and revisionist moulds. The film waters down the questions of *nanshi* and *sange* and builds heroes out of an actor, rather than of a brawny soldier, who grows into the leader of the theatre group. The 'win-win' scenario makes a fitting tribute to Tōhō's vision. The message of *ikigai* seized upon the socio-economic and political climate of the time. Yet the film remains problematic; it plays up 'Shūchō no musume' and downplays the questions of casualty in the name of entertainment and giving *ikigai* to the theatre group and the audience.

The 1995 adaptation: Clashes between *sange* and *nanshi*

The 1995 adaptation overhauled the 1961 film into a tragedy arising from the inherent dilemma of *ikigai*, *sange* and *nanshi* of the theatre group. The film amplifies the dilemma but ultimately endorses *sange* and censures the individualistic desire of *ikigai*. Upon release, the film failed to garner public attention despite using well-known actors. Part of its lacklustre recognition comes from it being a low-budget independent production. A more significant reason may lie in its quality. The strong acting does not fully compensate for the sometimes confusing plot structure that extends the film to 134 minutes. A more decisive blow came from a short and caustic review in Japan's premier film magazine, *Kinema Junpō*. Film critic Masubuchi Tsuyoshi decries the film as a disappointment that ruins the fine first adaptation and hijacks its original narrative with a blatantly anti-war agenda.[34] In response, the director and scriptwriter, Mizushima Satoru (1949–) explains that making a faithful rendition of the memoir or the 1961 film was not his aim. Nor was it his intention to make an anti-war film. The memoir and the 1961 film gave him the setting to explore the problems of 'post-war Japan from the perspectives of wartime' and not from the vantage point of the post-war era.[35]

In his defence, Mizushima cites two reviews that praise his adaptation. Both reviews agree that Mizushima's adaptation accentuated the paradox of entertaining soldiers in wartime and succeeded in complicating the simplistic binary of anti- and pro-war or victim and perpetrator narratives.[36] Mizushima's motivation and the reviews mirror the renewed debate over acts of aggression that Japan committed in the name of empire and the war (Chapter 1). Masubuchi's review and Mizushima's counter-response underscore the role of the filmmaker in bringing new perspectives and interpretations into the historical film. A re-evaluation through the prism of *ikigai*, *sange* and *nanshi* not only helps in comparing this film with the 1961 film but also helps to probe how far the 1995 film challenged the anti- and pro-war binaries.

The conflicting attitudes towards life and death hold strong significance for Mizushima's film. In YouTube commentaries posted in 2013 and 2015, he explains that he wanted to pit the ethos of post-war democracy against the wrath of the deceased soldiers.[37] Mizushima explains that the suicide of the novelist Mishima Yukio (1925–70) gave him the original inspiration. During the 1960s, Mishima grew concerned about the corruption of Japanese nationalism. He envisaged reviving the national military and the imperial sovereign according to the pre-war constitution. To achieve his aim, he founded Tate-no-kai (the Shield Society), a private paramilitary group. In November 1970, Mishima and four members of the Shield Society entered the Tokyo Headquarters of the Self-Defence Force and took a commander as hostage. Mishima demanded the Self-Defence Force servicemen join his cause and stage a revolt. His words got drowned out by the noise of a helicopter hovering above. Jeers and indifference from the servicemen brought Mishima to commit ritual suicide in honour of the emperor.[38] Yoshikuni Igarashi and Oda Makoto understand Mishima's suicide as an anachronistic demonstration of the *sange* principles that he had embraced. The suicide made little impression on contemporary Japanese politics and brought the swift demise of the Shield Society.[39] The suicide made the then 21-year-old Mizushima ponder what Mishima wanted to say about the place of patriotism in a post-war Japan where the collective mood had swung to one of individualism. Mizushima further explains that Mishima's suicide motivated him to portray the anger of the deceased soldiers in a way that they 'did not die to see the post-war Japan turning out in the way it did'.[40]

Mizushima's question spawned alterations and new features in his film. The main plot revolves around tension between two characters espousing *nanshi* and *sange*. The protagonist Sudō, modelled after Katō, values an intrinsic purpose in human life, identifying acting as his *ikigai*. Sudō comes to view the soldiers' deaths as *nanshi*. Cast as Sudō's antagonist is his superior Lieutenant Murai. He embodies the ideology of *sange* in the image of Mishima. New features of the film are the subplots in the opening and ending sequences set in the post-war era. The film opens with a group of Japanese veterans visiting a fictitious location in New Guinea long after the war. They have come to find and repatriate Colonel Sudō, who has remained in the jungle ever since the war. In the course of their search, a local militiaman hired by the visitors accidentally shoots Sudō. Two of the visitors, Kanaya, Sudō's best wartime friend, and his daughter, call for help and sit beside him while waiting for the rescue to come. Sudō then begins to explain to the Kanayas why he had remained in New Guinea this whole time. The film then goes to the middle section where Sudō recalls his role as the leader of the theatre group. The final sequences bring us back to the present when Sudō finishes his reason for remaining in New Guinea before drawing his final breath.

The middle section involves Sudō's recollection of the activity of the theatre group and develops the schism between Sudō and Murai. Their first altercation concerns the choice of play for their inaugural performance. Sudō suggests *Mabuta no haha* (The Mother He Never Knew). The cinematic adaptation, released in 1931 (dir. Inagaki Hiroshi), was popular, and would have been familiar to the soldiers during the wartime. This play, set in the late Edo period, centres on a lone-wolf *samurai* named Chūtarō and his search for his estranged mother. When he finally meets her, his mother rejects him. He abandons all hope of for reconciliation and resumes his solitary existence.[41] Sudō believes that the play is appropriate because 'what soldiers think of the most on battlefields is our mothers' and it is the affection for the mother that gives hope for survival and meaning for life. Murai hesitates because '"mother stories" may give too much stimulation to soldiers'. After a pause, Murai changes his mind: 'If they see that play, everyone will have kind feelings as Japanese. I want the soldiers to die wonderfully as Japanese deserve'. It remains unclear exactly what he means by 'too much stimulation' and 'kind feelings as Japanese' and why he changed his mind. It is possible that Murai initially imagined that the play could provoke homesickness that would dampen the soldiers' morale. What Murai saw was that the play spoke to the essence of *sange*. Chūtarō's mother's rejection could encourage soldiers to channel their devotion to leaders and the nation instead of the mother.[42] His subsequent comment reinforces his belief that soldiers should 'die wonderfully' for Japan:

> From now on, all the soldiers seeing plays here will go straight to the front line. Looking at the way we are now, I suspect no one will return home alive. That's why this place becomes the last place for the soldiers to remember their homeland.

A startled Sudō asks, 'Is this a place for death?' Murai responds:

> Ultimately, yes. We are soldiers. Someday we must die for our nation. … We do our best to make [fellow soldiers] laugh, cry and make them reminisce about their homeland and their families. Even for a short moment, I want them to be happy and proud to have lived as Japanese. Sudō, we have to convince ourselves that this war is for our land and our families. If we don't do this, we cannot die properly. That's why we make them reminisce about their homeland and their mothers. Sudō, let's do *Mabuta no haha*.

Murai has shifted his understanding of the theatre group's purpose from boosting the morale of the soldiers to giving meaning to their eventual sacrificial deaths. Sudō is stunned to hear Murai's statement and only gives a feeble 'yes' in agreement. Murai's rationale highlights the point Mori's cameo made in the 1961 adaptation, when Murai justifies the theatre as a device to give meaning to soldiers' imminent deaths and throws doubts about Sudō's innocent belief in the theatre giving meaning to life.

From here onwards, Sudō's questions about the theatre and *sange* build up. At the end of the inaugural performance of *Mabuta no haha*, Murai's aide congratulates the theatre group for their fine performance. Sudō then asks, 'Everyone in the audience today was wearing a combat uniform. Are they going on an offensive somewhere?' Murai yells at Sudō. Murai's aide calms Murai down and answers, 'Certainly, the troops were moved to tears today. They are going to a difficult battle in Sorong. I am afraid they will not come back here again. I have to thank you on their behalf'. The aide shows his loyalty to his superior and explains that the purpose of the performance is to prime soldiers to accept their death as inevitable. Murai's aide then orders the theatre group to prioritize performing for units that are about to embark on offensives. When he leaves, another member of the troupe, a singer, asks Murai, 'Are we telling our comrades "You are going to go and die well?"' Murai retorts, 'You bastard! Don't answer back! Don't ruin the morale of our Imperial Armed Forces!' He punches him so hard that he falls to the floor. The singer stands up and apologizes. Murai yells at him: 'Sing each and every song with your heart and soul!' This dialogue illustrates the clash between followers of *sange* and *nanshi* and reflects the hierarchy in the military. Together with Murai's insistence, the officers use the rhetoric of *sange* to justify the deaths of their subordinates as an inevitable consequence. The scene obscures the questions of their deaths as *nanshi* and imposes the doctrine of *sange* as the officer's command to the theatre group.

The Japanese flag in the nationalist theatre

The nationalistic purpose of the theatre manifests in features other than the plot and dialogue. The Japanese flag and its symbolism are silent yet noticeable elements of the 1995 film that the 1961 film seldom employs. One scene that makes this message clear is the performance of 'Shūchō no musume'. Like the 1961 film, the 1995 film features the performance as a short segment between theatrical pieces. The performance attenuates racial and sexual undertones and pushes the nationalist message within the broad framework of imperial conquest. As the curtain opens, seven men with skin covered in brown paint and wearing grass skirts sing the song and dance with exaggerated and robotic movements. As the song begins an *onnagata* dancer appears and takes the centre stage halfway through the song. Exciting the soldiers' sexual desires does not seem to be the primary objective of this performance. The dancer's muscular physicality is devoid of any eroticism and instead of a striptease, the costume is retained until the end. Next, the camera shows us the back of the *onnagata* looking towards the audience. In the background is a large Japanese flag hanging on the wall at the far end. As the song ends, the curtain comes down where we see a large Japanese flag stitched onto the front of it. The repeated appearance of the Japanese flag reminds the soldiers that they are first and foremost Japanese, and the theatre exists for the national and imperialist purpose of the war. The point becomes evident in the camera work that shows the audience as one faceless mass, a well-behaved crowd without the frenzied reactions of a few individuals.

As with the 1961 adaptation, the performance taps into the cultural roots of the Japanese imperial imaginary of the South Seas but emphasizes conquest. The seven men evoke minstrel performers seen in the West and like the Pacific islander males in Shimada Keizō's popular manga series *Bōken Dankichi* (Adventures of Dankichi, 1933–9). In a manner similar to *Robinson Crusoe*, it charts the boy-to-king growth of Dankichi following his accidental arrival on a fictitious South Seas Island. Dankichi recruits male islanders, defeats his foes and builds his kingdom. The manga earned its place as a made-for-boys iteration in the Japanese discourse of *nanshin-ron* (the South Seas advance) legitimizing the Japanese mandate of the South Seas Islands.[43] The seven male dancers are no mere symbolic nod to these cultural figures. The presence of the males further implies that Japanese men must subjugate the islander men before laying claim to the chieftain's daughter. The flag reminds the soldiers to take pride as the imperial representatives of a higher culture.

In addition to the actual flag, its symbolism acts as another silent prop in support of the nationalistic orientation of the theatre and the affect it had on soldiers. One such reaction comes from Corporal Shirane. Previously, his platoon went on an all-out mission that should have ended in everyone in the unit being killed. The survival of the unit meant Shirane's failure to fulfil the patriotic ethos and he became the target of ridicule. After seeing *Mabuta no haha*, Shirane thanks Sudō for providing him with the motivation to live without the shame of survival. Several months later, Shirane's platoon returns for another performance. Afterwards, Shirane tells Sudō that he has decided to lead his platoon on a mission to collect barrels of food from a submarine. Sudō knows that the mission is tantamount to suicide and tries to dissuade Shirane. Shirane responds that the play reminded him of home, his family as well as his dead comrades and motivated him to volunteer for the mission. If his platoon never returns, their families will know that their loved ones enacted the spirit of *sange*. Sudō cannot contain his dismay:

Sudō	[*Slowly*] You are decent soldiers. You are too decent. But I disagree [*Shirane interjects*].
Shirane:	Corporal, we are going on the mission. Please let us think that our deaths are valuable. Please. [*Looks Sudō in the eyes.*] We will not die in vain. We will fight hard so that we can come back.

Shirane's words border on naivety and betray Sudō's idealism. Shirane's conversion proves the nationalistic purpose of the theatre assailed Sudō's hope for what the theatre group could achieve. Furthermore, the camera work contrasts Shirane's assured face with Sudō's dismay. The following scene turns to the shoreline in the twilight. The wreckage of the vessels and dead bodies announce the deaths of the entire platoon. An aerial view of a dead soldier shows his body lying on the beach, without his left arm and left leg. Underneath his body is a large round white patch, presumably rice or flour. The blood from his head makes a round red patch which, when seen against the white background, evokes images of the Japanese flag. The dismembered body confirms Sudō's premonition about the mission ending in futile death. However, the imagery of the flag accentuates the sacrificial aspects of the mission. Shirane's change of heart and his platoon's death reinscribe the centuries-old and well-revered cultural trope of the tragic hero that 'recognized a special nobility in the sincere, unsuccessful sacrifice.'[44] The film makes a muted yet firm case of the theatre group succeeding in preparing soldiers for sacrificial deaths.

The final confrontation

The film moves quickly. Murai orders the dissolution of the theatre group as the news of the Japanese defeat reaches Dutch New Guinea. The next sequence brings Sudō and Murai into a final confrontation whereby Mizushima's endorsement to *sange* crystallizes. Murai fulfils his desire to die in the *sange* mould. Sudō bears the consequence of his personal ambition and settles for a life of consoling the spirits of his comrades. The two meet on a beach and discuss how best to console the souls of the dead. Murai regrets 'driving them beyond the limits of what humans can bear' and praises the soldiers for their obedience and fortitude. He then directs his anger at his superiors and commanders, whom he thinks are concerned about evading their responsibility and going home. He continues: 'I despise them. They praise the dead only in words. They are only thinking of how to live comfortably now. How many soldiers died as a result of my commands?' He decides to take personal responsibility for his part in Japan's defeat by killing the commanders first and having Sudō kill Murai. Sudō immediately rejects Murai's request and asserts that the appropriate way of consoling the spirits of the dead is to continue living on behalf of the dead. Sudō asks: 'Isn't this what the dead want us to do?' Murai responds: 'They won't be so kind to let us survivors leave [New Guinea]. They'll be angry and sad. They resent us and say, "What are you going to do!?" Sudō, around me are dead soldiers. Do you see them?'

After a long pause Sudō only mutters 'No'. Murai says he can see the dead beckoning him and the commanders. He resolves to kill the commanders himself. He explains:

'There are times when people choose death for certain causes instead of living for the sake of living. Choosing death is a way of living! Just like the soldiers who died in battles. Clinging on to life like rotten women is like insulting the heroes who died in battles!' Murai's insult provokes Sudō's retort:

Sudo: That's nonsense! Like you say, the dead soldiers cannot die properly even if they wanted to. [*Eyes tearful*] They're angry and screaming 'What are you going to do!?' Whatever people say, until yesterday, the soldiers died like dogs. They died pathetic and meaningless deaths. You can't use beautiful words to fool me.

Murai: That's why I, as a soldier, an officer, am going to die to take responsibility. This is my duty and responsibility.

Murai and Sudō come to a head. They perceive that the spirits of the dead are speaking to them in conflicting languages of *sange* and *nanshi*. Each believes that unless the living act on the wishes of the dead, they will not depart to the other world. Sudō's sympathy with *nanshi* develops into his newly found desire for *ikigai* towards self-actualization through purposeful living. Fulfilling *ikigai* matters to him and his comrades, as a more responsible way to respond to the dead's desire for the lives they have lost. Murai still disagrees. Sudō puts his gun down and continues:

> [*Slowly zooming in on Sudō's face*] I am an actor. I live to be watched, to be laughed at and to be cried at. It doesn't matter how pathetic I look. It doesn't matter if I am a coward, poor or hungry! [*Bursts into tears*] All I want to show in my acting is that life is wonderful! I don't want to act to glorify death! I don't want to see death anymore. I cannot let you have your way. [*Sudō aims the pistol at Murai*]

Sudō's assertion renounces his life as a soldier and the hypocritical rhetoric of *sange* and seeks to pursue acting to fulfil his *ikigai*. Murai remains unimpressed and commands Sudō, 'Shoot me ... This is war. Shoot!' Sudō shoots up in the sky and swears he will never kill his comrades and challenges Murai to shoot him instead. Sudō's word infuriated Murai as the former subordinate now takes the moral high ground and exposes the personal motive beneath the veneer of *sange*. He regains composure, grows silent and shoots himself in the temple. His sudden suicide sends Sudō into shock and then a coma. A voice-over by the older Sudō explains that on 18 August 1945 he escaped the barracks into the bush and had lived there by himself until now.

The confrontation signals different kinds of retreat into *sange*. Murai achieved his self-actualization of *sange* through his suicide; Sudō's retreat surrendered his personal ambition to the emotional pull of his comrades' spirits. Murai's death seems to pay homage to Mishima's, as was the imprint it had on Mizushima. However, the context makes the allusion tenuous. Mishima acted on his desire to restore Japan's imperial spirits in a changed Japan. Murai's suicide sought to preserve his dignity before he became an outdated and outmoded relic of the wartime. His reaction to Sudō's provocation relates to a finding by John W. Dower: Japanese soldiers committed suicide for reasons other than patriotic sacrifice, such as the fear of disgrace at home and killing and torture by the Allies captors.[45] Beneath Murai's claim of 'duty and responsibility' was his reticence to face an uncertain future. Murai's suicide fulfilled his wish and unleashed his anger at Sudō. His death sends Sudō into a coma and a hurried sequence of two scenes pulls Sudō into conflicting impulses. The first has Shirane and his platoon beckoning Sudō to stay behind to console their spirits and the second brings us back to the present, where he is still in a coma. Kanaya's daughter persuades him to return to Japan. However, Sudō refuses, saying 'everyone is here'. He then finds himself on a rescue helicopter with the Kanayas. Through the window Sudō sees snowflakes in the setting sun. He then regains consciousness, lying flat on a field with the Kanayas sitting beside him. Sudō mutters 'snow' and draws his final breath before the helicopter arrives. This denouement ultimately punishes Sudō for his conviction about the soldiers' deaths as *nanshi* and the pursuit of his *ikigai* as individualistic ambition.

From a cinematic perspective, the closing sequence rushes to the end and can confuse the audience. From a historiographical perspective, the scenes send a conservative message often found in Japanese war-retro films. Mizushima's adaptation smacks of the hit war film *Biruma no tategoto* (The Burmese Harp, 1950 and 1985). In this film, a Japanese prisoner of war in a British camp volunteers to persuade his fellow comrades who are still resisting surrender. Following his failed attempt, he sustains injury in an artillery attack. On his way back to the camp, he sees bodies of soldiers in the countryside and decides to stay in Burma to console the spirits of the dead.[46] Both films have their protagonists forgo their post-war personal lives and confine them in an imagined space during the wartime where they continue to dedicate their lives not to the emperor or the empire but to their vanquished comrades' spirits.

Conclusion

This chapter has demonstrated how memoir-to-film adaptations offer fertile insight into how memory travels across media and time. Each rendition of *Minami-no-shima* reflects the *zeitgeist* and the film-makers' interests. The characteristic becomes evident through in the ways the films address *ikigai*, *sange* and *nanshi*. The 1961 film retains the 'happy-ending' forward- and future-looking ethos of Katō's original memoir. The drama recasts Katō's discovery of *ikigai* as inherently desirable and endorses the transformation of the veterans of his rank and age in the post-war economic recovery. The celebration of *ikigai* characterized the ebullient mood of the 1960s and deviated from the thorny tension between *sange* and *nanshi*. The 1995 film is a tragedy that revisits and amplifies this tension through the figures of Sudō and Murai. The idealistic Sudō becomes 'the good Japanese' who suffers for his principles. Murai is the 'the military hero' who fulfils his desire for *sange* and maintains his dignity before he becomes an outmoded relic of the past like Mishima. The shock Sudō feels about Murai's suicide prompts him to stay on the island. This conclusion ultimately privileges a nationalist interpretation that honours the spirits of the dead and punishes Sudō for his ambition to pursue his *ikigai*.

One common limitation shared by the two adaptations is the sexist and racist residue of the Japanese empire and military masculine mindset. One striking example is the performance of 'Shūchō no musume'. The 1961 film masks its imperialist assumptions in the guise of light-hearted entertainment but legitimizes the racist and sexist nostalgia. The 1995 film replaces the prurient excitement with the nationalistic and even imperial mission of the war. This chapter has shown that *Minami-no-shima* is a malleable and versatile text deserving greater attention beyond the emblematic snowfall episode. Despite the differences, both films present the war and New Guinea as exclusively Japanese domains. Neither cinematic adaptation addresses the issues of Japan's wartime responsibility in relation to the local residents and the Allies. This lacuna becomes a focal point of the documentaries that the next chapter explores.

5

Documentaries as co-performative partnership: Framing and presenting testimonies of painful memories

In addition to feature films, documentaries are a vibrant historical medium that transports historical memories across temporal and geographical realms. The documentary is not simply a storehouse of historical information; its audio and visuals form a narrative vehicle which can pass down memories and opinions on the subject matter and maintain its own conventions and effects which written history may not adequately address. Of the many documentaries on the Asia-Pacific War made by Japanese-born film-makers, this chapter analyses four that focus on the New Guinea campaign. Three are made-for-cinema and available on DVDs: *Yukiyukite Shingun* (dir. Hara Kazuo, 1987, 122 minutes) and *Senjō no onna tachi* (dir. Sekiguchi Noriko, 1989, 55 minutes) and its English version *Sensō Daughters* (1990, 55 minutes). The fourth, *Nyūginia ni chitta 16-man no seishun* (dir. Ushiyama Jun'ichi, 1991, 96 minutes) is a television documentary available to the public at three archives.[1] This chapter asks how the documentaries function as a co-performative space between the film-maker and the subjects to elicit emotions from the viewers. Under scrutiny are seminal scenes in the four documentaries and how the film-makers frame and present testimonies with considerable variations. This chapter argues that the variations are manifestations of the film-makers' exercise of their creative input in projecting their views of history.

One crucial commonality shared by the four documentaries is the timing of the original releases and broadcast. These occurred during a pivotal transition period between Phases 2 and 3 as outlined in Chapter 1. Vital to this transition is the death of Emperor Hirohito in January 1989. It rekindled debates over his wartime responsibility and the positioning of soldiers in the war as victims or perpetrators and marked a watershed in Japan's long post-war period. This was clearly a significant moment in the trajectories of Japan's travelling memories, and many of the Japanese veterans and Papua New Guineans with direct war experience were still alive to share their testimonies. The film-makers were able to record their voices for future generations who will remember and interpret them as memories.

The question as to whether the documentary constitutes a legitimate medium of history leads us to clarify what a documentary is and does. Stella Bruzzi insists that the documentary can never represent the real world as if the camera were absent. She suggests that a more fruitful approach is to think of the documentary as 'the results of this collision between [filming] apparatus and subject' and 'a negotiation between filmmaker and reality and, at heart, a performance'.[2] Particularly useful in extending this understanding of a documentary is John Ellis's application of Erving Goffman's analysis of communication to the performative aspects of the documentary. Goffman asks, 'What is it that is going on here?' Ellis asks, 'What is it that is *really* going on in the framing of a documentary event, both when it is being filmed and when it is being watched?'[3] These questions prompt attentiveness to the way in which a documentary draws the audience into the film-maker's ambit. One method involves the documentary creating a rapport with the audience through its presentation of co-performance between the film-maker and the subject. Beinda Smaill extends Bruzzi's conception of the documentary to analyse expressions of pain by subjects of documentaries. Smaill stresses that representing pain as a subjective or objective experience is not an end in itself. Rather, engaging the audience's emotions has the social purpose of evoking the viewers' empathy towards the subject and prompting awareness of the issues. The audience reaction can help empower the subject towards self-actualization.[4]

Taken together, understanding what happens on screen and recognizing its performative character demands attention to three contextual aspects. First, it is vital to recognize that the subject performs on camera, however much or little the subject is conscious of the camera and the power it imposes on the subject. What matters here are the exposition, dialogues, facial expressions and gestures. Second, the film-maker exerts varying levels of directorial influence on the subject. To this end, wherever available, the analysis in this chapter draws on publicly available sources on the subjects and the film-makers. Third, the film-maker edits the recorded footage and mixes it with other sources to make a coherent narrative. The placement and sequencing of scenes in relation to the entire documentary are not arbitrary decisions. This process of drawing on multiple sources, selecting episodes or scenes and organizing them in a particular way, exemplifies how the production of the film-maker is in many ways analogous to that of the professional historian. Exploring how documentaries engage the audience and elicit their emotions requires a close analysis of descriptive details.

Yukiyukite Shingun: Excessive rage impeding engagement with painful memories

Yukiyukite Shingun (hereafter *Shingun*) follows the rage-riven Okuzaki Kenzō (1920–2005), a private in the 36th Independent Engineering Regiment, deployed to New Guinea in 1943.[5] The bulk of *Shingun* consists of Okuzaki's interrogation of ex-officers from his unit. He pursues the truth behind the execution of two soldiers for the offence of desertion in the face of the enemy (*tekizen tōbō*) that occurred twenty-three days after Japan's surrender. The ex-officers' reluctance and evasive and conflicting answers are remiscient of *Rashōmon* (dir. Kurosawa Akira, 1950) to viewers, but frustrate Okuzaki. He makes violent threats and bursts into not just one but two fights captured on screen. *Shingun* goes as far as implying that the officers executed the two soldiers for their reluctance to participate in cannibalism.[6]

Shingun impressed domestic and international reviewers. They praise Hara for exposing the limits of the victim narrative and provoking questions about the chain of command that goes all the way to Emperor Hirohito. Okuzaki's character divided the critics.[7] Yoshimoto Takaaki reveals his feelings towards Okuzaki as '60 per cent nauseating shock … 30 per cent confused shock, and 10 per cent refreshing shock', albeit without reference to the corresponding scenes.[8] In a different vein, Karatani Kōjin felt '100 per cent empathy' towards Okuzaki.[9] A full scene-by-scene study by Jeffrey and Kenneth Ruoff argues that Okuzaki's fanatical obsession for truth and justice prompt erratic and comical behaviour. The Ruoffs believe that Hara's concentration on Okuzaki's present life contributed to a portrayal of Okuzaki as a comic anti-hero lacking in psychological depth.[10] Ellis's question – what is happening in the framing of the scenes during the filming and as the final product – complements these other reviews, especially the Ruoffs's, and aids in reinterpreting *Shingun*. While many extant reviews revolve around Okuzaki's personality and antics, reading the film as co-performance can make a helpful intervention in these reviews that revolve around Okuzaki's antics. This analysis agrees with the Ruoffs's insight but looks into the ways Okuzaki's on-screen personality resulted from Hara's off-screen input.

Of several examples, the initial twenty-eight minutes are a fast-paced dazzling sequence that brings Okuzaki's eccentricity to the fore. Okuzaki attends a wedding where he hijacks an opportunity to give a speech. He announces that he spent a total of thirteen years and nine months in prison for three offences – two of which involved his shooting a slingshot at the emperor at the imperial palace and the other for distributing leaflets with pornographic portrayals of the imperial family. We see Okuzaki driving his car, equipped with a PA system, from his home in Kobe to central Tokyo on the emperor's birthday. He announces himself as a survivor of the war and continues with an impassioned speech in which he 'consoles the souls of soldiers victimized by Emperor Hirohito' and challenges the assembling police to apprehend him. The sequence then shifts the tone and reveals Okuzaki's tender side. He goes to Etajima in Hiroshima prefecture and meets Shimamoto Iseko, the mother of a deceased veteran. He chokes with emotion and weeps, as he recalls how her son was buried in New Guinea. Okuzaki sits beside her at her son's grave. He watches sympathetically as she sings a song about a mother going to a pier every day expecting her son's return from the war. Then, Okuzaki visits the graves of his comrades. As he pays his respect, he looks deep in thought at the grave and remains silent. The entire opening sequence not only hints at the gamut of Okuzai's emotions – rage, sorrow and grief – but also mesmerizes and entices the audience to learn more about what lies beneath Okuzaki's hatred of the emperor.

The sequence represents Hara's approach to film-making, what he calls the 'action documentary'. It resembles participant observation where the film-maker maintains a minimal presence and is largely absent from the screen whereby the camera follows the subject.[11] The film unfolds what turns out to be Okuzaki's personal mission – interrogating the ex-officers. Okuzaki turns up at the veterans' houses unannounced and well dressed in a suit and a tie to surprise them, like the grim reaper catching them unawares. His interrogation technique consists of continual pressuring the veterans to tell the truth on camera for the sake of the war dead. He occasionally erupts into anger to threaten them with violence. Hara strings these interrogations together with the minimal use of intertitles and without voice-overs to pass his judgement. *Shingun* challenges the audience to make sense of inconsistent and haphazard testimonies and work out the web of personal connections. Hara's conspicuous absence on camera can thus challenge the audience to work out 'what is going on' in the film and what drives Okuzaki's search for truth.

Hara's 'action documentary' method has an additional co-performative element. One could argue that Hara's camera encouraged Okuzaki to put on such a heated performance. During the course of filming, Hara found that Okuzaki became more difficult to work with. Okuzaki repeatedly insisted Hara capture him in the image of the action hero and even instructed him how to film Okuzaki. His demands grew so burdensome that Hara vowed he would not want to work with Okuzaki again.[12] One scene that illustrates this tension and polarized the audience's reactions is his confrontation with Yamada Kichitarō, an ex-Sergeant. The penultimate sequence of twenty-two minutes is the longest in *Shingun*. The sequence starts with Okuzaki visiting Yamada at his house with his wife, his associate and the crew. The scene inserts a vignette from the opening twenty-eight-minute sequence. Okuzaki visits a bedridden Yamada in the hospital and tells him that his recurrent illness was the work of divine retribution (*tenbatsu*) for his failure to confess his wartime deeds. Now at Yamada's house, the hospital scene gains clarity. Okuzaki believes that Yamada was complicit in the execution of soldiers for their reluctance to participate in cannibalism and demands that Yamada speak the truth as the best form of consoling the spirits of his dead comrades. By this stage, Okuzaki's technique has lost its freshness and become routine. Yet, what is different is that of all the ex-Sergeants Okuzaki confronts, Yamada puts up the stiffest resistance to Okuzaki's interrogation technique. Yamada states his point of view, and questions Okuzaki's violent approach as well as Hara's complicity in it. Conversely, Okuzaki repeats his accusation that divine retribution explains Yamada's recurrent illness.

As with the rest of *Shingun*, Hara's 'hands-off' approach sets the stage for Okuzaki's one-dimensional performance. Yamada's resistance adds new dramatic tension in a similar manner to the dialogue between Sudō and Murai seen in the previous chapter. Okuzaki and Yamada discuss the most conscionable way to console the spirits of the dead. Yamada refuses to speak because he has vowed to remain silent about certain matters. Yamada says: 'I make my offering to the dead in my way. You must be doing it your way. I do it my way'. He goes on to deny that his illness has anything to do with divine retribution for his alleged part in the war and his silence. Rather, Yamada's commitment to silence is a means to protect himself. Viewers may deduce the wartime left Yamada and Okuzaki in considerable pain. Hara's editing gives Yamada a greater claim to sympathy from the audience and contrasts with and even undermines the sympathetic responses Okuzaki has thus far garnered.

The next phase of the encounter between the two men illustrates a dynamic interplay of the subjects, situation and director. Okuzaki's aggression sets the agenda of the next sequence. Okuzaki's performance as a man locked into his own anger comes to the fore again. Just when Yamada has made his point, he begins to elaborate: 'Even if I went to the Yasukuni shrine'. At this moment Okuzaki loses control of himself and shouts: 'You think the spirits of the glorious dead will be saved if you go to Yasukuni, you bastard!?' Notable here is the change in the way Okuzaki addresses Yamada. Until this moment Okuzaki called Yamada *anata*, a polite and formal 'you'. However, at this juncture Okuzaki uses *kisama*, a variant of 'you' that implies condescension and contempt. He steps onto the floor with his shoes on – a major social *faux pas* in Japan – that signals his disrespect in deed as well as in word. Yamada's wife intervenes but to no avail. Okuzaki pushes Yamada down on the floor, throttles, kicks him with his shoes on, and injures both Yamada and Okuzaki's wife who has tried to stop the fight.

Yamada: [*Looking to the camera*] Can you see Okuzaki's being violent with me!? [*Yamada's grandson comes in but gets overwhelmed and retreats*]
Okuzaki: Why don't you say it!?
Yamada: You won't understand however much I say.
Okuzaki: You killed people! Tell the truth!

This second fight of Okuzaki in *Shingun* may polarize the audience and is likely to prompt sympathy for Yamada as a victim of Okuzaki's rage. Hara recalls that the turn of events was unexpected and gripped him with uncanny compulsion to continue filming.[13] His decision to continue filming at this point contributes to how Okuzaki's rage dominates this episode. This in turn hinders the development of more nuanced perspectives on Okuzaki's complex wartime memories.

What lies behind Yamada's incomplete sentence remains uncertain and Okuzaki never fully expresses himself. The closest Okuzaki gets to doing so occurs when he tells Hara to record him at a spirit consoling ceremony at Yasukuni where he assaults the staff.[14] John Breen argues that at the base of Okuzaki's revulsion are the different responses that Yasukuni elicits. Its defenders see Yasukuni as commemorating the soldiers' glorious sacrifices for the nation and absolving them of wrongdoing. The living can perform rites to find solace and relieve their trauma. The critics of Yasukuni contend that it denies the pain, suffering and death soldiers suffered and inflicted upon others in the name of war. Okuzaki may have deduced that Yamada also thought the soldiers sacrificed themselves for the nation, not as victims of the emperor and his subordinates.[15] Okuzaki's sudden outburst not only conveys the depth of his anger but also reduces him to an object of spectacle – as an anti-comic hero.

The next two scenes undermine the little empathetic capacity Okuzaki has shown so far and, correspondingly, may limit audience engagement. The progression of these scenes shows that Okuzaki's rage is the dominant motif of the documentary and thereby inhibits a creative rethinking of war memories. Initially, it appears as if Okuzaki has been able to calm his rage and gain a fresh understanding of Yamada's situation. When the scuffle subsides, Yamada reveals that other soldiers excluded him from the execution plans because he had valuable skills in bush craft and finding food. Then, the scene cuts to Okuzaki kneeling down and apologizing for his behaviour. Okuzaki's sudden change of heart shows his apparent contrition for making an erroneous assumption about Yamada's culpability. Okuzaki subsequently learns about the gravity of Yamada's health issues, and offers to take responsibility for the injury, as if to make amends for his earlier divine retribution comment. These gestures can demonstrate Okuzaki's respect for Yamada as a fellow victim of extreme privation and his integrity in abstaining from cannibalism. However, the next scene immediately sabotages his contrite gesture. Okuzaki and his wife are standing outside the hospital where Yamada has gone. Okuzaki looks into the camera, and expresses his regret about inflicting damage on Yamada, but maintains: 'As long as I am alive, by my judgement and responsibility, if violence can bring good results for humanity, I will use plenty of it.' His line of reasoning, told with a poker face, shows no moral or ethical qualms. In a review, Akira Iriye finds that Okuzaki's logic resembles that of Japanese officers' justification of violence on their subordinates as being the emperor's divine will and shows his inability to recognize or adapt to post-war democratic reforms. The residue of Okuzaki's wartime mentality brings Iriye to suspect Okuzaki's background had a part.[16]

Iriye's speculation amplifies the Ruoffs's critique and necessitates an exploration into Okuzaki's past. To fill the gaps, Yuki Tanaka looks into Okuzaki's writing to understand him from his earlier years to the 1980s. Born to a poverty-stricken family, he dabbled in Christianity as a youth and believed in an equal society where no one suffered from poverty or oppression. During the war, like many low-ranking soldiers, he experienced extensive bullying by his superiors. While many soldiers put up and shut up, Okuzaki hit back at the officers.[17] By July 1944, he was emaciated and had his right thigh and the little finger of his right hand injured in an Allies' attack – he subsequently lost the latter. He encountered sorry sights of corpses covered with maggots, emaciated soldiers begging him to kill them, and pigs eating emaciated soldiers. He had little energy left and decided to surrender. He was one of two survivors in his 350-troop company.[18]

This backstory can explain Okuzaki's on-screen violence-prone persona and accentuate another aspect of his character as a one-man social activist who addresses Japan's ills, like David taking on the Goliath. Hara thinks of Okuzaki's pursuit as 'monomaniacal' but concedes it as a plausible manifestation of his trauma and an equally plausible reaction to post-war Japan's sanitizing of historical memory.[19] This is an aspect *Shingun* has overlooked. As if to fill the void, Tanaka elaborates on how Okuzaki's utopianism developed into his fervent anti-Emperor stance. In 1956, he was convicted for murdering an estate agent. In ten years of solitary confinement, Okuzaki developed an eclectic blend of 'utopian anarchism and a vaguely Christian religious idea'.[20] Okuzaki saw the nation-state as evil, and the continuation of the imperial system and Emperor Hirohito in the post-war era as an embodiment of this inequality continuing into post-war Japan. Upon release from prison, Okuzaki expended his energy to challenge the legality of the imperial institution. Okuzaki's rage and his paradoxical behaviour captured on-screen mask his trauma and the evolution of his beliefs. *Shingun* has given Okuzaki too generous a platform that has ended up engendering a divided emotional engagement with the audience.

Senjō no onna tachi/Sensō Daughters: Co-performing victimhood and self-advocacy

Although overlooked in the mainstream Japanese media, *Senjō no onna tachi* (Women on Battlegrounds, hereafter *Senjō*) earned accolades from Japan's prominent film scholar Satō Tadao. He commended the film for presenting a 'very rare' portrayal of the Japanese as perpetrators and made this stance very clear to viewers.[21] *Senjō* and its English version *Sensō Daughters* (Daughters of War, hereafter *Daughters*) probe virtually unknown aspects of the New Guinea campaign: the operation of comfort stations in Rabaul in which comfort women served the sexual needs of the Japanese and where sexual violence was inflicted on local women.[22] Sekiguchi's documentaries argue that the women bore the brunt of triple discrimination based on race, gender and civilian status. The documentaries become works of co-performance between Sekiguchi and the women she interviews. The women represent themselves and fulfil the roles of social actors who articulate similar experiences of other women. Affective engagement with the women is the salient outcome and Sekiguchi's aim. Differences in editing and subtitles can bring about minor yet consequential variations in the responses each film engenders.

Sekiguchi's motivation for film-making is not a prominent part in *Daughters* or *Senjō*. However, her comments underline the importance of travel on her desire to make the documentaries. Sekiguchi was studying international relations at the Australian National University, when one of her classes screened a documentary, *Angels of War: World War II and the People of Papua New Guinea* (dir. Andrew Pike, Hank Nelson, Gavan Daws and John Waiko, 1982). It features testimonies of the brutal treatment by the Australians and the Japanese towards Papua New Guineans. What Sekiguchi admired about the documentary was that a team of Australians and Papua New Guineans subverted the benign view of the Australians as the liberators and presented the Papua New Guineans' perception of the Australians as invaders in disguise. She then grew motivated to make a documentary that probed the Japanese presence in the same vein while addressing the absence of females in *Angels of War*.[23]

Senjō and *Daughters* share many similarities in the footage and the structure, but this does not make them identical film. Sekiguchi believes that *Senjō* and *Daughters* are separate yet complementary works that she tailored to the English- and Japanese-speaking audiences.[24] Many variations, some clear and some less so, separate the two documentaries. For instance, the titles suggest nuanced differences in the portrayal of women's experiences. The Japanese title, *Senjō no onna tachi*, gives prominence to the hidden roles of women on the battleground such as those who were offering farm produce to soldiers and became prey to theft, violence and sexual assaults. The English version shows these themes too but bears a different title, *Sensō Daughters*, meaning 'daughters of war,' which juxtaposes with the Japanese word *Sensō* and the English word *Daughters*. The apparent mismatch implies that the war entailed the Japanese invasion of the villages. For instance, *Daughters* explains the difference between the Western perception of the Second World War and the way the Japanese remember the Asia-Pacific War, seeing the New Guinea campaign as a collision point between Japan and Australia. In *Daughters*, Sekiguchi makes greater use of voice-overs to create an additional subtext. She explains that making the documentary was a way to overcome her ignorance of the New Guinea campaign and was also a means to present female perspectives to counter the usual male-centred narratives of war. In *Senjō*, however, Sekiguchi has less of a vocal presence, but she gives prominence to Joseph Kanaka, a man in Bougainville who worked under the Japanese in his youth. He speaks a smattering of Japanese and praises the valiant efforts the Japanese put up against the Allies. Kanaka's loyalty to the Japanese makes a counter-narrative to the one of violence Japanese committed against PNG females.

Sekiguchi's commitment to co-performance comes most clearly in her attempts to give agency to her interviewees. An interview with Makunia Noira of Bougainville Island is one example where Sekiguchi makes her directorial intervention in the way she places different emphasis. In both documentaries, her testimony appears at the fortieth minute and lasts about nine minutes. The scene starts with Noira and another woman, Angela Pirigi, who translates Noira's vernacular into Tok Pisin, while they sit next to each other on the beach. Both women wear red dresses, seemingly exhibiting solidarity and preparedness to talk on camera. For the first time in forty years, Noira speaks about being coerced into a sexual relationship with a Japanese soldier, named Kojima, in Rabaul where Noira and her husband had moved to work on a banana plantation. Noira recounts that she fell pregnant to Kojima and had the baby. Noira's testimony underscores that sexual violence occurred in informal settings outside the more organized system of the military comfort women stations. Noira's recollection squarely places the Japanese male as the perpetrator, even going so far as to bringing up his name, and so undermines the more common narratives that viewed the Japanese as heroes or as victims.

Their performance, together with Sekiguchi's editorial role, prompts Ellis's question about what is happening during the filming and on the film, and invites attention to the self-presentation and the mediated presentation of a traumatized subject as well as the emotions that the documentaries can elicit. *Senjō* presents Noira speaking in her vernacular, her words are translated in the Japanese subtitles. In *Daughters*, another woman, Angela Pirigi, who sits beside Noira, translates Noira's words into Tok Pisin, which appear in English subtitles. In *Senjō*, Noira's speech is slow, steady and clear. Her eyes are mostly downcast and only occasionally does she look up:

> One day, when I was alone, [Kojima] came along, and suddenly held me tight. I said, 'Stop' and refused, but then I was held with a strong force (*tsuyoi chikara de dakarete*). [He said] 'I like you', and I got pushed down. But my son does not yet know that his father is Japanese. My father thinks that he [the son's father] comes from Buin, where I come from. Only I, the mother, know the truth – But my son's skin is not as dark as us. So, there were rumours. Several times I tried to tell the truth, but I couldn't, up to now – How would my son react if he sees this film? At any rate, he may be able to listen calmly if someone else told the story. I decided to come on this film. I wanted someone to research if the man is still alive.

Noira declares herself a victim of triple discrimination by gender, race and civilian status, but resists being a passive victim. She speaks to inform the viewers about the trauma she has lived with and wishes to set the record straight. In addition to her words, her face shows an emotion that is not anger but rather a poignancy laced with a determination to tell her story. Her restrained demeanour suggests that expressing anger to enlist the audience's sympathy is not her primary aim. Rather, what moves the audience is the quiet courage she took to break her forty-year silence and talk on camera. The audience will appreciate how nervous she is each time her shoulders move up and down, and her chest expands and contracts between sentences. Noira's testimony communicates the most private and awkward episode of her life and seeks clarity about Kojima. Her testimony also serves a public purpose of addressing Japan's historical responsibility in relation to the people of PNG as an example of Japan's wartime footprint across the Asia-Pacific War.

At the same time, close attention to Noira's personal story helps to uncover a tragic irony behind the name Kojima and accentuates the sorrow of Noira's painful memory. What the film does not mention, but what Sekiguchi explains in the accompanying book, is her attempt to identify Kojima through a veterans' association. The members told Sekiguchi that the association's register listed five men with the surname Kojima. Of these, two were dead and three were unidentifiable. Sekiguchi's uncle, who had fought in China, remembered that Japanese troops often used false names when raping women. She then suspected that Kojima could have been a false name.[25] Moreover, the name carries an ominous undercurrent. The most common rendition into *kanji* denotes 'small island'. For 'Kojima', it was but an escapade on a small island on the fringe of the Greater East Asian Co-Prosperity Sphere. For Noira, it was a life-changing event.

A significant difference in the narration of this episode in *Daughters* can influence how the audience perceives Noira. *Daughters* shows Pirigi translating Noira's words without any apparent signs of excitement or distress on Pirigi's part:

> [Noira] says that one day when her husband was away [the solider] came to see her and said, 'You want to live with me? Do you like me?' She was afraid and said, 'No. I'm too scared.' The Japanese man said [*Noira moves her right hand, puts her fingers against her mouth, and chews betel nut*] 'Don't be scared. What are you afraid of?' So, they started sleeping together.[26]

Following Pirigi's remark is a short segment, shown only in *Daughters*, that has Noira recalling she and Kojima 'did it only four times' and that she fell pregnant shortly afterwards.

There are crucial differences in the two testimonies about the nature of Noira's relationship with Kojima, in particular about Noira's degree of acquiescence to the situation. Noira makes it clear that Kojima forced her into a sexual relationship while Pirigi's translation reduces the coercion and

Noira's victimhood. Pirigi implies the relationship grew into a consensual one after Kojima convinced her to agree to 'start sleeping together'. In particular, the word 'together' in the subtitle implies some kind of consent. Without publicly available statements about Pirigi's translation, the precise reasons for this difference remain uncertain. A further clue comes from another segment that only *Daughters* features. Pirigi says Noira had the baby after the couple returned to Bougainville. Pirigi tells of the villagers' reaction to the birth of the baby: 'They were surprised and said "Goodness! It's a light-skinned baby". The people were astonished and afraid. Even its grandmother was afraid and said "Oh, my daughter. What will your brothers say about this baby?"' Here, Pirigi becomes animated as she describes the villagers' reactions with dramatic relish. However, what also matters are Noira's words and gestures revealing the burden of stigma that stained her relationship with her family and her husband over the past forty years.

Both films end the sequence with a short scene in which Pirigi speaks about her relationship to Noira. Sekiguchi's placing of Pirigi's remark at this point sheds light on the rationale for her translation. Pirigi reveals the son Noira had with Kojima is her husband. She further explains that listening to Noira's testimony solved a question about her husband's ethnic origins that she had pondered over for a long time. Given Pirigi's relationship to Noira and her son, Pirigi's translation possibly shows layers of compassionate concern for Noira and her husband. Pirigi has heard of Noira's painful memory and wanted her translation not to inflict more sorrow upon Noira than Noira already felt due to the opprobrium she and her son had had to endure.

Sorrow and empathy are not the only emotions Sekiguchi invokes as she also makes a strong point about Japanese soldiers' attitudes. Following Pirigi's revelation, both works move swiftly to two Japanese veterans: ex-corporal Miya Ichirō stationed outside Rabaul, and Gotō Yūsaku formerly in the Eastern New Guinea Army command. Sekiguchi asks these men about sexual relations between Japanese soldiers and local women. Both veterans deny that soldiers ever had sex with the women. Miya remarks, 'The women really stank in those days. Now they're clean and tidy, but then they weren't'. Gotō recalls that the soldiers found the females' skin condition repulsive, 'They were dirty things. I wouldn't have dreamt of sleeping with them [*wry smile*]'.[27] The comments of the veterans reveal their unexamined racist and sexist prejudices, their words alone can elicit strong reactions from an audience.

From the empirical standpoint of the historian, however, Sekiguchi's sequencing of those scenes may raise questions about the creative licence she has taken in juxtaposing the testimonies. In one earlier scene Miya claims although his posting was near Rabaul, he never went there during wartime. Gotō was in eastern New Guinea Island. Thus, it is possible to argue that the realities they recount might not have been the same as in Rabaul where Noira, her husband and Kojima were based. However, on a pre-filming research trip to Eastern New Guinea, Sekiguchi heard old women's stories that painted a different picture than that from Gotō's remarks. She wanted to record those women's testimonies on camera but the government rejected her application for a filming permit.[28] The on-screen performance of the two men defends their comrades from possible accusations of sexual inappropriateness and insulates the high command from questions about who permitted or failed to regulate the soldiers' conduct.[29] The remarks by Miya and Gotō follow the logic of discipline in the medical gaze (Chapter 3). In their eyes, soldiers who failed to exercise restraint belonged to a lesser class of men. Sekiguchi's placing of their statements moves the viewers to shock, anger, and contempt for the veterans' hubris. In this, she deploys Noira as a co-agent in foregrounding the racist and misogynistic attitudes Japanese soldiers and officers held.

The following sequence in Bougainville provides a subtle but different nuance to the expression of painful memories and agency. Mora Pisikei sits next to Josephine Diai who provides consecutive interpreting. Both films use near-identical footage with a thirty-second difference in duration (4 minutes 17 seconds in *Daughters*; 3 minutes 47 seconds in *Senjō*). Both women speak calmly without halting, although their pained expressions remind viewers of the depth of Pisikei's trauma and the challenges for Diai to listen and translate. Pisikei worked in a Japanese-run prison camp under a chief named Iwata. When the Japanese arrived, they put Pisikei and other unmarried women into a prison camp. Iwata charged her with the task of relaying his instructions to the other women in the camp. On Iwata's command Pisikei fed an Australian prisoner of war only to see Iwata executing the Australian in front of her.

Both films present Pisikei's relationship with Iwata as far from the one based on her free will. Pisikei's humiliating experience amply supports Sekiguchi's message that women bore the brunt of the war. Significant differences emerge in the Japanese and English subtitles to Diai's interpreted words and can evoke varying responses from viewers. In *Senjō*, the Japanese subtitle says, 'Because Mora [Pisikei] was made to be Iwata's woman, she passed on his orders to other women'. This implies that her semi-private relationship with Iwata, though coerced, coalesced into her official role as an interlocutor and implicates her in a more complex position in the hierarchy of power than a straightforward binary of the victim and the perpetrator. The English subtitle in *Daughters* replaces Pisikei's status as 'Iwata's woman' with Iwata putting her 'in charge of other women' which accorded Pisikei with a little more autonomy in her role than the subtitle in *Senjō* indicates.

These subtle differences anticipate a greater discrepancy between the two films that appears in Pisikei's descriptions of what happened to her and other women upon the arrival of the Australians. Diai translates how the Australians released the women from the Japanese camp and transferred them to an Australian camp. Apparent in both films is the distress revealed in Pisikei's facial and body language, and the pain Diai shows in translating her words. *Senjō* translates Diai's words as: 'Because I [referring to Pisikei] was the woman who worked for the chief [of the Japanese camp], I was raped by an Australian soldier. Afterwards I had a pistol put like this [*Diai gestures the pistol put on Pisikei's temple*]. I was threatened to be shot to death for co-operating with the Japanese army'. In comparison, *Daughters* features Pisikei's other words translated by Diai: 'The Australian soldiers molested them. They threatened them with guns, pointing them here like this [*Diai gestures the pistol put on Pisikei's temple*] and said, "We'll shoot you and you'll die."' Pisikei's comments mark a pivotal transition in the two films. While the end of the war changed the nationality of the perpetrator, the violence nevertheless continued.

While Sekiguchi tells the same story in both films, differences in the subtitles can have ramifications for the audiences' reception of Pisikei's self-presentation. *Senjō*'s rendering of Pisikei's first-person 'I' statements frame her experience of rape into a double victim of Iwata and the Australian perpetrator. In comparison, *Daughters* uses the collective pronoun 'them' and the term 'molested'. The broader implications shed light on a wider extent of sexual abuse beyond rape. Moreover, the statement implies Pisikei's complex position as the insider–outsider in relation to the other women. It remains ambiguous whether Pisikei was one of the 'them' who were molested. The only information that the audience will receive is the translations by Diai and the subtitles. Pisikei comes across as the spokesperson who escaped but witnessed the cruelty inflicted upon her fellow Bougainvillian women. She occupies an ethically compromised position caught between 'them', the Australians and the Japanese, an 'implicated subject' that shapes historical legacy and influences the transmission of historical memories (Chapter 1). The differences between the two films show how the differences in the co-performance of the testaments and the film-makers and are complicated further by the interpreters.

In the closing scene, only *Senjō* features Pisikei explaining how she feels towards the war. Both women speak slowly and softly, looking exasperated with sunken shoulders. Diai translates:

> By then I [hereafter meaning Pisikei] felt like 'Let it be'. Then, at last both the Japanese and the Australians went away. I'm fed up with war. We lost food and places to sleep. It's women who are made to feel like fools. We get threatened by troops and we get raped. We have to live day and night feeling the trembling.

This remark forms the core of Pisikei's pain. Even if the fear of the soldiers disappeared with the end of the war, the haunting and humiliating memories cast shadows over the women's post-war lives. *Daughters* omits this entire remark and replaces it with another that *Senjō* does not use. In *Daughters*, Pisikei recalls telling the Australians that her husband was in a Japanese camp. After the Australians released him, the couple began walking away. Then, the Australians stopped the couple, and asked Pisikei if the man was her husband. The soldiers took him away and shot him dead. Killing her husband and making her live with the sorrow and trauma was, for her, the price the Australians made her pay for her collaboration with the Japanese. The films, however, could offer grounds for moral equivalence for the Japanese defenders of conservative narratives and interpretations, arguing that the Australian behaviour was just as morally reprehensible as, if not worse than Japanese sexual exploitation.

Condoning violence and moral equivalence could not be further from Sekiguchi's objective. Her films point to the deep-seated militarized masculine culture in Japan as well as Australia. The awkward smiles and dismissive statements by the Japanese veterans comprise the flipside of those latent misogynistic attitudes that denied the humanity of PNG women. Moreover, Caroline Norma's recent scholarship argues that the Australian military culture acquiesced to underlying racist and sexist attitudes among the soldiers.[30] The final remarks in both films drive Sekiguchi's main point home: women on the battleground suffer the worst in war and continue to live in its shadow. Sekiguchi's films do more than exhibiting solidarity with the PNG women by drawing the audience's sympathy towards them. The films challenge major historical narratives in both Japan and Australia. The testimonies undermine the soldiers-as-victims portrayal in Japan and the male-centric Fuzzy Wuzzy Angels trope in service of the Australian 'mateship' narrative.[31] Notwithstanding the common purpose across the two films, the varied emphases and nuances in each film can engender subtle and even significant influence on the audience's emotional engagement with the past.

Ushiyama Jun'ichi: Countering the victim narrative by collecting New Guineans' voices

Of the four documentaries, *Seishun* puts the role of the director, Ushiyama Jun'ichi (1930–1997), most prominently as a co-performer in the making of the documentary, framing him as a kind of historian presenting his argument. The documentary's content revolves around showing the experience and memories of the Japanese soldiers. This analysis concentrates on the significant subplot that emerges in *Seishun*: how Ushiyama becomes affected by the New Guineans' suffering at the hands of the Japanese. Ushiyama presents these testimonies to counter the victim discourse prevalent in Japan and in support of his vision: the Japanese must recognize the damage inflicted upon the others. *Seishun* is the third and final annual documentary about the war that Terebi Asahi (TV Asahi) commissioned Ushiyama to direct and produce between 1988 and 1991. Compared to the critically acclaimed other two works in the trilogy, *Seishun* faded into obscurity. One major flaw is many topics it tries to address. Jumps in themes and subjects result in a failure to sustain the narrative thrust. However, an analysis of Ushiyama's subjectivity – his on- and off-camera performance and co-performance with the subjects as well as his editing – could salvage the standing of *Seishun*.

Seishun and his war-themed documentaries have deep autobiographical and professional roots. Ushiyama's formative years illuminate a sense of mission and curiosity about the peoples and the customs of Asia and New Guinea. During his adolescent years spent in Ibaraki prefecture, he had to work in a munitions factory with his peers in service of the Japanese wartime mission. He noticed how so many men were sent to New Guinea yet seldom did any of them return. Japan's defeat compelled him to question the credibility of Japan's mission of liberating Asia from the Western imperial yoke. To seek answers, he majored in East Asian history at university.[32] He began his career in the early days of television. In 1953, the year after Japan began TV broadcast, he joined Nihon Terebi (NTV), a national television network, and grew into a highly respected television documentary film-maker of long-running series such as *Nonfikushon gekijō* (1962–8) and *Subarashii sekai ryokō* (1966–90). Throughout his career, he insisted that documentaries bring out the essence of humanity and held that this approach rested on two principles. First, the documentary had to draw on thorough research and fieldwork on location. Second, it had to show the subjectivity of the documentary maker's pursuit of truth. His approach left a crucial legacy for Japanese documentary and documentary film-makers – including the auteur Ōshima Nagisa (1932–2013), of *Merry Christmas Mr Lawrence* (1983) fame. Ushiyama's career was not immune from controversy. In 1965, he produced a three-part documentary on the Vietnam War. The series got cancelled after broadcasting the first instalment. It featured a scene of South Vietnamese Marine Corp soldiers executing a Vietcong soldier.[33] The Terebi Asahi trilogy is thus significant for Ushiyama. It marked his return to war-themed documentaries after a two-decade hiatus, and let him fuse together his long-standing interest in Asia, PNG and the Asia-Pacific War.

Consistent across Ushiyama's Terebi Asahi trilogy is his reportage style and argument. To obtain the footage, he spent sustained periods of time on location. The three documentaries argue that the war grew out of Japan's imperial ambition in Asia and that the Japanese committed violence on civilians on foreign soil who suffered the most, a stance that broke a taboo on Japanese TV.[34] The film's title, *Nyūginia ni chitta 16-man no seishun* – 160,000 adolescents scattered in New Guinea – signals Ushiyama's standpoint as a junior contemporary witnessing the conscripts dispatched to die there. The opening sequence declares Ushiyama's position on the New Guinean campaign and the Asia-Pacific War. He is walking on the beach in Buna, with the subtitle, 'The site of the first mass defeat of the Japanese in New Guinea.' Ushiyama avers that Japanese contempt towards the peoples of the Asia-Pacific region resulted in an unrealistic war that killed many young men on the battleground and stresses how the contempt and the ensuing desperation turned the Japanese into perpetrators. *Seishun* then follows the journeys of Japanese veterans and bereaved families to PNG and weaves their testimonies to tell how the campaign wasted so many lives. Both his on- and off-camera work creates a co-performance in which Ushiyama stakes his pacifist stance through his sympathetic engagement with the veterans and the families who suffered as a result of Japan's imperial hubris. Meanwhile, he moves beyond the victim narrative and develops an equally sympathetic view of the New Guineans as the victims of Japanese aggression. This shift lends itself to the progressive interpretation of the war. Of numerous scenes, many of which display Ushiyama's on-camera presence, the most compelling is the fifteen-minute penultimate sequence that deals with the little-known massacre by the Japanese in Timbunke village. The sequence features villagers' recollections and invites the audience to empathize with their trauma. Entering later is ex-Captain Watanabe (né Hama) Masaichi who commanded the massacre and visited the village to seek forgiveness. Beneath the on-screen co-performance of Ushiyama, the villagers and Watanabe compete for emotional capital through their testimonies and dialogues.

The Timbunke massacre occurred in July 1944, in Timbunke located in the Sepik Region to the south of Wewak (Map 4). In May 1944, a unit led by Watanabe occupied Timbunke while deploying a small number of troops at Korogo – upstream on the Sepik River. The Japanese began exploiting the existing antagonism between Timbunke and Korogo and inveigled the Korogo men into collaborating with the Japanese. Moreover, following an Allied attack on the Japanese in Timbunke, Watanabe suspected that the Timbunke villagers were spying for the Allies. On 14 July 1944, Japanese troops and Korogo men killed ninety-nine men and one woman of Timbunke, but spared the children. Men from Korogo raped women in Timbunke and then took them as hostages back to Korogo. This massacre stemmed from Japan's divide-and-conquer strategy as well as of the heightened aggression displayed by Japanese forces when impending defeat was becoming a reality.[35]

At the beginning of the fifteen-minute sequence, we watch Ushiyama hearing about the massacre from the villagers and see his facial expressions of agony and anguish. The voice-over, by an actor, intensifies Ushiyama's reaction as it opines the massacre as 'the worst of all instances of Japanese cruelty the production team heard from the Papua New Guineans'. The scene moves to villagers' witness accounts, and then brings Watanabe to have him listen to other villagers. Watanabe's tall and slender build belies his age of eighty-three years. He dons a black beret and a camera slung over his shoulder. The voice-over adds that Watanabe had long wanted to apologize for the massacre, and seek the villagers' forgiveness, but he could not visit Timbunke until now. All through the years, Watanabe had recurring nightmares of the villagers catching him and sentencing him to death. What *Seishun* leaves out, however, is the result of the war crime trial. Watanabe had received a death sentence, which was subsequently commuted to twenty-five years of imprisonment. He was eventually pardoned in October 1946. The chief of Korogo, Mamba, pleaded for clemency after confessing to his part in the massacre. He was then executed.[36]

Two scenes show Watanabe sitting next to villagers in their bungalows and listening to them speak about their memories. Sitting beside the villagers is a risky exercise for Watanabe. The narrator says that a local parliamentarian has advised Watanabe that many villagers still resent the massacre and could assault him if they find out who he is. Watanabe chose

Map 4 The South Sepik River area. Map reproduced with the permission of CartoGIS Services, Scholarly Information Services, ANU College of Asia and the Pacific, The Australian National University.

to keep his identity anonymous and told the villagers he was an ex-soldier. In the scene, Sanguame Daniel relates her witnessing of the execution of her father and uncle. Through the interpreter, Daniel tells Watanabe, 'The Timbunke Massacre is something I will never forget till I die. The incident simmers in my mind forever.'[37] Daniel looks stern and resolute as she tells her story to the ex-soldier. The camera closes in on Watanabe's face. Beads of sweat appear on his forehead. He puts his left hand onto his chin and looks pensive, processing the emotional intensity of Daniel's resentment. Above all, Watanabe's discomfiture is evident in the lack of eye contact. The interpreter, who remains off-screen, asks Daniel in English 'Do you think there are so many people who have the same feeling – as you have?' Daniel replies, 'Yes, I believe everyone in the village has' and remains silent for a few seconds, which impresses her anger on the viewers. Watanabe leaves the bungalow, looking exhausted, anxious and even shrunken in stature.

The subsequent scene reinforces the dynamics between the victims' trauma and the perpetrator's guilt. Watanabe goes to another bungalow and meets two women. One of them, named Takwaren, lost her husband and three male siblings in the massacre. Without shedding a tear or shouting, she speaks firmly and contends that PNG became the unwitting host of the Australians and the Japanese. She reminds Watanabe and the crew that the massacre occurred in the dry season and tells them that her mood sinks whenever the dry season nears. The narrator empathizes that the timing of the visit amplified her sorrow, and states, 'She raised her children without remarrying. Her words pierced Watanabe's heart'. Similar to Sekiguchi's documentaries, this narration indicates Ushiyama's clear intervention as the director by shedding light on the female and foreign victims of Japanese aggression. Augmenting the commentary is the camera work, which zooms in to Takwaren. She continues: 'You [the Japanese] have not given us any compensation. If I die, I'll tell you in the other world: you did not do anything.' Her eyes are wide open and tears well up. Throughout, Watanabe looks contrite while listening to Daniel. What confronts the viewers is the conflicting distress of the trauma the villagers have carried since the massacre, and the burden of guilt very obviously descending on Watanabe. Watanabe leaves the bungalow and walks slowly to the middle of the village. As the TV crew looks on, he walks forward to a cross that reads, '1943 Jap's [sic] killed 100 people here in Timbunke'. He lays a bunch of flowers and offers his prayer together with the Japanese crew and Ushiyama.

The interaction reveals both the agreement and tension between the two men to the viewers and challenges them to appraise the views that each espouses. After Watanabe finishes his prayer, the voice-over says, 'I suggested Watanabe Masaichi say words of condolences as the person responsible for the massacre'. Although the voice-over is not Ushiyama's voice, the use of 'I' thrusts his directorial presence to the fore. He leads his discussion with Watanabe and directs his actions. The emotional and intellectual investment of Ushiyama and Watanabe in *Seishun* is not always identical. Watanabe faces the cross: he looks fragile but musters the courage to say:

Watanabe: I think that war was really fierce for both [PNG and Japan] and the peoples involved. However, I think that this should be the basis for the Papuans, the Japanese, and the Australians – and all humans – to wish, sincerely, to restore and maintain peace. [Inaudible] As a Japanese who rushed to this land, I am left with a feeling that [*As his speech slows down, Ushiyama walks up towards Watanabe from behind*] I cannot forget forever. I sincerely hope peace prevails upon both nations. I conclude my statement. [*Looking exhausted and gives a shallow bow*]
Narrator: Watanabe's words of condolence resonated quietly.
Ushiyama: [*Looking impassive*] Mr Watanabe, as the person responsible for the Timbunke incident, you should apologize to those who died.
Watanabe: Um, well, you are right.
Ushiyama: [*Firmly*] Please say just that.
Watanabe: [*Nervously*] Yes.
Ushiyama: Yes, you are not an ordinary visitor. [*Looks up*]
Watanabe: [*Looking down on the ground*] Yes, that's right. Er, considering the matters at the time, as the main culprit, I have deep regret – Please forgive the crime I committed in the past. From the bottom of my heart, I hope that each one of you rests in peace. [*Bows*]
Ushiyama: Thanks. I am sorry that I said those things to an eighty-four [*sic*]-year old man. But after all, I think that every Japanese ought to have this sort of feeling.
Watanabe: [*Feebly*] Yes, that's right.
Ushiyama: I also feel the same way. I am also guilty of the same crime, because I am also a Japanese, don't you think?

Watanabe: Yes.
Ushiyama: But –
Watanabe: [Inaudible, *Bows down*] I apologize profusely. I did cause trouble.

Ushiyama positions himself as a Japanese citizen who feels the burden of his intergenerational inheritance of guilt for Japanese wartime violence. This closely follows Ienaga Saburō's belief that those born in Japan as Japanese should face up to the responsibility for the war even though they did not actively participate in it.[38] Indeed, in the terminology of Michael Rothberg, Ushiyama is an 'implicated subject' in the war diachronically, that is, over the trans-war span of time, in that he believes he bears the burden of Japan's imperial and wartime legacy as a Japanese. Ushiyama is also 'synchronically implicated' in the complex web of Japan's wartime mobilization of human resources.[39] His awareness of the age gap with Watanabe kept Ushiyama on polite behaviour but did not impede him from asserting his position.

Ushiyama's candour sets the stage for a co-performance with Watanabe. Ushiyama finds Watanabe's apology not sincere enough and coaxes him into making a greater effort to apologize not only as an individual, but also as a representative of the Japanese. This theatricality of Ushiyama's nudging and Watanabe's obliging is in keeping with the latter's motivation for appearing on *Seishun*. After all, Watanabe's decision to keep his part in the massacre a secret from them undermines his original purpose of seeking villagers' forgiveness. However, Ushiyama has handed down an opportunity to do so in the village and on camera.

The ensuing dialogue turns a corner when Watanabe begins to explain his position. When he has had his say, Ushiyama says:

Ushiyama: Well, even in war, you would not kill civilians, would you?
Watanabe: Yes, but –
Ushiyama: How were you feeling at that time?
Watanabe: Well, in the end, I must say that I understood deep down that we should not have killed the unarmed.

By now quiet tension builds up between the two and Ushiyama lets Watanabe have his say. Ushiyama's question 'even in war, you would not kill civilians, would you?' comes from his empathy for the villagers and challenges Watanabe to demonstrate a more self-critical and self-reflexive stance. Watanabe's 'Yes, but' remark resists his manoeuvre. Then Ushiyama interrupts him and lets him explain himself. From here Watanabe continues to describe what went through his mind just before ordering the massacre while Ushiyama listens. Watanabe presents himself as caught between two choices: of executing the villagers or not. Inside himself he felt 'hostility burning up'. Meanwhile, two of his subordinates encouraged him to enact the reprisal whereas a medic advised against it. While Ushiyama listens, Watanabe remembers, 'But then I could not stop. Because it was war. I was military personnel. I could not help executing it because it was an act in war'. Watanabe accepts responsibility for his actions, but stresses that this was what he perceived as a do-or-die situation. This is Watanabe's appealing to Ushiyama not to judge his actions according to the contemporary moral compass, begging viewers to empathize with him as a victim of the circumstances at the time.

By this stage, Watanabe's speech flows well and he regains his composure. In fact, his 'narrative' is identical to an essay he published in 1972. In it, he accepts his responsibility for the massacre but maintains that he was a mere cog in the vast machinery of the war.[40] Undeterred, Ushiyama reiterates his position:

Ushiyama: As a fellow Japanese, well, I hear veterans visit to commemorate the deaths of their comrades. But really, it is the local people who got caught up and became casualties. [*Putting his hands in prayer*]
Watanabe: Few people think that far.
Ushiyama: I think that we ought to have the feeling that we mourn for such people.

The dialogue ends with Ushiyama having the last word to convince the audience of his position. To this effect, he shifts from his position of empathy with the villagers to 'a fellow Japanese'. Watanabe makes a qualified concession to Ushiyama's argument. This gesture reinforces his motivation to appear on TV in the first place. In this brief and silent sequence, Watanabe prostrates before the cross. He then stands up, walks away, and gives a backward glance at it. His contrite gesture makes a symbolic yet ineffable departure from the past into the present. The sequence returns us to Ushiyama's core argument – that ordinary civilians suffered the most under Japanese imperialism. Ushiyama wavers from being a proxy for the villagers to a spokesperson for his generation. Yet, Watanabe's response still shows the unbridgeable gulf from Ushiyama's positions. The subsequent and closing sequence reiterates the main theme of the lost youths of the Japanese soldiers. Still, *Seishun* ends with enough impact on the viewers to ponder about the lost youths of New Guinea.

Conclusion

This chapter has analysed the ways three film-makers, in four documentaries, elicit the audience's emotional responses to bolster their historical arguments. Applying Ellis's approach has helped tease out the ways the film-makers frame and edit the dynamic, or co-performance, between the film-maker and the subjects that occurs both on- and off-screen. Adding to the variation are the ways the film-makers exercise their control and input in the editing and processing of their footage. In *Shingun*, Hara's action documentary method yielded his on-screen presence the least visible of the three film-makers analysed. Hara's strategy evokes conflicting responses to Okuzaki ranging from sympathy to disgust but impedes meaningful exploration of the origins of his rage. Hara's orientation towards the present-day action, however, falls short of adding depth to Okuzaki's troubled past that lurks beneath his oft-violent outburst. In this regard, outperforming Okuzaki was ex-officer Yamada's revelation of his troubled relationship with his painful memories. The partnership between Sekiguchi and the female interviewees is arguably the strongest achievement of the three directors. She empowers the women to tell the world about their traumatic past. While Sekiguchi limits her on-screen presence, it becomes most visible in the subtle differences in subtitles, editing and footage. In particular, statements focussing on the individual can elevate the subjectivity of the speaker but can limit the advocacy role that the person assumes for the other victims. These amount to divergent portrayals of the subjects' identities tailored for intended audience of the two films.

While the co-performative partnership remains significant, the film-makers play critical roles as historians through their directorial input and interventions. These determine how the subjects see themselves and their war experiences and how the audience responds to them. Of the three film-makers, Ushiyama plays the most noticeable role as the film-maker and historian both on- and off-screen. The testimonies of the Papua New Guineans reinforced his long-held conviction that the Japanese were the perpetrators in imperial ambition and wars. The dialogue with Watanabe exposed the deep divide between not only the opposing positions but also across generations. Crucial here is the conciliatory concession Watanabe made which renders a theatricality of its own. This seems to derive more from his motivation to appear on TV than Ushiyama's crafting of 'winning the argument'. Thus,

Seishun ended up putting the two men's historical views under a brighter spotlight than the Papua New Guineans' concerns for redress. The more the audience appreciates the performative nature of historical documentary and the film-maker as historians, the more it gains its position as a historical medium on the process of travelling memory. Implicit in this chapter are journeys the film-makers took to various locations to unearth the emotions hidden in the sediments of memoryscapes. Part 3 analyses travel and travelogues and probes the influence travel can have on historical narratives and interpretations.

Part 3
Travelogues

6

From a soldier to a best friend forever? Manga artist Mizuki Shigeru and the villagers of New Britain Island

When manga artist Mizuki Shigeru (1922–2015) looked back at his frenetic activity at the height of his commercial success in the 1970s, he drew images of himself suffering from a condition that he called *Nanpō-byō* (South Seas syndrome).[1] Mizuki recalled that *Nanpō-byō* gave him an insatiable yearning for New Britain Island and the people of Namale village, on the Gazelle Peninsula of the island. For many days, Mizuki daydreamed about Namale and had his family watch and listen to dances and songs he recorded on his previous trips much to their annoyance.[2] His *Nanpō-byō* says more than his self-caricature and gives insight into his nostalgia for the fond memories amidst his otherwise arduous wartime. He served as a private in the 229th Infantry Regiment of the 38th Division from November 1943 to March 1946.

Life after repatriation was difficult for Mizuki as he struggled to make ends meet as a fledgling manga artist. Eventually, by the mid-1960s his perseverance paid off and he rose through the ranks to attain a status equal to other contemporary giants in the manga world such as Tezuka Osamu (1928–89), best known for the series *Testsuwan Atomu* (*Astro Boy*). Mizuki established two creative niches, one of which was *yōkai* (supernatural creatures rooted in ancient folklore and legends). Series such as *Akuma-kun* and *Gegege no Kitarō* became wildly popular and have been remade into anime and repeated on television and in cinemas for several decades. The other niche consisted of fictional and factual manga on the subject of the Asia-Pacific War. Mizuki spoke from a distinct first-person voice of pacifism. His subsequent autobiographies and historical manga repeat his pacifist messages.[3] However, they seldom explore what lay beneath Mizuki's *Nanpō-byō*.[4] This absence raises questions about Mizuki's *Nanpō-byō* and how he found a remedy for it. Mizuki's malaise reveals the depth of his emotional entanglement with the villagers that grew out of his lasting heavenly and nostalgic visions.

This chapter recasts Mizuki as a traveller to New Britain with changing profiles: initially as a soldier, then an adopted villager and later as a visitor. Under scrutiny are Mizuki's manga and prose essays in which he discussed his journeys to New Britain in multiple publications and forms. Insights from Nanyō-Orientalism, Japan's perception of the South Seas Islands, and travel writing studies inform the analyses. This chapter argues that Mizuki remained susceptible to the lasting influence of Nanyō-Orientalism which he seemed unable to disavow completely. Looking into Mizuki's *Nanpō-byō* raises the issue of Mizuki's lesser-known life as a traveller to New Britain. This complements his other well-known profiles as a manga artist and a war veteran. Mizuki visited New Britain more than ten times between 1971 and 1994, ostensibly to alleviate his *Nanpō-byō*. He wrote numerous accounts in manga and prose, many of which have been republished with new or revised structures, text and drawings. The multiple iterations of Mizuki's journeys provide a window into the dynamics of 'travelling memory'. How he, as a veteran, negotiated personal memories of the war along with the impressions gained from post-war journeys back to the same community mirrors the trajectories both Japan and PNG followed in the post-war era. Moreover, applying the trans-war perspective helps to place Mizuki's life and travel in the broader contexts of the Japanese imaginative construct of the South Seas Islands that preceded and followed the war.

The repeated journeys that Mizuki took to the islands are not uncommon. Veterans have paid repeated visits to erstwhile battlefields to pay tribute to their comrades and collect the remains of unidentified deceased soldiers. Sabine Marschall names this type of travel 'personal memory tourism' whereby the traveller visits and revisits sites bound up with 'key moments in a person's life and the deliberate return to sites associated with one's own past'.[5] Whether these moments and locations induce happy, tragic or traumatic memories, the traveller partakes on these trips with the intention to search for answers about personal identity. Personal memory tourism thus becomes as 'an extension of the process of remembering towards the travellers' autobiographical projects of imagining, negotiating and realizing their identities'.[6] Post-war journeys by veterans constitute a type of personal memory tourism and their writings a subgenre of the travelogue. Many are short essays about their journeys published in veteran associations' newsletters and magazines or self-funded publications.[7] Mizuki's journeys and writings intersect these categories. However, his writing contrasts with those of many other veterans in three crucial respects. First, he paid repeated visits to the same village over three decades and met the same people many times. Most travel writers generally form their impressions from a single journey and a single encounter with the people with whom they interact. Second, he seldom discusses commemorating his Japanese comrades and predominantly recounts his impressions of the villagers. Many veterans acknowledge receiving acts of kindness from the local population during wartime and express their gratitude on their post-war journeys, but never to the extent of Mizuki. Third, he wrote and published multiple accounts of his travel and, at times, multiple versions of the same journeys at length. Mizuki's approach in his travelogues has commonalities with the historical, autobiographical and war-themed manga in which he offers multiple reflections on seminal events. Roman Rosenbaum's writings on Mizuki's autobiographical works on his war experience contend that Mizuki's rewritings speak of his attempts to revisit his memories and reinterpret the same events.[8] This chapter stretches Rosenbawm's insight further to Mizuki's travelogues including his initial 'travel' as a soldier and his post-war travel as a veteran.

Mizuki's travel recollections relate to two scholarly genres: Nanyō-Orientalism and travel writing. Nanyō-Orientalism, a term coined by Naoto Sudō, denotes a set of literary tropes expressing 'fears and desires that arose from Japan's imperialist expansion and its concern over the activities of other powers in the Pacific region'.[9] Sudō argues that Nanyō-Orientalism recreates a hierarchy between the hegemonic Japanese and the subordinate Pacific Islanders, while at times challenging such assumptions. His conceptualization stems from Mary Louise Pratt's *The Imperial Eyes*, which treats the travelogue as a text speaking for or against the prevailing ethos of European imperialism. At the core is the metropolitan traveller's portrayal of what Pratt has termed 'travellees': the people the traveller visits, meets and writes about. Pratt argues that the traveller does not always denigrate the travellees or champion metropolitan values, but sometimes holds the travellees as mirrors to criticize the excesses of urban society.[10] Put differently, Nanyō-Orientalism helps to identify Mizuki's desires and motivations for visiting Namale and its people, and the traveller–travellee relationship illuminates the pattern of Mizuki's interactions with and his portrayals of the villagers.

Mizuki's multiple renditions of Namale chart the path of admiration, disillusionment and resolution in four phases. The first is the period he spent there during the wartime, in which he envisions Namale as a kind of heaven

Table 6.1 Four Phases of Mizuki's Travelogues

When the Journey Took Place	Main Event	Mizuki's Interpretations	Villagers' Responses
Phase 1 Wartime	Mizuki befriends villagers	Village as heaven/paradise	Villagers accept Mizuki as a member
Phase 2 The 1970s	Mizuki revisits Namale	Disillusionment and pragmatism. Mizuki satisfies his nostalgia and draws artistic inspiration	Villagers demand payment or donation from Mizuki
Phase 3 1989	Mizuki presents a pickup truck to villagers	Mizuki provides three different narratives of the truck	Topetoro acknowledges belated gift
Phase 4 The 1990s	Topetoro dies; Mizuki sponsors Topetoro's funeral	Mizuki grows more sensitive to the villagers' circumstances and Topetoro's spirit; Mizuki demonstrates his loyalty to the villagers and Topetoro	Villagers participate in the funeral

(*tengoku*) or paradise (*rakuen*). The second phase concerns his journeys in the 1970s, during which he becomes disillusioned. The third phase covers multiple narratives told over several years about a single journey Mizuki took in 1989. The fourth deals with trips Mizuki made in 1992 and 1994 after the death of the village headman, Topetoro. Mizuki had met him during the war when he was a boy and considered him his best friend in the village. Topetoro hosted Mizuki on his many visits and later, Mizuki sponsored and attended his funeral (Table 6.1). The analyses into the last two phases employ insights from gift exchange, a theme that has animated anthropology and sociology for decades.

Phase 1: Wartime – between hell and heaven

Mizuki's travelogues as a soldier set a pattern of alternating between hell and heaven. The contrast differs from other veterans' writings that saw the New Guinean campaign as endless hardship (Chapters 2 and 3). What made the war hell for Mizuki was the habitual physical punishment, mostly slapping, that he received from the officers for his clumsiness and continual disobedience. All of the officers were merciless automatons who demanded their subordinates follow the orders from above unconditionally. By contrast, he perceived the villages as heaven, with the people there living in harmony with the abundant bounty of nature.

Mizuki's heaven-and-hell binary has its roots in his vision of 'the South' under the strong influence of Nanyō-Orientalism. As a child, he was a fan of *Bōken Dankichi*, a popular boys' comic set in a fictional South Seas Island (Chapter 4). Developments in his family life cemented his fascination with the South. His father followed Mizuki's paternal grandfather to Java for a short stint in commercial enterprise. He returned with a fortune that elevated the family's financial standing.[11] Another significant influence came during his late teens. Following the outbreak of Japan's war with China in 1937 and the mass mobilization towards the war effort, many youths sought refuge in philosophy and literary classics to confront questions of life and death. Mizuki was an avid reader. One book that made the strongest impression on him was Johann Goethe's *Conversations of Goethe*, a book Mizuki encountered in his late teens. He took it to Rabaul, read it repeatedly until he memorized it, and considered it his lifelong anchor.[12] In it, Goethe extols the people of the South Seas for the purity of their lives especially in contrast with what he sees as the false veneer of so-called civilized societies:

> Every one [sic] is polished and courteous but no one has the courage to be hearty and true, so that an honest man, with natural views and feelings, stands in a very bad position. Often one cannot help wishing that one had been born upon one of the South Sea Islands, a so-called savage, so as to have thoroughly enjoyed human existence in all its purity, without any adulteration.[13]

The contrast between the pure but putatively uncivilized South Seas and the civilized but tainted West and Japan was the mindset Mizuki formed. It was the mindset that he brought to the Army barracks upon conscription in March 1943, at the age of twenty-one.[14] Early in his military training, he realized that he was ill-suited to life in the barracks and volunteered to serve abroad. His superior asked him bluntly, 'North or south?' Mizuki's immediate reply, 'South', resulted in his being sent to New Britain in October.[15] His response was not a spontaneous one; it was premeditated with multiple roots in his upbringing and held a pragmatic angle too, as he hoped to make the best of the hell he would spend in the army.

By the time Mizuki arrived in New Britain, the tide of the war had turned against the Japanese. Japan had lost the battles of Midway and Guadalcanal.

The death of Admiral Yamamoto Isoroku in Bougainville in an Allied attack in April 1943 dealt a further blow to the Japanese troops' morale. The announcement of the zone of absolute defence in late September 1943 practically left the Japanese soldiers abandoned and exacerbated their conditions. Mizuki recounts his journey to hell and back in at least three epic manga works. *Sōin gyokusai seyo* (1973) is a 350-page war memoir focussing on his time in the Zungen Battalion. *Komikku Shōwa-shi* (1988–9) is an eight-volume manga that intertwines a history of the Shōwa era (1926–89) with Mizuki's autobiography. A three-volume autobiography *Kanzenban Mizuki Shigeru den* (2004, hereafter *Kanzenban*) follows the same formula of *Komikku Shōwa-shi* but puts greater emphasis on his autobiography over history and extends the chronology beyond the Showa-era (Table 6.2).[16]

Mizuki was one of around 500 troops assigned to Zungen Point, south of Rabaul, to provide a frontline defence against the Australians.[17] In *Kanzenban* and *Komikku Shōwa-shi*, Mizuki writes how he heard a rumour that Zungen was a heaven-like land replete with tropical fruits. He then features a character called Nezumi-otoko (Rat Man), a cynic who often appears in Mizuki's *yōkai* manga. Nezumi-otoko opines that the rumour could not be further from reality, describing Zungen as 'a place from which one could go to heaven', with enemy attacks, hard labour, hunger, tropical disease and natural hazards.[18] Before departing for Zungen, superiors urged the soldiers to go to military brothels for their final experience of sexual intercourse. Mizuki decided that waiting in long queues was futile and ventured out to a local village instead. The villagers welcomed him for his curious mind and unassuming demeanour.[19] His straying off underlays his inclination to find paradise on his own terms.

Arguably, the most profound experience shaping Mizuki's outlook on war was his deployment to Baien, around 100 kilometres south of Zungen, over five days away on foot. One day a raid on his barrack killed all of ten plus troops in his detachment, except Mizuki, who happened to be outside on watch. On his way back to Zungen, Mizuki experienced extreme hunger and privation and narrowly escaped being ambushed by local men who were apparently collaborating with the Australians.[20] His return to Zungen in May 1944 provoked his superiors into telling him to kill himself, since they had already reported to Rabaul the deaths of the entire detachment. Mizuki's survival would embarrass them for their apparent failure to enforce honourable suicide. His manga, essays and interviews continually refer to this incident and

Table 6.2 Mizuki Shigeru's War and Travel-Related Books[a]

Original Year of Publication[b]	Title	Notes
1973	Sōin gyokusai seyo (Published and translated into English as Onward towards Noble Death)	Predominantly a memoir of Mizuki's military experience in New Britain.
1982	Neboke jinsei	Prose essay that covers his childhood to post-war life, including his travels to New Britain.
1985	Mizuki Shigeru no musume ni kataru otōsan no senki	A prose essay mostly about Mizuki's wartime experience, accompanied by illustrations.
1988–9	Komikku Shōwa-shi (8 vols.) (Published and translated into English as Shōwa, 5 volumes)	A historical account of the Shōwa era (1926–89), intermixed with Mizuki's autobiography.
1994	Mizuki Shigeru no Rabauru senki	Contains original pictures and prose created between 1946 and 1948. Some illustrations come from Musume ni kataru otōsan no senki.
1995	Rabaul jūgunkōki: Topetoro tono 50 nen	A prose essay recalling Mizuki's wartime experience in and postwar travel to Namale, as well as his friendship with Topetoro. Ends with Topetoro's funeral.
2000	Karankoron hyōhakuki	Collection of manga and prose essays published in a weekly magazine.
2004	Kanzenban Mizuki Shigeru den (3 vols.)	Originally published as Bokuno isshō wa gegege no rakuen da (2001).
2008	Watashi wa gegege: shinpika Mizuki Shigeru den	A condensed autobiography, using previously published material.
2015	Sensō to dokusho: Mizuki Shigeru shussei mae shuki	Original pictures drawn and diary written before and during the wartime, ca. 1945–6.

Note:
[a] Mizuki authored more works, but this table includes his works cited in this chapter.

[b] The years correspond to the initial publications and may be different from the republished editions cited here.

stress the disappointment and anger he felt at the scant respect the officers had for human life.[21]

Mizuki's return from Baien opened what became his decades-long friendship with the Namale villagers. Back in Zungen he developed malaria and lost his left arm following a raid by the Allies. In July 1944, Mizuki was transferred to a field hospital in Kokopo and then in February 1945 to a second hospital in Namale, both near Rabaul. A medic there advised Mizuki to trade his army-issued goods with the local villagers for food. This piqued his appetite for the villagers' lifestyle. One day, Mizuki slipped out of the camp and headed for Namale. As he approached, Mizuki encountered Ikarien, the village matriarch, who allowed him to enter the village. The villagers' offer of food delighted the sick and hungry soldier so much that he devoured everything, even the portions intended for other villagers. He returned on another day with army-issued cigarettes and blankets to recompense them. In turn, he received more food and began befriending the villagers. Meanwhile, the soldiers who did not barter with the local residents continued to deteriorate. It is no surprise that Mizuki felt indebted to the villagers' kindness for restoring his health.[22]

One constant theme Mizuki repeats in his writing is his superiors' growing hostility towards the rapport he struck with the villagers. Each visit Mizuki paid to 'heaven' was followed by punishment from his officers for violating the prohibition on fraternizing with the locals. Undeterred, he continued to frequent Namale. The villagers welcomed him. Mizuki claims that they liked his unassuming manner and sensed that he had a genuine interest in them as human beings while many Japanese held racist attitudes towards them.[23] They even adopted him as a *kandere* (a matrilineal family member) and gave him a patch of land to grow food and shell money, the last item bearing significant symbolic value in New Britain. The villagers found his reading the Bible aloud so amusing that they nicknamed him Paulo. Mizuki appreciated how the village became heaven to him and relates two episodes marking his rebirth. First, he noticed a smell like a newborn baby emanating from the wound on the stump of his severed arm and regarded it as a sign of hope for survival. Second, Mizuki boasted to other soldiers that he could obtain fruit from village children. One soldier dismissed this claim as impossible, stating that no one would do favours for Japanese troops. Mizuki responded, 'I am Paulo. I am a man of the forest'. The next frame has a village boy delivering food in the torrential rain.[24] Mizuki says little about his moniker. However, Michael Dylan Foster identifies Mizuki's christening as a pivotal moment of spiritual rebirth.

It parallels the New Testament apostle Saul changing his name to Paul upon conversion.²⁵ The village heaven led to Mizuki's physical and metaphysical rebirth and laid the foundation for his special relationship with the villagers.

Mizuki's survival and acceptance makes a heart-warming story verging on the sentimental. Indeed, in most publications, Mizuki projects himself as an eccentric ne'er-do-well soldier staying outside the strictures of the military. He rarely tells how much he knew of the political dynamics underlying his relationship with the villagers during the wartime. In a few publications he recognizes that the necessities of the wartime shaped villagers' acceptance of Mizuki. A one-off account in *Neboke jinsei* (1982) notes that the villagers had their own motives; he suspected that they befriended him so that he could mediate on their behalf when disputes with other Japanese soldiers came to a head. Such disputes, usually pertaining to the theft of potatoes from the villagers' plots, arose after soldiers learnt of his friendship with the local people. Mizuki recalls that the task of mediation put him between a rock and a hard place.²⁶ In the early days of the Japanese occupation of Rabaul, the Japanese tried to build cordial relationships by cultivating patronage and fostering loyalty, but as the war progressed and Japanese supplies ran low, they turned to coercion, torture and execution to extract food and labour from the local residents.²⁷ For the Namale villagers, accepting Mizuki served the triple purposes of demonstrating their loyalty to the Japanese, protecting themselves from violence by the Japanese and training a sympathetic Japanese negotiator. By the same token, the Japanese officers might have tolerated Mizuki's fraternizing with the villagers because he served a unique purpose in resolving disputes. Yet, the romanticized tales of heaven outnumber the background issues and bring focus to Mizuki's self-portrayal of the harmonious traveller–travellee relationship.

Later, the paradisiacal experience Mizuki enjoyed with the villagers came to a poignant end. Following the Japanese surrender, Mizuki informed the villagers of his imminent transfer to a prisoner-of-war camp away from Namale. Saddened by the news, they encouraged him to stay and promised him a house and a vegetable plot. Mizuki told his superiors of his intention to remain; however, an army doctor, Sahara Katsumi, persuaded him to seek appropriate medical treatment in Japan for the wound associated with his severed arm. Mizuki changed his mind and promised the villagers that he would return in seven years. He repeatedly drew images of himself and the villagers looking tearful as they shook hands. Behind them were Japanese soldiers looking bemused by their sadness, evidently unable to comprehend their special bond.[28] The soldiers' facial expressions accentuate Mizuki's eccentricity. Unlike many soldiers, Mizuki formed meaningful connections with the villagers and fulfilled his original intention to find his 'South Seas paradise' amidst the hell soldiers experienced.

Mizuki's tears represent the dilemma of Nanyō-Orientalism. He almost always recalls how his decision to leave the village was a difficult one that involved choosing between the village and his long-held ambition to become a painter back in Japan. Only in *Neboke jinsei* did Mizuki admit that he had harboured doubts about fully 'going native'. No matter how much he enjoyed the villagers' company, he still perceived of himself as civilized and the villagers as primitive and he looked forward to his eventual repatriation.[29] His later narratives present varied reasons for his repatriation to Japan. In his prose-and-manga essay *Karankoron hyōhakuki* (2001) and his autobiography *Kanzenban*, Mizuki inserts a flashback of an accidental encounter with Epupe, a woman to whom he was deeply attracted, although he relinquished thoughts of romance when he learnt that she was married. While walking to Namale to announce his departure, he saw Epupe naked, bathing by a waterfall. Mizuki recalls that she smiled and he suspects that this was an invitation to make love to her. Mizuki regretted walking away from a once in a lifetime opportunity but admitted his concern about contracting a sexually transmitted disease. He also wondered whether he could become a manga artist if he fathered a 'mixed-blood child'.[30] His anxieties epitomize the essence of Nanyō-Orientalism. Epupe represented irresistible temptation as in the song 'Shūchō no musume' (Chapter 4) yet posed the risk of disease and entrapment – emotional or otherwise – and of thwarting his ambitions in post-war Japan. The farewell scene, which he relates numerous times, can evoke sorrow in the reader. Such a poignant tale is possible only if Mizuki keeps his reasons for returning to Japan private. A reader aware of these motivations may, of course, interpret the situation differently. Mizuki's tears can represent not just the sorrow of departure but also the anxiety of the challenge his life could throw at him after returning to Japan.

Phase 2: Paradise revisited

Mizuki returned to New Britain Island and Namale in December 1971 for the first time in twenty-six years. Mizuki's absence lasted significantly longer than the seven years he had initially promised the villagers. Little did Mizuki anticipate that the Japanese government would prohibit foreign travel for most ordinary citizens until 1964. For decades, foreign travel remained beyond the reach of many. Meanwhile, Mizuki struggled to establish his career and to attain financial security.[31] His success brought unrelenting demands and afflicted him with the self-diagnosed *Nanpō-byō*. He saw himself as a tormented misfit in post-war Japan and identified with writer Robert Louis Stevenson, painter Paul Gauguin and sculptor-turned-folklorist Hijikata Hisakatsu, all of whom made the Pacific Islands their adopted home.[32] What finally made Mizuki's return journey possible was a chance encounter with Sergeant Miya Ichirō, a former superior in Zungen and a fellow sufferer of *Nanpō-byō*. Miya asked Mizuki to accompany him and Ishibashi, another veteran, to commemorate their comrades who had died in New Britain.[33] Towards the end of their journey, Mizuki split from his companions and managed to locate Namale with the aid of a local driver that he hired. Many of the villagers recognized 'Paulo', and Mizuki met his best friend among them, Topetoro. By 1971, Topetoro had a family and had become the village headman. He hosted Mizuki as a guest for the night. Mizuki also met Epupe and found that although she had lost her beauty, she had retained her graceful manners.[34]

His accounts of his visits to New Britain Island in the 1970s and 1980s express his ambivalence and growing disillusionment. Mizuki's praise of the villagers following his December 1971 'homecoming' was not as emphatic as that of during the war. The first comment he made regarding his December 1971 journey appeared in an interview with the *Asahi Shinbun* in September 1973, a month after the publication of *Sōin gyokusai seyo*. In the interview, he expressed his pleasure at having reacquainted himself with the people and the landscape but lamented the intrusion of 'civilization' that continued to undermine the Namale villagers' lifestyle. Mizuki noted that Namale had become more like Japan: the cash economy had damaged the carefree lifestyle where villagers used to 'eat, sleep and dance'.[35] Mizuki attributed these adverse effects to Japanese businesses 'selling goods, felling trees and scattering the poison of civilization'.[36] Conversely, he equated the villagers' harmonious relationship with nature to that of the Jōmon era (ca. 10500–300 BCE) in Japan and referred to the villagers as *dojin* (indigenous people). This term is now deemed highly offensive. However, he employed its literal meaning of 'people of the earth' to praise their living off the land without having to work too hard.[37] What Mizuki witnessed was that the intrusion of modernity spoiling the very sociocultural fabric that created and sustained the lifestyle that had attracted him. His admiration of the villagers parallels Marshall Sahlins's notion of the original affluent society. Sahlins argues for a reappraisal of the hunter-gatherer society as a civilization on its own merit and dismisses its treatment as being inferior to industrialized society.[38] However, Mizuki remained oblivious, at least in this interview, to the benefits he accrued from Japan's economic recovery, as it enabled him to travel and fulfil his promise to return to Namale.

While the visit to Namale satisfied Mizuki's nostalgia and validated his respect for the villagers, the trip left him with an ambivalent aftertaste as he felt he had planned his return too late. His sentiment exemplifies what travel writing scholars call 'belated arrival'. The term denotes occasions when a traveller has failed to fulfil the hope of experiencing authentic culture because it is disappearing, or has already vanished, as a result of foreign intrusion. Consequently, the traveller's disappointment develops into a wistful and apologetic sentiment and a lament for the corrosive effects of foreign influences on the local culture, especially where the traveller's own nation is responsible.[39] This is a sentiment Mizuki developed later in *Neboke jinsei*:

> The only place in Japan where people can relax is in the coffin. As long as you are alive, you remain anxious and busy. The natives [sic] often remind me about how the Japanese work too much. They have a point. In their view, happy people are the people who do not work. So, the Japanese are unhappy. I work very hard and don't like the cold. I don't really like working and want to lead a relaxed life. My personality makes me want to head to the South.[40]

Just as the young Mizuki saw the South as a zone of escape from the army barracks, in the post-war years he continues to see the South in the similar trope of a paradise that affords escape from onerous regimen. Mizuki's repeated criticism towards Japan reinforces the sorrow of his belated arrival in a changed New Britain and his yearning for the way the heaven he enjoyed but which can no longer be experienced. The gap between the realities in Japan and New Britain puts Mizuki in a state of perpetual and incurable *Nanpō-byō*.

Later Mizuki recognized that the specificity of wartime skewed his perspective of the village. In an essay *Mizuki Shigeru no musume ni kataru otōsan no senki* (1985, hereafter *Musume*), he recalls how he felt before embarking on his search for the village on his first return trip to New Britain

Island. *Musume* is one of Mizuki's most candid accounts. The title announces his private intention to tell his wartime experience to his daughters, or to follow Narita Ryūichi's model of transmission from Generations A to B (Chapter 1). The change of scenery in New Britain brings him to muse about his views of Namale as paradise during the war being due to his youth and the scarcity of food at the time. He admits, 'The heaven was heaven only in my mind.'[41] Indeed, Mizuki realizes that the village he held in his mind diverged from the village he saw in the post-war years. His descriptions of the food and accommodation mark Mizuki's shifting perceptions. On one occasion, Topetoro prepared a large meal of boiled potatoes because he remembered that Mizuki had a hearty appetite. Mizuki found the potatoes, cooked in oily water, so bland and hardly edible. He decided to hide them from the villagers' sight. He got up in the middle of the night to throw them out into the bushes. As he began to move around in the hut, he felt human flesh under his feet. He saw a dozen people sleeping on the floor. One even had rat faeces in his open mouth. The sight not only repulsed him but also made the visitor admire the villagers' ability to sleep in rough conditions and to coexist with nature.[42] At breakfast the next morning, Topetoro made instant coffee. Mizuki found the coffee tasted strange. When he finished drinking it, he noticed mosquito larvae at the bottom of the mug. He accepted that larvae-filled water was normal in Namale and kept drinking Topetoro's larvae coffee during the following days and in subsequent trips over the years.[43] His willingness to tolerate some, but not all, discomfort elevates his self-image to that of an adaptable traveller and rekindles his affinity with the village.

A more crucial difference in Mizuki's account of his return visit concerns values. In *Musume*, Mizuki tells his daughters that he struggled on his return trip in 1971 to sustain conversations with the villagers. With his limited Pidgin and English, he shows the villagers his manga books and explains how he made his living. The villagers' clumsy handling of his books and blank responses prompt him to deduce that publications and his profession are alien to them. He realizes that he and the villagers have grown apart. The pathos fans his nostalgia for an untainted primitive culture that he could no longer find. Nonetheless, he did not give up on the hope of recreating this heaven. He still fantasized about relocating to Namale with his family. To convince his family to emigrate, he reasoned that the clean air made everyone equal and the simple lifestyle was worry free. The family remained unwilling.[44] Mizuki's first return journey gave him an inkling of the irreversible changes to the villagers and Mizuki himself as did the changes to Namale and Japan.

Five years later, in 1976, Mizuki paid another visit to Namale. He recounts this journey in great detail in a chapter titled 'Ushinawareta rakuen' (Lost paradise) in *Neboke jinsei*. A key theme of this chapter was that the Namale of his memory had disappeared. He found that the time-honoured lifestyles and values of the Namale residents had changed and concluded that staying in the community had now become awkward for him. He saw drastic changes to the landscape: tar-sealed roads had replaced dirt roads, the boats now had motors and general provision shops dotted the roads. What disturbed him most was the villagers' loss of free time as cash crop farming replaced subsistence farming. Mizuki noticed that Topetoro now spent long hours husking coconuts for the paltry price of six-thousand yen for 40 kilograms. Mizuki felt that he could no longer relax in the village due to his sense of obligation to help Topetoro with his work.[45]

His disillusionment remained until his final autobiography, *Watashi wa gegege* (2008). Mizuki notes with sadness that the villagers had ceased living off the land and had instead started buying canned food and importing rice with the money they earned from selling copra. Mizuki originally travelled there to escape the demands of work in Japan only to witness the villagers had come under the pressure of a cash economy. The situation left him wondering if this was the end of paradise.[46] Such poignancy highlights the paradox of belated travel but permitted him to cut a figure of a melancholic traveller afflicted with *Nanpō-byō*. Underlying it are two conflicting impulses. His affinity for the villagers initially led him to reify them in the images he held. Conversely, he could not disentangle himself or even reconcile with the unstoppable forces of modernization in the village.

Mizuki's disappointment affected his behaviour towards and the impressions of the villagers. Amidst his mounting frustration on this 1976 trip, Mizuki vented his growing antipathy towards the Namale villagers. On one occasion, Topetoro's brothers offered him chickens, a highly valued food item in the village. The brothers then abruptly requested that he invest in a local cocoa factory and donate a farm vehicle. Mizuki found them brazen and annoying.[47] The biggest disappointment on this trip came from Epupe. When Mizuki gave her a wristwatch, she retorted, 'I would have preferred a radio'. However, she continued to play host and served him a meal of chicken. Afterwards, she demanded that he buy her a beautiful *laplap* (a sarong-like cloth) as payment for the meal. Mizuki disparaged Epupe for turning into 'a greedy old hag'.[48]

What we see in the accounts of his 1971 and 1976 trips is a changed Mizuki in a changed Namale and its villagers. The former trip left Mizuki ambivalent about the gap between the village as he remembered it during the wartime and in 1971. The latter trip confronted him with changes in the villagers themselves. Their interactions with Mizuki suggest that his novelty as a long-lost friend had worn off by 1976. The villagers had come to see him less as a *kandere* and more as a paying guest from an affluent country. His irritation indicates a creeping hubris: a traveller feels entitled to expect travellees to offer the same unconditional hospitality as they had during the wartime period. His various writings bring home the irony that the more Mizuki tried to cure his *Nanpō-byō*, the more he had to tolerate the unsavoury realities of contemporary Namale. *Neboke jinsei* and *Musume* vent Mizuki's bitterness. Mizuki finally abandons his relocation plan. Instead, he decides to return only for short-term visits to gain artistic inspiration and to reminisce.[49]

Mizuki's new resolve promises a departure from his agonizing *Nanpō-byō*. It also touches on the essence of Nanyō-Orientalism and the traveller–travellee relationship. On the one hand, Mizuki champions the villagers' carefree and innocent character and unassuming lifestyle, which he deployed to counter the prejudice Japanese readers may have had towards the South Seas Islanders, viewing them as 'primitive' peoples. Mizuki's inability to interrogate his own presence in Namale in the post-war era resembles postcolonial, that is, post-1960s, travelogues of the industrialized English-speaking world. Debbie Lisle argues that such travel writers substitute an apolitical celebration of cultural diversity for the overtly racist idioms of imperialism when describing the former colonies. She finds it troubling that travel writers fail to ask themselves what their travel means to continuing global inequality.[50] As the shared memories of the war grew rarefied, Mizuki had to adjust his expectations and tip the balance from personal memory travel towards leisure travel. The new attitude of the villagers shifted their relationship from the personal realm to traveller–travellee interactions on an international level between Japan and PNG.

Phase 3: The end of Mizuki's long wartime: A pickup truck in three narratives

Mizuki's pragmatic stance led to a reckoning with *Nanpō-byō* and Nanyō-Orientalism following a trip he made in 1989. On this trip, he donated a pickup truck to the villagers. Travelogues in Phase 3 retell the same episode with new contexts, functions and meanings of the truck in three narratives. The variance suggests Mizuki's attempts to reinterpret the gift of the truck and his relationship with the villagers (Table 6.3). Mizuki's writings touch on the theme of gift and exchange and how his views affected his perceptions of himself, Topetoro and the villagers. The practice of gift and exchange stimulated rich debates among and has grown into an interdisciplinary field. A seminal text by Marcel Mauss, *The Gift* (1925), attempts to formulate universal principles across history and cultures, including societies in Oceania. His thesis holds that gifts create bonds between individuals and groups but lock them into mutual obligations of repayment. The gift can be a tangible object or an intangible act. The donor gives with altruistic intent or economic self-interest. The receiver pays back financial and moral debt or even pays forward in anticipation of arger returns in the future. Following

Table 6.3 Mizuki's Narratives of Gifting the Pickup Truck

	Year Published/Medium/ Target Audience	Role of the Truck	Effects/Symbolism
Narrative 1	*Kommiku Shōwa-shi* (1988–9) and *Kanzenban Mizuki Shigeru den* (2004) Graphic novel Adults	Initially unstated; repayment for past generosity.	Private gesture of long-term friendship with Topetoro and the other villagers. The end of the Shōwa era.
Narrative 2	*Sensō to Nihon* (1991) Graphic novel Juveniles	Apologize and compensate for Japan's past atrocities.	Obligatory compensation. Reaffirms special friendship. Public role as a grassroots ambassador, with an international outlook.
Narrative 3	*Topetoro tono gojū-nen* (1995) Prose essay General audience	Payment for house.	Apologizes for embarrassment or guilt. Compensation for the house Topetoro built for Mizuki.

Source: Modified from Ryōta Nishino, 'Better Late than Never? Mizuki Shigeru's Trans-War Reflections on Journeys to New Britain Island', *Japan Review*, no. 32 (2019): 116.

Mauss, economics-leaning scholars frame gift exchange in the transactional logic of the market economy. Scholars with sociocultural backgrounds treat gift exchange as the basis of human bonds, even proposing that they maintain an intangible or inalienable spirit between individuals and groups.[51]

Mizuki's musings on his gift and his portrayals of himself and the others illustrate the dynamics of the traveller–travellee relationships. In the first narrative, Mizuki recognizes the truck has settled a moral debt to Topetoro and the villagers and marks the closure of his long wartime relationship with the village. The second narrative turns the truck into an olive branch to the villagers on behalf of Japan. The third narrative reveals his personal motive for the gift. More than other episodes in Mizuki's travelogues, the multiple accounts of the truck illustrate Rosenbawm's point about Mizuki's continuing writing to work out the meanings that a single episode sparked.

The first narrative told in *Komikku Shōwa-shi* (1989) has a meandering flow leading up to the gifting of the truck. Mizuki draws two meanings behind the truck but leaves some elements for subsequent retellings. Mizuki opens with the deaths of Emperor Hirohito in January 1989, which marked the end of the Shōwa era (1926–89). The accession of the new emperor and the transition to Heisei (1989–2019) compelled Mizuki to reflect on his past and future. Mizuki wonders if his life has meaning outside of his work. He draws a dialogue in which *yōkai* persuade him to give them due credit for their nurturing him and the success his *yōkai* manga provided. Then, Mizuki draws another scene whereby Topetoro and villagers ask him, 'Are you sure you want to live with us? We've built a house for you with the little money we've got.'[52] Back in Japan, Mizuki finds himself perplexed amidst conflicting demands from his publishers expecting more manga and his family telling him to slow down and reduce his workload.[53]

His ambivalence towards competing impulses brought him back to Emperor Hirohito. Mizuki pours out his feelings towards the emperor in four frames that take up two whole pages.

150   *Japanese Perceptions of Papua New Guinea*

Figure 6.1 Mizuki reflects on the death of Emperor Hirohito. Mizuki, *Shōwa-shi* 8, 248–9, (a) and (b) respectively. © MIZUKI Productions.

In the four frames, Mizuki says as follows:

> Frame 1 (a. Top left): As we moved from the Shōwa to Heisei era, somehow my mind became calm. I felt as if I were liberated from my pent-up anger.
> Frame 2 (a. Bottom left): During the war, everything was done in the name of the Emperor. Soldiers got bullied in his name. So, I had this anger I could not express.
> Frame 3 (b. Top right): I am sorry to say this, but for some reason or another I was getting angry at "the Emperor" unconsciously. Now, he is no longer around.
> Frame 4 (b. Bottom right): Ever since I was a child, I loathed having my freedom taken away. This is why my strange anger at the war was bound to be stronger than other people's.[54]

The candid words combined with sophisticated drawings form an unequivocal expression of his sentiments towards the emperor and the war. The dead soldiers left abandoned in the wilderness accentuates the cruelty and absurdity of the war and their meaningless deaths.

In Frame 1, Mizuki makes a pun on the name of the new era 'Heisei' by substituting an identical-sounding word meaning calm or tranquil (*heisei*). The name Heisei stands for 'peace all around'. It vests a hope for the peaceful future in the new era for Japan and a breakaway from the tumultuous Shōwa era. Mizuki's pun follows the ethos of the new era but adds his personal desire to achieve calmness in his mind. The following frames unfold Mizuki's catharsis. This is a rare political statement, even more daring than Okuzaki Kenzō's open criticism of Emperor Hirohito (Chapter 5). A case that most clearly demonstrates the sensitivity around the question of Emperor Hirohito's wartime responsibility is the repercussions of a statement by the mayor of Nagasaki city, Motoshima Hitoshi. On the anniversary of the Pearl Harbor attack, 7 December 1988, Motoshima stated that the emperor bore responsibility for the war. This statement caused a furore in the Japanese media who handled this issue with great restraint. In January 1990, a year after Hirohito's death, right-wing extremists shot Motoshima in the back; he survived the attempted assassination.[55]

Mizuki's visit to Namale in the wake of Hirohito's death marks his openness towards the villagers. On this trip, he takes Topetoro's family member, Eparom, out to lunch before buying Topetoro a truck. He sees Eparom putting her left-over lunch into a plastic bag to take home and feed her family later. Mizuki realizes the severity of poverty in Namale. He buys a truck from a local car dealer and paints Kitarō, the character from Mizuki's best-known manga, *Gegege no Kitarō*, on the bonnet, and donates the truck to Topetoro. In turn, Topetoro holds a ceremony to celebrate with Mizuki and the villagers. Topetoro announces, 'I am happy because what I did [for Mizuki] came back'.[56] Topetoro's remark, though brief, surprised and humbled Mizuki. Because he had learnt that Topetoro had dementia. Yet the more lasting reaction was embarrassment. Mizuki regrets using his delirium from malaria as an excuse for forgetting the finer aspects of their interactions. As far as Mizuki can recall, Topetoro's comment is the first of its kind; he had never asked for anything in return for his hospitality despite the deteriorating poverty in Namale. Topetoro's modesty compels Mizuki to form an even fonder impression of Topetoro.[57] The ceremony ends with Mizuki and Topetoro shaking hands in front of the vehicle, surrounded by the villagers. Mizuki's portrayal of Topetoro's faraway eyes hints at his good grace in accepting Mizuki's gift. By contrast, Mizuki looks humbled for having ignored Topetoro's long-held wish.[58] Mizuki then brings together two meanings for the truck: 'This [gift] possibly marks the demise of my

Shōwa. Maybe the end of Shōwa put an end to me, too. Indeed, it was a tumultuous era. I had a firm handshake with Topetoro and said goodbye to him.'[59]

Topetoro's response and Mizuki's counter-response highlight the gap in their perceptions of reciprocity in their relationship. Mizuki's reaction points to his assuming the relationship rested on what Sahlins names generalized reciprocity, often found in close families and friends. Sharing and giving goods and resources without explicit expectation of return. However, when, in what form, and by how much the receiver reciprocates remains unclear. This ambiguity rests on mutual trust and can, in David Graeber's words, sustain the relationship more like 'open-ended responsibility' in which people help one another on the assumption that the others will do likewise in times of need.[60] Mizuki assumed that the wartime bond and his status as *kandere* kept him and the villagers in generalized reciprocity. In contrast, Topetoro sees the truck as an overdue repayment for the service he and the villagers offered to Mizuki. Topetoro's ceremony represents what Sahlins calls balanced reciprocity. The receiver reciprocates the gift with goods and resources of equal value. Balanced reciprocity, or 'closed' reciprocity in Graeber's term, implies ending or the possibility of discontinuing mutual commitment. Yet, when the return gift comes with greater value than the previous gift, the return gift can indebt the receiver and extend the relationship.[61] After the ceremony, Mizuki bids Topetoro farewell, without the promise of return or the vow of renewed friendship. Mizuki thinks that Topetoro's ceremony has equalled the balance between them and left either party without reason to give or receive. Mizuki then extends the closure to the idea of 'his' Shōwa. In Mizuki's mind, Hirohito was a paradoxical figure who epitomized the wartime hell and motivated Mizuki to seek his paradise. However fraught and traumatic, the war nevertheless gave Mizuki an identity, to the point that he even developed *Nanpō-byō*. Mizuki's belated gift to the village marks the end of hell and of paradise. Be it war, its memory, or work, Mizuki needed hell to keep his paradise.

The second narrative is a 23-page manga essay, 'Sensō to Nihon' (1991) included within *Shōgaku rokunensei*, an 'edutainment' magazine aimed at children in the sixth year of primary school, aged eleven and twelve years.[62] 'Sensō to Nihon' follows the formula of his autobiographical manga that interweave the origins and the course of the Asia-Pacific War with Mizuki's personal experiences as a soldier. A distinctive angle of this essay, found in no other works by Mizuki, is that Mizuki positions the truck as compensation and a peace offering for the past atrocities the Japanese committed towards the Namale villagers. Mizuki tells about his personal transformation from a soldier to a veteran, and from a friend of the villagers to a grassroots ambassador seeking reconciliation with the travellees. 'Sensō to Nihon' has a narrow focus but his travel to New Britain figures as an event that changed his perceptions of the villagers and the war.

'Sensō to Nihon' advances an international and political agenda. Mizuki takes a clear stance in which he identifies the Japanese as the perpetrators in the empire-building project and the ensuing war. Mizuki avers 'inhuman deeds' carried out against the peoples of Korea, Southeast Asia and China.[63] In the final three pages, he relates his recent travel to New Britain. One villager comments that the Japanese executed the chief of the village for refusing to cooperate. Other villagers join in and tell Mizuki that the Japanese executed two more village chiefs, one of them Topetoro's uncle. In quick succession, Topetoro reassures Mizuki, 'Don't worry, you are different'.[64] Mizuki adds that this is the first time he has learnt of the Japanese atrocities from the villagers directly. His belated discovery of his own complicity, however indirect and distant, validates his appreciation of the villagers' kindness towards him.[65]

'Sensō to Nihon' then moves to a scene where Mizuki gifts the truck to Topetoro and the villagers. Mizuki writes, 'I think that they had big hearts like human beings should. Right away, I gave them a used truck. But this won't erase the wartime guilt'.[66] In the following and concluding four frames, he reiterates the injustice and cruelties the Japanese committed in Korea and China and asserts that 'only when the Japanese express sincere contrition for these past events can they stand tall as world citizens'.[67] Mizuki refocuses on his compatriots' violence inflicted on the people of New Britain. The killing of the village chief and two leaders has him reassess his positionality in relation to the war and the villagers. Mizuki's truck comes from the place of contrition and compassion for the people who expended considerable largesse on him in spite of their gross suffering. The truck assumes metaphorical significance. As well as a peace offering for the villagers, the truck becomes a vehicle carrying Mizuki's future-oriented vision for the Japanese youth to practise when they grow older and interact with people from other countries.

Mizuki draws symbolic significance from the truck as a vehicle transporting him back to his past journeys. While 'Sensō to Nihon' leaves his relationship with the villagers underdeveloped, two subsequent writings mark Mizuki's re-examining of his past journeys through the eyes of the villagers. Both writings appeared in 1995 when the fiftieth anniversary of *sengo* was high on the public agenda. One is a new epilogue to *Musume* and the other is a retrospective essay on his friendship with Topetoro, included in *Mizuki Shigeru no jūgunkōki: Topetoro tono gojū-nen* (1995; hereafter, *Jūgunkōki*). Mizuki made few public comments on the anniversary, but the year 1995 was crucial for his personal memory. The year marked the first anniversary of Topetoro's funeral, which Mizuki sponsored and attended as the chief mourner.

Along with 'Sensō to Nihon', these writings draw on his journeys to form his position on the war, but go even further. He reframes his past trips through the optics of the villagers. In one episode, Mizuki reconsiders the night he threw away potatoes Topetoro cooked for him. He found the whole hut replete with the villagers sleeping on the floor. Mizuki now speculates that Topetoro sent the villagers to the hut to protect him from men who still resented the Japanese. What he once thought of as an innocuous oddity turns out to be the result of Topetoro's thoughtful gesture. Mizuki comes to appreciate Topetoro even more as a friend.[68] Moreover, Mizuki further learns that Topetoro feared that other villagers might attack or even kill him. Mizuki now understands that such hostility was plausible because he learnt that the Japanese had killed many islanders.[69] The two episodes indicate the rift in their opinions on the Japanese among the villagers. Mizuki enjoyed reception by Topetoro, the village headman. This alone was not sufficient to allay the hostility and suspicion other villagers held towards the Japanese. Rather, Mizuki's presence dredged up the division among the villagers that Topetoro had to deal with. Mizuki could not continue isolating himself from the historical memories simmering in the villagers' consciousness. These two writings inform us of the symbolic value of Mizuki's truck that spurred his retroactive recollections of his past journeys.

The third narrative, appearing in *Jūgunkōki*, elaborates on the first narrative and couches the gift in Mizuki's personal motivation. Crucially, Mizuki answers one question the other two narratives provoke but have left unaddressed – why the truck? Mizuki's answer has bearings on the notions of gift exchange and reciprocity. The third narrative starts with a trip to Namale that Mizuki made in the 1980s. On this trip, he discovers that Topetoro had built a house for him on the understanding that Mizuki still intended to settle in Namale.[70] In *Jūgunkōki*, Mizuki admits more clearly than other writing that the news surprised and troubled him.[71] The house also made Mizuki anxious about the letters he had written to Topetoro over the years: Mizuki made vague promises to return to the village, but never informed Topetoro that he had in fact ruled out retiring to Namale. Mizuki realized that Topetoro and his family believed that Mizuki would indeed retire and live out his life in Namale. Eventually, Mizuki recalls that Topetoro had long wanted a truck and giving one would serve as adequate compensation for the house.[72]

Jūgunkōki throws new light on the meaning of the truck and reciprocity – Topetoro's decades-long acts of kindness as an intangible gift, in the mould of the generalized reciprocity. The house is a different kind, a tangible gift that Mizuki needed to reciprocate with a counter-gift, in the manner of balanced reciprocity. For Mizuki, settling in Namale could have presented him with the same dilemma of Nanyō-Orientalism he encountered in the wake of Japan's defeat. Still, refusing to accept Topetoro's offer to live in the house would cause a loss of face for both parties and leave Topetoro in financial debt. Yet, Mizuki still wanted to visit the community on a temporary basis for his South Seas 'fix'; squaring the debt for the house could pre-empt, mitigate or repair any potential damage to himself and his relationship when he next visited the village. The truck also carries the moral purpose of apologizing for the myriad costs that Topetoro and his family had borne as a result of Mizuki's equivocation or bad faith. The gift of the truck is not an arbitrary or spontaneous act of generosity or compassion, but a calculated decision.

What became of the truck? After the trip, Mizuki received a letter from Topetoro's family. One of Topetoro's sons, Tami, had driven it into a ravine under the influence of alcohol but had come off unscathed. An accompanying photograph showed the truck was a total write-off. Mizuki and his wife deduced that Topetoro's family expected a replacement from Mizuki. On his wife's advice, Mizuki decided not to respond to the letter. The Mizukis grew reticent to have themselves embroiled in the continuing chain of gift exchange and became suspicious that Topetoro's family could take advantage of Mizuki in the future. Mizuki then put his plan for the next visit at abeyance.[73] The demise of the truck meant the loss of its practical value for the villagers' day-to-day life. For Mizuki, the news announces an additional closure of his symbolic investment as his avatar, as seen in his drawing and the signature on the bonnet, to maintain his bond with the villagers.

Phase 4: Closing the circle

The donation of the truck turned out to be the last time Mizuki and Topetoro met. Two subsequent trips Mizuki made with his two daughters, magazine editors and assistants in 1992 and 1994 make up Phase 4 of his travel. Following the news of the wrecked truck, Mizuki received letters from Topetoro's family in 1992. The letters notified him of Topetoro's sudden death and urged him to visit soon. Mizuki arrived in Namale in July but saw little indication of a funeral. The villagers told him to return two years later. Mizuki duly returned in July 1994 and he sponsored the full funeral of Topetoro for the villagers as the chief mourner. In travelogues recounting these journeys, Mizuki fulfils his loyalty to Topetoro as his friend, but, more crucially, his social responsibility as a *kandere* to the entire community. Beneath his decision was Topetoro's spirit directing Mizuki to hold the final rites. Nonetheless, Mizuki's reflections fall short of interrogating his personal incentives to satisfy his underlying yearnings for the good old days.

Mizuki's growing sympathy to the villagers foregrounds a significant shift in his attitude before his trips in 1992 and 1994. In *Jūgunkōki* (1995), he realizes his lack of consideration throughout the decades, to the point of describing himself as 'a little stupid' for taking Topetoro's hospitality for granted.[74] Mizuki admits that only after he turned sixty-five in 1987 did he appreciate how much effort the villagers had made to accommodate him in the post-war era as well as during the war.[75] Furthermore, the death of Topetoro made Mizuki aware that the villagers gave him so much more than he ever did, even though they had so little. Previously, he believed that small gifts were sufficient tokens of appreciation and gave Topetoro no cash for accommodation, because he assumed they lived off the land and needed little else.[76] Mizuki's admission makes a rare apology for his moral shortcomings and obliviousness to the penetration of the cash economy in Namale. His humility carries the residue of Nanyō-Orientalism that fixed Mizuki's gaze at Namale as an economically self-sufficient heaven.

The most significant event in Mizuki's 1990s journeys is his unexpected sponsoring of the funeral. The lead-up to it offers an insight into the gaps between how Mizuki and the villagers perceived one another. The 1992 trip made Mizuki wonder about the villagers' intention. When he returned in 1994, he found the villagers had not made any plans for the funeral. Only then did Mizuki learn that Topetoro's family faced severe financial difficulties and could not afford the funeral – a major blemish against the family of the headman. Mizuki then decides to sponsor it. Mizuki's sponsoring aligns with James G. Carrier's understanding of friendship in Melanesia, which includes PNG. His ethnography in PNG, complemented with other anthropologists' work, suggests that Melanesian people form and perceive affective ties in different ways from the West. Namely, people in the West tend to make friends based on mutually shared values and attributes. In Melanesia, the core of the interpersonal relationship lies in 'the effects one has on others, the ways they respond to one's actions' in shared social situations and structure.[77] Taken together, Mizuki's repeated visits or stays in the community do not constitute affective ties. While his donation of the truck compensated Topetoro's immediate family, it left the rest of the community expecting Mizuki to do something worthy of his stature as a *kandere* and as Topetoro's guest of honour. Mizuki's sponsorship fulfilled these obligations and enabled him to renew his bond with the villagers.

One important feature of Mizuki's Phase 4 travelogues is Topetoro's spiritual presence in Mizuki's mind. This is where Mizuki's lifelong fascination with *yōkai* meets his travelogues. In the 1990s, Mizuki visited many places to study *yōkai* around the world. He travelled to Namale in the 1990s with a renewed sensitivity to the world of *yōkai*. On his 1994 trip, Mizuki claims the spirit of Topetoro possessed him and inveigled him into sponsoring the funeral. In particular, *Kanzenban*, in its manga form, offers a graphic representation of the spirit of Topetoro. Mizuki and his Japanese assistant visit Mr Paivu, a former mayor of Rabaul and an acquaintance of Mizuki's. The three discuss the type of funeral they should hold. Paivu proposes a simple service but just as Mizuki agrees, the spirit of Topetoro appears and floats besides Mizuki. Mizuki goes into a sudden fit of excitement and insists, 'if there is no *tumbuan* [the traditional mask of the Tolai people of New Britain, used in ceremonial dances], then we can't say it's a funeral!'[78] Paivu's eyes glint; he agrees to assist if Mizuki pays and even suggests Mizuki be the chief mourner. Mizuki's assistant grows concerned about the steep cost. Mizuki, too, recognizes 'an eerie feeling as if he were turning into someone else'.[79] All he recalls was the vague feeling that lasted until the end of the funeral, but vividly recalls him 'getting pulled by someone'.[80]

Mizuki's claim of the supernatural experience in *Kanzenban* heralds his desire to extend his friendship in the spiritual and posthumous realms. As the negotiations continue, the spirit of Topetoro points his finger at Mizuki's head, as if to show his issuing of a command to Mizuki.[81] In subsequent sequences, Mizuki depicts himself, in both words and images, as being immersed in the traditional funerary rites and the *tumbuan* dance, relishing the happy memories of the wartime and his earlier post-war journeys. As Mizuki peers through his window on the aeroplane back to Japan, the spirit of Topetoro appears in the sky and closes his journey.[82] In *Jūgunkōki*, Mizuki reiterates the profound impression the funeral made on him. He muses about how the ideal humans are those who live in harmony with nature, and this makes him yearn for people like Topetoro.[83] This is Mizuki reaffirming that Topetoro built the bridge between

Mizuki's hell and heaven, and Topetoro's spirit sustained Mizuki's emotional bond to his fellow villagers.

This 1994 trip was the last trip Mizuki made to Namale. In 1995, Mizuki learnt that a volcanic eruption in Rabaul had destroyed many villages, burying them or turning them to ash. The news not only worried Mizuki but also led him to conclude that his relationship with Namale had come to its natural conclusion.[84] By then, Mizuki had mellowed and grew more self-reflexive than he had been in the 1970s and the 1980s. Still, from the point of view of the traveller–travellee relationship, Mizuki's sponsoring asserts his privileged position as the traveller able to buy off the villagers' performance. The sponsorship brought mutual benefits. The community gave Topetoro a long overdue ceremonial farewell. The dance gave the last injection against Mizuki's *Nanpō-byō*. The power relationship is a recurrent issue in Japanese travellers' travel to the nation afflicted by a war that was not of its making, which is addressed more closely in the next chapter.

Conclusion

In his manga and prose, Mizuki provided multiple renditions of his visits to Namale from the wartime period through the mid-1990s. What began as a search for utopia amidst wartime hell evolved into his decades-long friendship with the local residents. Nanyō-Orientalism coloured his initial perceptions and affinity with the community. In the post-war years, *Nanpō-byō* accelerated his nostalgic yearning for the paradise he relished. Mizuki's relationship with the villagers went through enchantment, disillusionment and resolution before its eventual closure. The deaths of Emperor Hirohito and Topetoro impelled Mizuki to recognize changes within himself and reassess his relationship with the villagers. Among Mizuki's travelogues, the three accounts of the truck bring Mizuki's exercise of authorial agency into sharp relief. After the mid-1980s, Mizuki grew more empathetic towards the villagers and disavowed his ignorance and arrogance so much so that he reciprocates the gift of life he received from the villagers during the wartime. His sponsoring of Topetoro's funeral marked his delayed participation in their communal life and cemented his status in Namale more than when he was Topetoro's guest.

Dismissing Mizuki's belated admissions of his flaws and his multiple writings as self-serving rationalization is a fair point. The people of Namale and the many Mizukis we encounter represent the images Mizuki has crafted. Still, such criticism misses the more amorphous, enduring and even insidious power of the Japanese imperial imagination. Nanyō-Orientalism shaped Mizuki's life from his youth to his old age. *Nanpō-byō* both troubled and delighted Mizuki and the villagers in varying degrees. These by-products of the Japanese imperial imaginary put Mizuki in a paradox. Nanyō-Orientalism not only shaped and saved his life in ways few could imagine but also kept him captive and even vulnerable to the very imagination that made him.

7

Vicarious consumer travel and the performance of emotional awakening in travelogues

The rise of international travel in post-war era Japan has boosted the variety and the volume of travel, travellers and travelogues. Of the many genres of travelogue published, narratives of journeys to former battle sites of the Asia-Pacific War comprise a niche in the publishing market. PNG has never been a major tourist destination for the Japanese in the post-war period. Yet, as with other Pacific Islands, veterans and families of deceased soldiers visit PNG, often on multiple occasions, to conduct *ireishiki* (spirit-consoling services, in a similar manner to a pilgrimage) and to grieve and console the spirit of the dead in accordance with the Japanese Buddhist custom. Some also engage in *ikotsu shūshū* ('bone collection') to recover and repatriate the remains of deceased soldiers.[1] These travellers come close to what Sabine Marschall terms 'personal memory tourism'.[2] The travellers under scrutiny in this chapter are an overlooked group whom I call vicarious consumer travellers. They visit sites of historical events and, to borrow John Urry's words, 'consume places' that are bound up with historical memory.[3] Moreover, the travellers' vicarious imagining of the past, occasioned by the virtue of 'being there', can add something new to their visions of the past, present and future that could not be possible without seeing the site with their own eyes. Looking into the writings of vicarious consumer travellers can elevate the importance of travel as a part of travelling memory, a conduit between the different temporal realms, and as a historical, a means of reconstructing and a mode of representing history.

This chapter asks how these travellers develop their perspectives on the war during and after their journeys. The application of vicarious consumer travel helps to analyse the travellers' empathetic engagement with the past and the historical interpretations they develop. What this chapter finds in the travelogues analysed is that vicarious consumer travellers can influence the sentiments the travellers form, but it may not necessarily overturn their previously held beliefs and values or open them to alternative visions. With whom and which historical narratives the travel writers identify depend on multiple considerations. The traveller's personal background, values, modes of travel, and the sociopolitical and cultural contexts of their journey play important roles. The travelogues analysed here tend to reimagine and represent the foreign warscape into an exclusively Japanese memoryscape in which the local residents remain on or off the margin of the travellers' consciousness.

The notion of vicarious consumer travellers expands on the oft-used Japanese word *tsuitaiken*. Its literal translation, 'experiencing in the footsteps of someone else', parallels what Peter Hulme names 'footstep travel' in its purpose and nuances. In the long lineage of Japanese travel writing, generations of travellers retrace the footsteps of preceding travellers and their writing.[4] Where *tsuitaiken* provides motivation for travel and sets the agenda, vicarious consumer travel pays additional attention to the performative character of travel and travelogues. As with the previous chapter, the power of travel on the travellers' perception of the place, history and even their life, remains a continuing and underlying theme. Travel forms part of the heterogeneous feedback loop of memory- and history-making. The consumption of places and history, the (re)imagining and (re)production of history and articulating historical interpretations in non-academic domains underlines the publicness of history.[5]

This chapter looks at seven commercially published travelogues by six vicarious consumer travellers that appeared between 1962 and 2009. This period offers a cross section of the travellers' responses to the changing sociopolitical and cultural landscape in Japan and PNG that led to reinterpretations of the war. The selection is by no means exhaustive or representative, but shows sufficient variations in the styles of journeys undertaken (alone, with friends or local people), and in the traveller's identities, such as their gender, age and occupation (see Table 7.1).[6] The age of the authors indicates their generations (as discussed in Chapter 1) and prevailing *zeitgeist* at the time at which they were socialized. Age is but one factor that influences their individual values and beliefs. One crucial criterion for selection is availability: all are commercially published books sold at bookshops (brand new, second hand, online and physical) or held at public libraries. None of the travelogues have, to my knowledge, enjoyed commercial success or critical acclaim. Those by travel journalist Kanetaka Kaoru, photographer Yasujima Takayoshi and journalist Makino Hiromichi were published by well-known

Table 7.1 Profiles of the Travel Writers

Name and Year of Birth	Occupation	Year of Travel	Purpose	Dominant Narrative*	Post-travel Inspiration
Kanetaka Kaoru (1928–2019)	Television travel journalist	1961	Work; travel programme	Victim	Strengthened her pacifist outlook, but no strong identification with the Papua New Guineans as victims
Kawaguchi Kizuki (1958)	Office worker	1990	Leisure travel	Victim < Perpetrator	Wrote the book with substantial historical research; joined an NGO after travel.
Makino Hiromichi (1935)	Journalist; lecturer	2001 and 2007	Journey 1: Work; journalism Journey 2: lecturer on war sites for a training trip for Shinto priests	Heroes	After the first journey he resigned from the Sankei newspaper and became a freelance writer and a guide to war-related sites.
Miyakawa Masayo (1942)	Journalist	1983 and 1984	Work; journalism	Perpetrator	Resolved to re-examine her life and to speak with her father. Introspective.
Tsumori Takudō (1933)	Buddhist monk	1976	Officiating at spirit-consoling ceremonies	Victim > Perpetrator	Pursued his theological occupation
Yasujima Takayoshi (1959)	Photographer	2008–9	Work: photography	Victim	Continued with his photography and activities

Note: *The symbols > stand for 'more than' and < 'less than'

Japanese publishers, but not with any large print runs. The modest reputation and circulation do not undermine the inherent value of the publications. The availability to the public entails the authors' perspectives going into the public arena and joining in the collective exercise of history-making.

As seen in the lasting effects of the war on those involved, vicarious consumer travel presupposes that the traveller will reflect upon their travel after the completion of their physical journey. The current trend among travel writing scholars is to hold self-reflexivity as a vital indicator of how travel informs the travel writers' worldview. In sum, self-reflexivity refers to a critical examination of the travellers' purposes of their travel and of the influence of their presence in the foreign land on the global asymmetry of socio-economic power. In her examination of post-war English-language travelogues, Debbie Lisle concludes that the travelogue is a generally conservative genre. What she finds most problematic is the absence of self-reflexivity. The travel writers abandon the idiom of imperialism and racism and adopt that of diversity and tolerance instead. Yet, the travel writer ultimately exercises the power of the pen.[7]

Lisle's caveat speaks to the vocabulary of 'being implicated in history' and the modes of commemoration as discussed in Chapter 1, and ties them up with the politics of travel and the travelogue as an everyday and textual manifestation of international relations. The connections contemporary citizens have with the past, as Tessa Morris-Suzuki and Michael Rothberg have elucidated, share common grounds with the contention by Geoffrey White and Eveline Buchheim. They argue that travel does not necessarily deliver the commonly held benefits of broadening the mind and stimulating self-reflection, but rather may have the opposite effect of reinforcing the traveller's ideological leanings.[8] These assertions call to mind Hiro Saito's distinction between nationalist and cosmopolitan commemoration and the further addition of national commemoration (Chapter 1). Where national and nationalist commemoration privileges the memories of the compatriots, the latter transcends national boundaries to mourn the suffering and the deaths of the 'foreign' others. Both heroic and victim interpretations presuppose Japan as the underlying site of commemoration. By contrast, the perpetrator discourse upholds cosmopolitan commemoration that seeks to transcend ethnocentric biases to foster compassion across national and ethnic boundaries.[9] Vicarious consumer travel cannot offer solutions but can help to analyse the extent to which travel can facilitate the traveller to question and explain how they are implicated in the war and how they draw their conclusions about history.

The war that never leaves us

The earliest travelogue analysed here is *Sekai no tabi* (1962) by the television travel journalist Kanetaka Kaoru. This travelogue derived from a filming trip that Kanetaka and her two-person crew made to Australia and the southern Pacific Islands in 1961 for a weekly television programme of the same title, which aired from 1959 to 1991. The series gained immense popularity shortly after its debut in 1959 and Kanetaka soon became an iconic figure among her contemporaries and with younger women.[10] The programme began at a time when foreign travel was restricted in Japan. Even when the Japanese government lifted the restrictions in April 1964, foreign travel still remained unaffordable for many.[11] Each 30-minute programme had a light ethnographic and educational touch, which was appropriate for a family-friendly Sunday morning slot. Kanetaka's awakening to her ignorance of wartime history led her to identify with the victim discourse of the Japanese defeat and with pacifism, in line with the liberal politics of the day.

Kanetaka began her imaginative journeying back into the war period at the town of Lae, where the Japanese landed in March 1942 and established a base. The Allies isolated the Japanese by attacking their reinforcements and supply vessels. A prominent incident was the Allied attack on Japanese vessels in the Dampier Strait while they were *en route* to Lae from Rabaul, in March 1943. During her visit to Lae, Kanetaka and her crew hired a local driver, who remained anonymous throughout. Her interaction with the driver influenced her personal reawakening about the war. The driver was twelve years old when the Japanese occupied and established their base in Lae, making him Kanetaka's near contemporary. He also claimed to have attended a Japanese-run school for two years. His Japanese, initially halting, flowed a little more easily after they conversed for some time. He pointed to the sky and said *hikōki* (aeroplane) and referred to a flowerpot made from a disused bombshell as *bakudan* (bomb).[12] He even sang Japanese children's songs. Kanetaka felt more embarrassed than surprised to hear his Japanese. The driver asked a film crew member if he knew a military officer, Mr Hamazaki, who spoke good Pidgin English, adding, 'Was he a good man or a bad man? No comment'. The driver then offered to pay Kanetaka to buy and send him tins of corned beef that Mr Hamazaki used to give him, and to have a watch, that Hamazaki had given him, repaired. Kanetaka was troubled by his request for her to do errands.[13] The driver's wartime memories left her in a morally ambiguous position for dealing with wartime memory.

The driver's recollection of the wartime upsets the traveller–travellee hierarchy (Chapter 6). The moneyed traveller assumes superiority over the 'service provider' who relies on income from the traveller. The driver's 'no comment' keeps the upper hand by withholding the full details of his experience, which accentuated the subtlety of his remark in conveying his subordinate position and even ill-treatment by Hamazaki. The driver expects her to function as a conduit between the two men. Equally, the driver's request for her to perform errands, and his anecdotes about receiving food from the Japanese, shows that he achieved sufficient credit in wartime and maintained emotional ties with the Japanese after the war. Up to this point Kanetaka describes the interaction without expressing her feelings. Her subsequent account registers her emerging sentiments about the war.

The disturbing presence of the past came to the surface when the driver took Kanetaka and her crew to a beach. The travellers saw the wreckage of the *Myōkō-maru*, a Japanese transport vessel sunk by the Allied forces.[14] Kanetaka felt the stark contrast between the natural beauty of the sea and the rusted and decayed shipwreck. At the beach, one of the film crew suddenly recalled his friend who had died in the war, and he wept. The sight jogged her memory of a previous assignment to East Berlin. There she saw a wartime government building with its ceiling and windows destroyed and bullet marks on the walls. She dismissed the building as 'the relics of warriors' dreams' and even felt 'a sense of aversion because the building was in an area where wartime ringleaders met'.[15] She admitted that the wreckage of *Myōkō-maru* provoked a different reaction:

> The transport vessel was a harrowing sight. Around 4,000 soldiers and crew perished in the sea near here in 1943. I felt intense anger at those who pushed the powerless to sites of death. People preach the virtue of keeping harmony and good manners. But everything changes once war breaks out; they demand hatred and victory. I felt we were weak to have been dragged along by those people.[16]

Kanetaka's anger registers a candid and coded endorsement of the victim narrative she probably could not express on TV. Her anger went not towards the Allies, however; she saw the hypocrisy of the Japanese military elite and officers. Behind the rhetoric of peace and harmony, they stoked jingoism and animosity and pushed the Japanese public into war. Her comment is coded, as she accused military strategists for the loss of lives and eventual defeat. What mattered more than nationality was the status of those occupying the building and the vessel. She identified the soldiers and the crew on the *Myōkō-maru* as victims of the war and held the military elite in contempt. Though Kanetaka did not join the dots to form or articulate her position clearly, her reaction has traces of cosmopolitan commemoration.

Kanetaka's reaction indicates personal background as a vital, if not definitive, ingredient of vicarious consumer travel. Kanetaka grew up in a comfortable middle-class household and attended an Anglican mission school. She benefited from a liberal education while state-funded schools came under wartime control. Kanetaka studied for two years at the University of California, Los Angeles in the early 1950s, and recalled experiencing little animosity or discrimination for being a Japanese citizen. Back in Japan, she put her bilingual skills to good use and launched a career in journalism.[17] *Sekai no tabi* enabled Kanetaka to polish her international outlook and to project a public image of a woman of the post-war era with 'traditional' and 'modern' sensibilities. In the early years of the programme, she wore a *kimono* when filming, even in New Guinea, to stress her Japanese femininity. Behind the TV screen, she enjoyed an unparalleled autonomy her contemporaries could only dream of: she planned her trips, led the all-male crew, and directed, edited and narrated the programmes.[18] The trip to New Guinea confronted Kanetaka with raw and unexpected reminders of the war. Age and a privileged upbringing did not shield her from the legacy of the war and even stimulated her to examine her conscience.

Kanetaka's emerging disposition reiterates how sentiments travel across national boundaries. It highlights the central trait of vicarious consumer travel: the traveller confronts the legacy of the past and informs their evaluation of the past, present and future. The intense anger that Kanetaka felt drove her to criticize herself as a complicit bystander, although only a teenager, as a result of her 'weakness'. She then assumed a pacifist stance to make restitution for her own perceived weakness and to contribute to sustaining the ethos of the pacifist post-war constitution that prohibited Japan from engaging in warfare. Kanetaka's opinion resonated with the rhetoric of pacifism that had risen to prominence during the early post-war years. The high point of this rhetoric was the bitter struggle over the ratification of the US-Japan Security Treaty of 1960. Peace campaigners and the intelligentsia voiced their opposition to what they perceived as Japan's backwards step into war and the consolidation of Japan's subordinate status to the United States.[19] Readers older than Kanetaka might have found her criticism naïve because she failed to recognize the severe control and repression of wartime. As if to counter this criticism, her witnessing of her colleague's reaction brought her close to the raw grief of wartime and gave her the authority to speak her view. She accepted her moral responsibility to prevent war from recurring. Kanetaka's vicarious consumer travel forged a pacifist vision on a hopeful note.

On the surface of the travelogue, Kanetaka's empathetic imagination did not extend to the New Guineans. She describes a light-hearted gesture that her driver made. He suddenly picked up a stone from the beach and slowly started writing *Dai-Nihon* (Great Japan), shorthand for the Japanese Empire, in big *kanji* script on the hull of the shipwreck, not just once but twice. Then, he turned to Kanetaka and smiled at the travellers.[20] Kanetaka made no comment or offered no explanation as to the driver's thoughts or actions, and left readers to draw their own conclusions. Her description can reduce him into an inscrutable other who bordered on ignorant of the grief Japanese felt. Still, her account underlines her confusion about the driver. His apparent pride in his past association with the Japanese presented Kanetaka with an irony that a foreigner embodied the vestige of Japan's delegitimized military ethos.

A subsequent encounter with another local person also illuminates Kanetaka's empathetic capacity. Kanetaka visited Goroka and met a New Guinean coffee plantation owner. His attire, identical to that of European plantation owners, and his fluent English, not Pidgin English, immediately told Kanetaka that he had received a western education. After the initial pleasantries, the plantation owner broke into Japanese: 'While I was in Rabaul, I was hired by the navy for four years'.[21] His command of Japanese shocked Kanetaka. She thought his Japanese was far better than the driver's. The plantation owner claimed to have learnt Japanese while working as an interpreter under the Japanese for four years. When Kanetaka heard him say, 'Come here!' in the commanding tone of a military officer while he was showing her his plantation, she got 'an eerie feeling'.[22] To Kanetaka, the man represented a paradox. If his western dress and 'proper' English signalled his status as a member of the indigenous elite, then his military Japanese revealed another layer to his cultural repertoire. This military speech was presumably the only variety of Japanese he had learnt. His unwitting display fifteen years after defeat reminded Kanetaka of the deep imprint of wartime discipline upon him.

Kanetaka's reactions demonstrate the unevenness of vicarious consumer travel. Her filming trip evolved into a history lesson of sorts that continually challenged her with unexpected and unsettling reminders of the war. The sadness of the wreckage and the crew's reaction prompted her anger at the wartime militarists, which, in turn, informed her pacifist vision. Where her vicarious imagination fell short was her reaction to the driver and the plantation owner. These men were living witnesses of a wartime experience that the Japanese would find embarrassing and would rather forget. Tempting as it is to criticize her lack of sensitivity towards these men, her surprise, embarrassment and confusion, at least on the pages, registers her inchoate anxiety about the wartime she did not know. Her encounter with the memories of the war exposed the fragility of an ostensibly upbeat mood of the early 1960s that she came to represent.

Tangible reminders of an intangible presence

The travelogue by ordained Buddhist monk Tsumori Takudō, published in 1980, records his six journeys across Southeast Asia and the Pacific Islands in the mid-1970s. On these trips, he accompanied veterans and their families and officiated at spirit-consoling ceremonies. Tsumori's travelogue largely substantiates White and Buchheim's claim that travel reinforces existing beliefs. However, Tsumori's account presents a glimpse into the ways travel can stimulate an alternative understanding of war history. Tsumori's brief autobiographical account hints at his pacifist beliefs. He was born into the family of a Buddhist monk and his upbringing in wartime and later experience of the subsequent defeat taught him the futility of war and reinforced his Buddhist belief that harm should not be inflicted upon sentient beings. Later, his Buddhist faith led him to participate in anti-Vietnam War rallies while studying at university. He subsequently volunteered to officiate at pilgrimages for Japanese veterans and their families.[23]

Tsumori visited Wewak from late August to early September 1976, a journey that was to have a significant impact on him. This was his second journey to the Pacific Islands, and the first to PNG. Wewak had been the site of a major Japanese airbase. Allied attacks between August 1943 and May 1945 considerably undermined the Japanese presence and cut off the Japanese supply lines to the rest of the country.[24] On the way to a commemoration site in Wewak, Tsumori found a metal flask beside a path, which he ascertained was of Japanese military issue. He subsequently found over thirty flasks scattered around. He collected them in a fit of excitement, with the aid of the local residents, put them in a van and brought them back to his hotel. Tsumori told a fellow pilgrim about his intention to return the flasks to the soldiers' families. The pilgrim doubted that the families would want to accept them. Tsumori stared at them, and saw the images of soldiers in them:

> [The soldiers] had been waiting for the very day to return to Japan for these long thirty-three years. And the day is tomorrow. How would I feel if I died here? I would probably want to go home. These water bottles know the hardship of every one of those soldiers. ... Yes! I decided to take them no matter what. ... At any rate, if we had travelled a day later, the river would have been too full for us to cross. We could not even have collected the flasks. Yes, the fallen heroes were watching us. The moment I had this thought I felt so much lighter.[25]

This was Tsumori's *satori* moment – a moment of spiritual awakening and sudden enlightenment. Although Tsumori's decision to bring the flasks back seems presumptuous, irrational and impractical, it symbolizes his commitment to give appropriate final rites to the soldiers and their families in accordance with Japanese funeral customs. As anthropologist Namihira Emiko documents, funeral customs in Japan require the mourners to see the dead person before sending them off to the realm of the dead. The mourners then cremate the body and put the ashes in the family grave. Thus, for a bereaved family, not seeing their loved ones and not knowing their whereabouts is tantamount to leaving them in the unconscionable halfway zone between the living and the dead.[26] During the war, the Japanese military had little capacity to repatriate bodies and remains. The compromise was to send an empty box to the family containing a note acknowledging the soldier's service and sacrifice, and sometimes sand or seashells from the beach were included as a substitute for the body of the dead. The military reasoned that the sand contained the spirit of the deceased. Many families found no solace in this: they felt deprived of their chance to perform their final rites for the dead.[27] Tsumori felt that this gesture was a meagre substitute for not being able to bring back the actual remains of the soldiers, but he convinced himself that small efforts like these were necessary to build peace. He brought all the flasks home, much to the astonishment of the customs officers in Japan, and delivered several of them to the soldiers' families.[28]

Tsumori did not elaborate on exactly how bringing the flasks home would lead to peace. What mattered to him was the gesture that symbolized his spiritual sensitivity for communing with the fallen soldiers, and further promoted his role as a spiritual conduit between them and their families. This was his pacifist vision cultivated through his vicarious consumer travel. These claims, however, brought about an imaginary reconquest of the islands. When Tsumori decided to take the flasks home from Wewak, thunder struck and rain began to fall. Tsumori became convinced that the thunderclap represented the soldiers' spirits dancing with joy.[29] While this may sound sentimental and outlandish, what matters is the individual's receptiveness towards and belief in these phenomena, that is, in the ability to suspend their rational and scientific mindset in order to commune with the dead. Tsumori's interpretation of the thunderclap is not an isolated claim. Ordained Buddhist priest and anthropologist Nakayama Kaoru officiated at spirit-consoling services in PNG between 2001 and 2012. He repeatedly witnessed the pilgrims relishing their encounters with the ghosts and spirits of the dead, which gave their journeys greater emotional depth.[30] Encounters with the supernatural and the surreal provide opportunities for visitors to claim that their trips are worthwhile and even authentic for attaining spiritual unity with the dead.

Tsumori's account comes with political implications of marginalizing the local people, especially for how he turns Wewak into an exclusively Japanese zone of commemoration. Nonetheless, as his journey progressed, Tsumori began to recognize the perpetrator narrative after hearing a story told by a veteran, a Mr Takahashi, to fellow pilgrims at a dinner at a hotel in Wewak. One of Takahashi's purposes was to look for a village vice headman who had assisted him and his troops with food and other materials.[31] Takahashi managed to find the vice headman and both men were delighted to see each other for the first time in over thirty years. The vice headman returned the Japanese military currency that Takahashi had given him as payment for his kindness that saved him and his troops. Takahashi was immediately embarrassed that he had paid in a currency that had no value in New Guinea. He returned to the hotel and gave most of his belongings to the vice headman in appreciation of his past generosity and to recompose the inadequacy of the payment in military currency. The two men parted with tears, promising to meet again. Takahashi ended his tale with a twist: New Guineans such as this vice headman 'had had a difficult time' for helping the Japanese.[32] Tsumori reflected on the position of the New Guineans, 'I had heard stories about New Guinean chiefs who had been put on trial and sent to prison for assisting the Japanese during the war. I realized that these were true stories. As a Japanese I must not forget that the New Guineans are also victims of the war! I'd like to commemorate their deaths if time permits'.[33]

Tsumori's inclusion of this episode augers his emergent identification with the perpetrator narrative of the war in Japan. Although Tsumori's reflection above was a one-off comment, his sympathy for the New Guineans suggests the influence of the intellectual underpinning of anti-Vietnam protests he participated in earlier. Writer Oda Makoto (1932–2007), who was a leading figure in Beheiren, the Citizens' Federation for Peace in Vietnam, criticized

Japan's rearguard support for the United States in the Vietnam War. He claimed that it repeated the Japanese citizen's complicity during the Asia-Pacific War that sanctioned the violence on others. Oda's objection stemmed from his conviction that the Japanese were no mere victims of the Asia-Pacific War and the militarized state but also the perpetrators.[34] Whether he found the time and space to commemorate the deaths of the New Guineans remains uncertain. Even though his style of travel likely caused him to tune more into the voices of the Japanese, Tsumori's travelogue signals the possibility that travel can encourage a cosmopolitan imagination for the suffering of the foreign others.

Photography as occupation and its imaginary reoccupation

Like Tsumori's book, the professional photographer Yasujima's travelogue describes unexpected encounters with supernatural and surreal phenomena. Arguably, the occurrence of this mystical experience is more noteworthy in the case of Yasujima who, unlike Tsumori, claims to have little spiritual inclinations or religious background. We find two incidents jolted Yasujima's secular frame of reference and made him susceptible to spirituality. These incidents reinforced his empathy for the Japanese soldiers. For Yasujima, travelling to war sites to take photographs was close to his heart. In 1995 he began travelling throughout Japan to photograph war sites, and exhibited his works domestically. From the mid-2000s he shifted his attention to war sites across the Pacific Islands. His travelogue, *Aruite mita Taiheiyō Sensō no shimajima* (2010), recounts his Pacific Island trips in reports complemented by photographs, historical accounts and interviews.[35] By the time of his Pacific Island trips, Yasujima had formed his anti-war stance, defined the purposes of his travel and identified that his lifelong work was to exhibit his photographs to convey the cruelty of war.

While his background indicates Yasujima's pacifist views, *Aruite mita* charts his engagement with war history and memory. In April 2008 he visited PNG, and he followed this with a trip to Biak Island in West Papua in February 2009. On the PNG trip he visited the Japanese memorial in Wewak, along with a group of pilgrims, that Tsumori had visited some thirty years earlier. It was the middle of the night and he recalled seeing 'the belongings of Japanese soldiers and used weapons left lying around randomly. These gave me chilling sensations'.[36] Yasujima felt so unnerved that he could no longer notice the balmy temperature. He admitted that until then he had never believed in ghosts or spirits. The raw power of the objects compelled him to suspend his doubt. He began trusting what he saw before him and what he felt inside himself. As with Tsumori, Yasujima's spiritual dimension of vicarious consumer travel, his experience of a heightened spiritual sensitivity not only forged a greater solidarity with the dead soldiers, but also elevated him above non-travellers who cannot feel such sensations. Reports of such spiritual encounters become another means of travellers' performance of vicarious consumer travel for national commemoration.

Another significant moment of Yasujima's spiritual 'rite of passage' happened on Biak Island. He was attracted to this island because of the marginal public recognition of the campaign here against the Allies between late May and August 1944 in which only 500 out of 10,000 Japanese survived.[37] Yasujima visited Biak Island for ten days with a group of seven men who were siblings or children of Japanese soldiers who had died there. What impressed Yasujima about the pilgrims was not just their willingness to continue commemorating the dead but also their determination to recover and identify the remains of the fallen. After reaching a spot suspected to be a battle site, the pilgrims' group and local guides began excavating and found bones, skulls and jaws with teeth, as well as personal items. In Biak, a large proportion of the deceased remains buried beneath the ground and unidentified.[38] The group then conducted a memorial service to honour the deceased soldiers, and proceeded with an impromptu spirit-consoling service:

> As soon as the remains of the bodies were found, the pilgrims conducted a memorial service. However, it was extremely difficult to determine the identities of the dead. Nevertheless, they were soldiers who fought for the nation on command by the nation. I cannot utter a word when I come to think about the unknown soldiers' 'sleeping' in this land with their regrets.[39]

These vivid reminders rendered Yasujima speechless and gave him goose bumps; he even felt chills, despite the tropical heat. He then felt 'the chagrin of the unnamed soldiers who are laid to "rest"'.[40] Compared to Kanetaka and Tsumori, Yasujima's brief expression of anger can seem restrained and even clichéd. It may also be ambiguous because he does not identify who he feels upset about. What is clear is that his sympathetic reimagining of the fallen soldiers as victims bolstered his anti-war stance.

To what extent do his photographs convey his historical consciousness as a result of his travel? In a subsequent interview with a magazine, Yasujima acknowledged that his approach to photographing the war relics changed when he went overseas. In Japan, he preferred to let the relics and sites speak for themselves. Abroad, he imagined what had occurred on the battlegrounds, but found it difficult to reconcile how the Japanese were both perpetrators and victims.[41] Despite these comments, the ways Yasujima's photographs employ the local setting and people result in this imaginary reoccupation. Many of his photographs feature relics of the war with the local landscape in the background. In one photograph, Yasujima captured a group of five of the Japanese men, facing the remains and praying for the dead soldiers while surrounded by tropical vegetation. At the back of the frame are about ten local residents whose faces are almost too small to see. The vegetation and the local people convey the 'foreignness' of the ceremony but are mere props: the Japanese group dominates the frame. Yasujima used a similar technique in a photograph of a Japanese-constructed observation post in Rabaul. The palm trees and the branches convey the incongruity of the Japanese installation in the tropics, and the composition accentuates the subject matter and suggests the folly of a war that transported materials and manpower to a faraway location. The photograph implies the foreignness of the pilgrims' experience of meeting their loved ones in a faraway location like Biak. It relegates the local people and contexts to the backdrop to emphasize how far the travellers had gone to travel and formed closer emotional ties to the dead soldiers. Yasujima's photography reinforces a national commemoration. The composition reflects his style of travel that resulted in placing the Japanese objects and people in the centre.

An inner journey

Over two decades after Kanetaka's journey, travel writer Miyakawa Masayo wrote *Papua Nyūginia rekuiemu* (hereafter *Rekuiemu*) following two trips to PNG in the 1980s. Miyakawa adopted two alternating roles: an investigator of war history and a participant-observer in a Japanese pilgrimage. She used written and oral sources on Japanese and New Guinean wartime history to provide historical context to her journeys. Miyakawa's encounter with Japanese pilgrims in PNG began with a chance meeting. On her first visit in September 1983, Miyakawa came to Wewak on an assignment to cover the anniversary of PNG's independence. In a hotel where she stayed, she happened to meet a group of Japanese pilgrims who came to commemorate the deaths of their comrades and loved ones. This coincidental contact prompted her to recognize her ignorance about the war and ask her father about his wartime experience, which he had never related to his daughters; her mother did not want to talk about the war either. Miyakawa grew up in this silence without developing any interest in the war. After returning from her initial trip, she asked her father about the war for the first time and he told her about how he had served in the Inspectorate General of Military Training (Kyōikusōkan-bu). Although he did not fight in the New Guinea campaign, his work took him to Salmi, Dutch New Guinea, on a brief assignment between January and February 1944. There, as a non-combatant, he observed the conditions to gather materials for a military manual. Miyakawa grew interested in 'filling in the blank of the past' and began reading up on the New Guinea campaign.[42] She joined a Japanese pilgrimage tour and returned to Wewak in July 1984 to report on these Japanese pilgrimages.

Miyakawa's desire resonates with what Marianne Hirsch calls postmemory, whereby the second and subsequent generations grow up in the shadow of parents with traumatic experiences. In the family, it is not only words and emotions that parents communicate but also the unspoken behaviour and images that form the children's perceptions of these traumatic events. Direct and indirect transmissions of traumatic memory are so profound that it creates memories of their own.[43] It is this silence that shaped Miyakawa's understanding of the Japanese soldiers and drove her to get to know what her father was really like. While her initial journey gave her a direct impetus to investigate the war, Miyakawa also travelled at a time when the questions of Japan's wartime aggression had resurfaced in Japan and escalated into international controversy. In 1982, the Japanese Ministry of Education inspected school history textbooks and recommended that one publisher revise its original description of the Japanese 'invasion' of China by using the more euphemistic word 'advance' in its place. The Chinese and Korean governments, as well as domestic critics, protested. This incident exposed, *inter alia*, the official reluctance to recognize conflicting interpretations of Japan's imperial period.[44]

Miyakawa's return visit marked a pivotal transition in her perception of the war and her personal life as a whole. Although she travelled with a Japanese group, her main purpose was to investigate what the local people thought of the Timbunke massacre of July 1944 (Chapter 5), which she had learnt about earlier.[45] One morning, Miyakawa told the tour coordinator, Mr Honma, of her intention to visit Timbunke on her own while the group visited another site. Honma urged her to write her will before departing, and to leave it at the hotel. She reassured him and the group that she was leaving her personal belongings, such as her passport, cash and the key to her suitcase, at the front desk of the hotel. Beneath a confident exterior she was anxious about what would happen to her: 'Even 40 years after [the massacre], I am going to the village where the

Japanese, my compatriots, killed so many people. I'm a woman and I'm going alone'.[46] This was a bold gesture, since Miyakawa had made no prior arrangement with the villagers to stay overnight. She knew the risk of venturing into an area seeped in Japanese violence; the local residents might give her a hostile reception. Upon arrival, she began looking for accommodation for two nights. At the local church, she announced herself as a Japanese person wanting to learn about the village – without mentioning the massacre. The clergy and the staff at the clinic attached to the church were standoffish and told her they had no spare beds. She wondered if they declined her request because she was Japanese. Their manners were not openly hostile, but the cool reception and responses made her speculate that the cruelty of the massacre was greater than she had imagined.[47] Her anxiety subsided when she met Francesca, a woman in her mid-twenties working as a nurse at the village clinic. Francesca let Miyakawa stay in the clinic's staff house. Her polished manners and impeccable English brought relief to Miyakawa. Francesca did not come from Timbunke, but promised to introduce Miyakawa to her colleague Annamarie, a 21-year-old resident. Francesca expected that Annamarie would introduce Miyakawa to her grandfather, Boembu, who had witnessed the massacre.

The meeting with Boembu and others on the next day confronted Miyakawa with eyewitnesses' accounts of the massacre by the Japanese. In the presence of other villagers, Boembu talked about his work under a Japanese unit. When another unit, led by Captain Hama (later Watanabe) Masaichi, arrived and announced the end of the war, Boembu narrated how he felt compelled to flee Timbunke. Suddenly, his facial expression grew serious. He said very slowly, in English, 'Fighting no good. War no good'. A middle-aged woman nearby suddenly began speaking about witnessing the massacre as a child. Japanese troops had rounded her up into a hut with many others. She had peered through the cracks of the wall and watched the Japanese troops strip the men naked, tie their hands, and finally shoot them. Miyakawa asked Annamarie for her opinion. 'Just scary' was her short-but-firm response. Then she added, 'If you were at the scene, you would not feel hatred. You would only feel scared'. Her face suddenly turned solemn for the first time; Miyakawa sensed the weight of Annamarie's comment. The middle-aged woman continued to talk about her mother, who had remarried after her husband was shot dead in the massacre. Miyakawa listened with her face downcast: 'I felt as if everyone was expecting me to say something. I could not lift my face'.[48] The woman's testimony disturbed Miyakawa and humbled her into an awkward silence, in recognition of the gap in memory between the residents, who remembered the massacre as victims, and the Japanese traveller, who had grown up without knowing about it. The silence that pervaded the villagers and Miyakawa represented the intersection of travel and personal and collective consciousness of the memory of the wartime violence.

The meeting culminated in Miyakawa's awakening and her rethinking of her attitude to the war and its impact on the New Guineans. After some moments had passed, Annamarie broke the silence: 'We are Christians. We have to forgive everything'. Only then, Miyakawa admits, was she able to lift her face.[49] Annamarie's words reassured Miyakawa that the initial responses she received did not represent the opinion of the entire village. She conjectured that the niceties directed towards her were the result of the passage of time and of Christian teaching.[50] While visibly distressed Miyakawa took comfort in Annamarie's graceful manner and how she made the villagers' collective moral stance clear. The village woman and Annamarie made it necessary for Miyakawa to apologize on behalf of the 'bad' male Japanese troops and to serve as a 'good' female Japanese grassroots ambassador. Annamarie played the stronger hand: she humbled Miyakawa with the memory of a massacre that remained vivid for the villagers but of which few Japanese were even aware. In *Rekuiemu*, Miyakawa grew even more sympathetic towards the New Guineans who were caught between the Allies and the Japanese: 'The deaths of the New Guineans are not honourable deaths. ... Amongst the most brutally killed are the 100 in Timbunke'.[51] Hearing the voices of the villagers was Miyakawa's mode of vicarious consumer travel. Not only did it give her immediacy to a massacre that she had only heard about, but it also engendered a new recognition of the Japanese soldiers in the perpetrators' camp.

Hearing the residents' testimonies led Miyakawa to put on the journalist's cap. She starts thinking about the present-day relationship between the Japanese and the residents and relationship among the residents. What sparked her imagination was Annamarie's comment, 'The Japanese come here sometimes and give us gifts. And then they leave'.[52] Miyakawa conducted an interview with a Japanese veteran, former warrant officer Hirakawa Yoshio. The interview sharpened her understanding of the New Guineans' response to Timbunke, and to the differences in the perspectives of the New Guinean elite and the broader populace. Hirakawa took part in the Timbunke massacre and even shot fire at the young people. In post-war years, he paid ten visits to PNG, but Timbunke was not his destination. The guilt from the massacre weighed on him so heavily that he could never muster the courage to visit Timbunke. In 1982, he joined a group of Japanese pilgrims and visited Timbunke. Assisting the group was Father Cherubim Dambui, whose theological training and university education gave him significant status. Dambui's grandfather had been shot dead in the massacre. Hirakawa remembered that Dambui was delighted to host the Japanese, but the villagers' reception was cold. For two hours in the village no one discussed the massacre. Then, suddenly, a man confronted Hirakawa. He claimed that during the massacre Japanese soldiers had shot him in the right shoulder. The man smirked at Hirakawa and demanded compensation. Hirakawa pleaded that he had nothing to give; he had already given gifts to the villagers in a memorial ceremony conducted earlier by his group. In a panic to avoid trouble, he handed over two pairs of shorts, and hurried back to his tour bus. Back on the tour bus was Dambui. He reassured the veteran and the entire group that 'the war is a thing of the past'.[53]

Hirawaka's recollection forms a basis for Miyakawa to compare how they perceived her. Miyakawa recalls Annamarie's reporting an exchange she had with the villagers. They asked Annamarie about Miyakawa; Annamarie told them she was Japanese and had come to pay her respects at the cross commemorating the massacre.[54] The villagers' questions disturbed Miyakawa, but made her aware of a split between different groups of local people. As seen in Chapters 5 and 6, her realization points to the conflicting views of the Japanese. On the one side were ordinary residents who formed the majority. They harboured historical grievances and expressed them in various ways. On the other was a small group of future-oriented people such as Dambui and Annamarie. They had received advanced education, spoke English and practised the Christian-inspired virtues of forgiveness and reconciliation. Miyakawa knew that Annamarie and Dambui '[did] not represent the opinion of the whole village. I sensed this with my own skin'.[55] Miyakawa's conclusion does not fall back on the minority's rhetoric. Rather, her empathy for the grief-stricken villagers indicates her cosmopolitan commemoration.

The two trips to New Guinea culminated into Miyakawa's coming of age moment. As she was leaving Timbunke on a truck, she brought her mind back to where she began:

> What I saw with my eyes and heard with my ears [in PNG] were things my father, a career soldier, did not know. Between he and I, we never discussed the war. Once I return to Japan, I would certainly like to meet my father and tell him everything, not just Timbunke, but also the retreat by the Japanese soldiers, starvation, cannibalism, prisoners of war, returned soldiers and bereaved families. I want to talk about everything. I am sure my father would like to hear it.[56]

Miyakawa's resolve exhibits a high degree of self-reflexivity. Grasping the depth of the wartime memory on the minds of the Timbunke residents was not enough. Miyakawa's awakening aligns with the notion of the silent transmission of war stories in the family that Hirsch alludes to in her discussion of postmemory. The trips Miyakawa took convinced her of the necessity to address the long-term silence about the war that pervaded her relationship with her father. *Rekuiemu* ends on an optimistic note, mentioning how the discomfiting encounter with the past ultimately gave Miyakawa the confidence to change the course of her life.[57] We do not know exactly what became of her inner journey but it seems that she decided to keep her family matters private.[58] Nonetheless, Miyakawa's PNG experience demonstrates the potential of vicarious consumer travel in spurring not only the re-examination of history, but also that of unravelling her embeddedness in history.

A *sarariiman* abroad: From ignorance to action

Another traveller that charted the path of cosmopolitan commemoration is Kawaguchi Kizuki, a *sarariiman* (office worker) and a self-proclaimed 'travel nut'. Before travelling to PNG in January 1993, he had travelled extensively inside and outside Japan. He decided to visit PNG by himself to satisfy his curiosity about exotic destinations; visiting battle sites and commemorating the war were not his main purposes. What began as incidental encounters with war history became a springboard for historical research in his travelogue and would later motivate his participation in a nongovernmental organization dedicated to PNG. Kawaguchi's trip began on the New Guinea Island and from there he headed to Rabaul on New Britain Island. At the former Japanese navy building, he met an old man who guided him to various sites, and saw the idyllic lives the local residents led. Like the New Guinean driver Kanetaka met in 1961, the old man recalled Japanese words and asked after a Japanese officer he knew. After seeing the relics of the war, Kawaguchi told him 'War is not good'. The man nodded in a pregnant pause.[59] After they parted, Kawaguchi visited a memorial built on a hill by the Japanese government. He lingered there and cast his eyes down toward the ocean. He could not help but imagine soldiers feeling alienated, anxious, scared in this faraway land with its tropical climate and scenery and gradually becoming averse to fighting. He then found himself placing the palms of his hands together in prayer.[60]

What strikes one as a gesture of national or nationalistic commemoration took a sharp turn. Kawaguchi realized how bizarre it was to see traces of Japan in Rabaul, and how much trouble the war had caused for the local people. He wrote that the local people had lived happily before the advent of German and Australian colonialists and Japanese troops. The images of the old man and the villagers were evidently in his mind. To remind his reader of the legacy of the Japanese, Kawaguchi quoted the inscription of the memorial: 'We [the Japanese] commemorate those who died in battles on Southern Pacific Islands and the adjacent seas in the Second World War. We erect this monument with the hope for peace'.[61] Kawaguchi found the words represented 'the imperialist tradition that does not care for others'.[62] Indeed, the text delimits the subject of commemoration to the combatants who 'died in battles' and fails to acknowledge the local casualties.

Kawaguchi's belated discovery led him to pursue research on the New Guinea campaign after returning to Japan. He lamented the inadequate attention to modern history in Japanese schools and stressed that the Japanese should learn more about the Japanese wartime aggression inflicted on the peoples of the Asia Pacific; importance should be placed, he felt, on not thinking only of the victimhood of Japanese people who fell prey to the oppressive measures of the military regime and the Allied attacks.[63] To rectify this imbalance, he introduced the little-known life of chief Karao, based on sources that include a Japanese veteran's memoir and a journalist's reportage.[64] Kawaguchi wrote that Karao had seen many Japanese soldiers suffering from starvation and illness and found the sight intolerable. Karao acted on his sympathetic feelings to help the Japanese soldiers until they died or departed. After the war, the Australians, who resumed the civil administration of PNG, put local chiefs suspected of collaborating with the Japanese on trial. The Australians sentenced Karao to death for assisting enemy combatants, and executed his wife and two sons. However, they released Karao after three years' imprisonment, and left him to live with his third son until his death in 1972.[65] Kawaguchi resisted the temptation to make what John W. Dower calls 'evocations of moral (or immoral) equivalence',[66] that is, to argue that although the Japanese were 'bad' the Australians were equally 'bad', if not worse, so we should not single out the Japanese as the sole perpetrators. This sort of rhetoric excuses both these nations and shifts the focus away from the violence committed against people like Karao. For historians specializing in the New Guinea campaign, the New Guineans' collaboration with the Japanese and Allies is a well-known aspect.[67] Kawaguchi's writing about Karao testifies to how vicarious consumer travel continues after the physical journey – in this case, in the form of his historical writing.

Was his discovery-to-writing trajectory a completely novel result of his travel, or did his travel affirm his previously held opinions or ideological inclinations? As with other travellers, the absence of 'before and after' statements makes it difficult to determine whether Kawaguchi's visit reinforced or transformed his views. Before reaching Rabaul, he had developed an affinity with and appreciation for the Papua New Guineans that had predisposed him to think of himself as a foreigner in a foreign land, rather than a traveller returning to an erstwhile war zone that his people had once occupied and fought over, even under the pretence of war. His pre-visit interest in PNG and his style of travel provide helpful insights. The fact that he travelled alone, and not with another Japanese person or a group of Japanese pilgrims, meant that his encounter with the places he visited was direct and personal. His travelogue devotes much space to his interactions with the local people, their heritage, culture and customs, which reveals the pleasure he derived from experiencing the exoticism that he had sought in his journey. Furthermore, Kawaguchi travelled at a time when Japan's wartime violence and questions about Japan's post-war responsibility had become matters of public debate. This led to the re-emergence of the perpetrator discourse and undermined the heroic and victim narratives of Japanese soldiers. These variables offer useful, if not definitive, contexts for considering the effects on the traveller.

One noteworthy aspect of Kawaguchi's travel, not found in most travelogues, is his willingness to relate his opinions on his post-travel life. The impression gained from his trip informed his view of the Japan–PNG relationship and motivated him to act. In closing his travelogue, Kawaguchi conjectures how the past has influenced the present. He criticizes post-war Japanese businesses for viewing PNG as a territory whose natural resources existed for Japan to exploit. He contends that this attitude stemmed from the wartime occupation of PNG and the disparity of political and economic power between the two nations in the post-war era. This remark corresponds to his reaction to the Japanese memorial in Rabaul, 'the imperialist tradition that does not care for others', in his understanding that the legacy of imperialism continues, with Japan damaging PNG in different guises. Kawaguchi asserts that the Japanese have a 'duty' to learn about their wartime actions in order to think about PNG differently rather than as simply an exotic curiosity.[68] Subsequently, Kawaguchi joined a nongovernmental organization, Friends of PNG in Japan, and paid repeated visits to undertake volunteer work for the people of PNG.[69] His travelogue charts his growth from pre-travel curiosity for 'the exotic others' to a post-travel appreciation for PNG and its wartime past. In view of travel and travelogues by Miyakawa and Kawaguchi, White and Buchheim's analysis of travel as inevitably reinforcing existing beliefs does not hold for all travellers.

Travelling in the footsteps of fallen heroes

The analysis of the five travelogues indicates a shift in thinking by all of their authors, although the changes differ in manner and extent. A contrasting example is the two travelogues by journalist Makino Hiromichi. The first travelogue, *Senseki o aruku* (2002) chronicles his thirteen trips to war-related sites inside and outside Japan between February 1999 and June 2002. On his first trip to Rabaul, in May 2001, he accompanied a group of Japanese who travelled there to commemorate Japanese soldiers. His sequel, *Senseki ni inoru* (2007) records, among other destinations, a trip to New Guinea Island and Rabaul in which he gave lectures on war history to a group of Shinto priests from Japan in their thirties and forties who had no apparent ties to soldiers. His personal and political reflections are brief, but sufficient to show he follows the *tsuitaiken* mould whereby he imagines himself as treading in the footsteps of Japanese soldiers. Makino's motivation and style of travel turn his travelogues into records of nationalist commemoration. He describes interactions with fellow travellers and military operations from the standpoints of middle- and high-ranking officers. His family background could explain his emphasis. His father was an army lieutenant who died in the Leyte campaign in the Philippines in 1944.[70]

Honouring Japanese soldiers as *eirei* (fallen heroes) is one telling example of Makino's deference to the heroic interpretation he develops in his writing. On his second trip to Rabaul, in February 2005, Makino describes his tour group conducting a memorial service at the Japanese monument, which Kawaguchi visited previously. Makino comments that it commemorated '118,700 deceased in the areas including Rabaul, Bismarck archipelago and Solomon Islands'.[71] Makino expresses no qualms about nationalistic commemoration. He even explained to the priests after the service that the high casualty rate did not necessarily mean that the Japanese defeat was absolute as the Japanese had won a few battles. He conceded that the vast difference in the capacities between the Allies and the Japanese meant that the former would replenish their supplies more readily than the latter, but averred he did not 'want to hear words like "continually defeated". If we do not tell the next generation how well the soldiers on the frontline fought, then we cannot imagine [the efforts of] the fallen heroes'.[72] Makino uses his concession to elevate his respect for soldiers' efforts to make heroic sacrifice and discounts the strategists' failure that put the soldiers in dire circumstances.

A more significant undercurrent in Makino's nationalist commemoration is his reduction of the local residents to a nuisance. On his first trip to Rabaul in May 2001, Makino joined a spirit-consoling tour with a photographer friend. The tour group went to East Rabaul airfield, which the Japanese had used during the war.[73] Makino then followed Mr Nakaiwa, a former aircraft mechanic stationed at Rabaul during the war. Nakaiwa found a spot for a makeshift altar and placed *sake*, *ofuda* (talismans) from the Yasukuni shrine and mineral water on it. All tour members paid their respects to dead soldiers.[74] Afterwards, one member suggested that they look at the wreckage of a Japanese bomber in the palm tree bush nearby. When Makino struggled to find the path to the site, two local young men turned up and offered to take the visitors. Makino writes: 'They more or less imposed their service as guides on to us. But this kind of thing happens everywhere. Then we were told to pay them two kina (around 100 yen) as a thank-you.'[75] Makino refrained from disparaging the local youths' demand of payment but his annoyance is palpable. He regarded the local youths' gestures as a gratuitous and an inevitable nuisance even though it aided the group to locate the wreckage. Perhaps his most significant oversight is that the land belongs to the local people, not the Japanese. To the local people, the Japanese were the guests, visitors or even intruders to their land. Makino's reaction clearly follows the logic of Western imperial imagination. Mary Louise Pratt has convincingly demonstrated how travel writers' imaginary cartography reproduces ethnocentric worldviews and erases, negates or, at best, marginalizes the indigenous people from the landscapes.[76] Makino's glaring obliviousness reflects his desire to keep the Japanese occupied warscape as an exclusively Japanese memoryscape, which can exacerbate the gulf between the traveller and the travellee.

Makino's dissatisfaction with the local people remains evident in the description of a subsequent incident. Early next morning, Nakaiwa returned alone to the airfield to offer his prayer at the makeshift Shinto altar but was dismayed to find that it had completely disappeared. An hour later he returned to the hotel where he reported his shock. Makino saw the distressed Nakaiwa and provided this explanation:

> It seems as though no one is watching but the locals are watching from somewhere. I can understand their taking the *sake*, but I wonder what they do

with the *ofuda* from the Yasukuni shrine. They just take anything. It is regrettable that no one explained this local information to Mr Nakaiwa.[77]

Whether the group obtained permission from the local people or not, the Shinto altar made the airfield a sacred ground from the perspective of the Japanese. This all-Japanese group in a former Japanese-occupied territory gave Makino an illusion of visiting an extraterritorial enclave of Japanese war memory. Makino sympathizes with Nakaiwa's disappointment and criticizes the local residents' covert surveillance to 'take anything' without any respect for the significance of the altar. The only item the locals appreciate, Makino implies, is alcohol. Together with Nakaiwa's naivety, Makino assumes an entitlement to an exclusive right to commemorate only for and by the Japanese. The paucity of meaningful interaction that he has with the local residents denies him the opportunity to listen to their war stories that could enrich and broaden his perspectives. His nationalistic vicarious consumer travel endorses White and Buchheim's caveat.

Conclusion

This chapter applied the notions of vicarious consumer travel to analyse how the six travel writers (re-)imagined and (re-)made histories and memories of the New Guinea campaign. Most authors acknowledged that the travel spurred them to reflect on the war and developed their opinions on the war. This is the feedback loop when inspiration from sites, fellow travellers and local people stimulate trans-war and transnational imagination in the travellers' minds. Nevertheless, Buchheim and White's caution – against overstating the effect of travel on changing travellers or opening them to new values – is a valid one and demands further scrutiny into the travel writers' backgrounds and styles of travelling. Testing situations arise when disturbing histories confront travellers. Kanetaka's response to Japanese militarists is a visceral one and incorporates recognition of the local people in a mostly national paradigm of the victim discourse. The imagination Miyakawa and Kawaguchi exercised led them to identify the Japanese soldiers as perpetrators and drove their post-travel pursuits in opposing directions. Their cosmopolitan vicarious consumer travel stems from the manner of their travel. Kawaguchi travelled alone and interacted with the local people more than those who accompanied spirit-consoling groups. Miyakawa deviated from such a group and ventured into Timbunke by herself. Tsumori and Yasujima largely identify with the victim discourse as they formed strong bonds with the bereaved families that they accompanied. A spiritual encounter with fallen soldiers entitled them to a claim of authenticity of 'being there' but also to an ethnocentric rendition of the foreign land. Makino's travelogues record decidedly stronger expressions of this nationalist commemoration and vicarious consumer travel.

This chapter has found that travel can influence the sentiments the travellers formed, but it does not necessarily spur complete negation of their previously held beliefs and values or open them to alternative visions. To a large extent, the travellers' views reflect particular experiences during the visit and the author's previous conceptions about the war and their political persuasions. The travellers who accompanied Japanese pilgrims tended to reimagine and remake history through an ethnocentric lens. The travellers who interacted with the local residents acquired more of a cosmopolitan disposition and raise questions about the Japanese military occupation and campaigns in a way that subverts the putatively hegemonic position of the traveller over the travellee. The travelogue has become a medium and a site of vicarious consumer travel for travel writers to perform and legitimize their positions in debates about history, memory and commemoration.

8

Conclusion: The road behind and ahead

This book has explored Japanese perceptions of PNG through the historical representations of the New Guinea campaign. Of the plethora of historical representations available in the public sphere, this book takes a deliberately narrow selection of memoirs, films, documentaries and travelogues as its focus. This selection does not denigrate the vast array of 'historicals' – tangible and intangible works and artefacts to tell their stories for themselves and posterity. Rather, the rationale for this selection was a pragmatic one, as it allows for close readings of the works in question. The significance of the New Guinea campaign in the mainstream post-war Japanese imagination has ebbed unlike in PNG and Australia. Its low profile in Japan stemmed, in part, from the Japanese headquarters designating New Guinea outside the absolute zone of national defence (*zettai kokubōken*) in September 1943. Even more significant was the colossal scale and rate of attrition of the Japanese combatants.

The circulation of the historicals about the New Guinea campaign mirrors the broader dialogues about the Asia-Pacific War in Japan. We have seen narrative tropes and historical interpretations permeating across the historicals examined. The inordinate suffering the Japanese experienced in the New Guinea campaign disturbed the heroic narrative of the war and the political implications that followed. The suffering the Japanese inflicted on others negates the ethnocentric claims of Japanese victimhood that had dominated many narratives of the campaign. The heroic and the victim narratives are instrumental to national or nationalistic commemoration. Conversely, the resistance, inability, or failure to imagine the suffering the Japanese caused to others can hinder not only international reconciliation but also an understanding of the state mechanism and militarism that led to the horrific deeds the Japanese committed in the name of the empire, emperor and the war. Even if PNG may not occupy a prominent spot in today's mainstream Japanese imagination, the works critiqued in the book should attest to the diverse, rich and continuing production and circulation of historical memory across time, space and media.

As outlined in Chapter 1, with fewer than twenty-five years before the centenary of *sengo* (post-war), questions such as who speaks for whom and in what form demand that we take a look at the generational shift and critical phases of the transmission of memories of the Asia-Pacific War. Generational shifts from the wartime generation to postmemory generations (or Generations A, B and C under Narita Ryūichi's model discussed in the introduction) anticipate movement towards historicizing the war as opposed to the previous modes that were comprised of narrated experience, testimony and memory. Today, the inevitable moment when the last person with living memories of the Asia-Pacific War (Generation A) passes on is looming. Generation B, the children of Generation A, are growing older. The demographic shift leaves Generation C, the second postmemory generation, to take the helm of reinterpreting and transmitting memory for posterity. This book has shown that veterans and citizens, historians of several descriptions and the cultural industry continue to create a range of historicals. The authors and the creators ranged from veterans of the campaign to those with little personal connection to it and its former combatants. In view of the generational shifts, it is important to pay attention to who created the historicals and when the historicals are created if we are to question modes of relaying from experience, testimony, memory and towards history. More often than not, every act of transmitting and receiving stories entails slippage, rupture and multiple resonances that the story imparts to the sender and the receiver. What, then, can we learn from re-examining those accounts?

This conclusion ties together various visible and opaque threads in the previous chapters and makes three observations. The first concerns the importance of continuing productions of historical representations in the current political climate in Japan. The second brings out subtexts running across and beneath the chapters. The body, emotions and performance comprise additional threads that bind the sources analysed. The interplay of these subtexts with the narrative tropes of the hero, the victim and perpetrator augers new readings and novel interpretations for future readings. The last is the significance of the implicated subject in sharpening our awareness of how we are bound to the public and the private discourses of the past. Here I offer my personal experiences which led me to write this book. In no way do I assume any of these insights to be final or definitive. Rather, this conclusion suggests potential avenues for rethinking, reimagining and recreating historical memories.

Combining the framework of travelling memory with that of intergenerational transmission of historical memory can offer an effective counterweight to calls from some quarters to settle historical debates. These calls carry resonance with the politics of history and the teaching of Japan's imperial and wartime era in Japan's schools. Japan has witnessed several incidents where history textbooks became a focal point of contestation, dealing with what kind of historical 'facts', wording and whose interpretations should feature in the history textbook, and pedagogical approaches teachers could use in the classroom. The politics of the history textbook seems to have cooled down since the mid-1990s and the early 2000s, when it dominated headlines in domestic and international media. Meanwhile, educational reforms have continued, with former prime minister Abe Shinzō (in office 2006–7 and 2012–20) acting as one of the main drivers during his two terms. His educational reform has garnered relatively minor attention compared with other issues such as the economy, constitutional amendments, diplomacy and defence. This deficit should not, however, belie the potential long-term effects on the ways future generations of Japanese perceive the past and shape their identity.

Abe's educational reform came under his broad rhetoric of 'normalizing' Japan that rested on two prongs. The first was the policy-driven 'cast off the *sengo* regime' (*sengo rejīmu kara no dakkyaku*); the other the emotionally charged 'beautiful Japan'. With the former, Abe contended that the *sengo* regime impeded Japan from taking an active role in international military affairs in closer alignment with US military interests. The centrepiece of the *sengo* regime he wanted to change was the constitution, which prohibited Japan from possessing a military with combat capacity and the ability to engage in war. His call for a constitutional amendment enjoyed support from hard-right nationalists. However, he met stiff opposition from liberal quarters and even some dovish members within his own party. He fell short of changing the wording of the constitution but managed to change the interpretation.[1] In contrast, his 'beautiful Japan' campaign aimed at fostering pride in Japanese traditions and history among the populace, particularly the youth. The mantra of 'beautiful Japan' subsumed educational reform. What warrants emphasizing is that since his early days as a parliamentarian in the mid-1990s, patriotic education remained central to his agenda, and he has subscribed to historical revisionism that promotes nationalism.[2]

Under his premiership, the Ministry of Education, Culture, Sports, Science and Technology reformed school curricula that saw the acceleration of nationalistic content in history and moral education. Recent history textbooks, approved for classroom use by the ministry, emphasize ancient Japanese tradition and culture and curtail expositions of Japan's colonialism and war. Abe's educational reform drew considerable rebuke from his critics. They charge that the reform was tantamount to shutting out decades of intellectual labour towards Japan's modern and contemporary history out of the classroom, and undermines the constitutional guarantee for academic freedom.[3] In the 2018–19 academic year, moral education was upgraded to an official subject by which teachers evaluated pupils' performance. The approved textbooks featured stories of the Asia-Pacific War. Felix Spremberg's analysis finds that these stories amplify the virtue of self-sacrifice and stress the suffering of the Japanese while omitting the historical context of the Japanese colonization and war.[4] In other words, if history education and textbooks form the front door to nationalistic (or nationalistic-leaning) historical consciousness prized in revisionist historiography and nationalistic history education, then moral education becomes the backdoor. The textbooks, however, mirror the resurgence of historicals about the Asia-Pacific War in Japan in the 2000s and the 2010s. Fukuma Yoshiaki finds that popular films, battle sites, tourist sites and museums privilege Japanese soldiers' honour and sacrifice for the nation. These representations, he finds, downplay historical contexts such as the suffering the soldiers experienced and inflicted on others. The reduction of the historical elements can make the historicals vulnerable to the political, sociocultural and even commercial imperatives of the present.[5] Although we cannot expect how each student receives or rejects the classroom instruction, formal education still has its civic role to teach students multiple ways of appraising and interpreting historical events and figures. This caveat could not be truer for those lacking in cultural, social and economic resources from their family and community.

Despite the public's concern, it would be too simplistic to dismiss Abe's education reform as choking off storytelling and history-making. The framework of travelling memory affords us a long-term and cross-media perspective on storytelling and history-making. It compels us to rethink and remodel how we 'do' history, both as consumers or users and producers of the historicals. Particularly telling is the candid opinions of writer Amamiya Karin (1975–) and sociologist Furuichi Noritoshi (1985–) both part of Generation C. Both respect the impassioned pleas by the wartime generation against the cruelty of the war and for pacifism, but sense that their message falls flat on

Amamiya and Furuichi's generation. Furuichi alludes to the dual shifts in the nature of war and demography. The changing nature of armed conflict occurs as the new generations have less or no direct experience or memory of the war. In the post-1945 world, we see more regional conflicts and terrorism under evolving geopolitical dynamics instead of full-scale wars between blocs of nations. Continuing technological sophistication has made attack and defence less dependent on face-to-face combat.[6] As the wartime generation (Generation A) diminishes in number, Generations B and C and even their children have and will have rather different perceptions from previous generations. Plausibly, they may oppose war, but the weight placed on this reasoning can vary from personal experience ('not to repeat what I went through') to concerns for the local and global community ('no more foreign war that involves my country'; 'no war for oil'; 'no war for exacerbating globalization and the North-South gap'). Conversely, justification for armed conflict comes with a different emphasis, be it liberation from oppressive regimes, a country's quest for sphere of influence, or a collective defence against common threats to sovereignty. This reasoning reflects not only standpoints but also shifting perceptions and sensibilities of distance from the war experienced by different generations and raises questions about the utility of *sengo* as an episteme in which we tell and receive stories. The narratives of the hero, the victim and the perpetrator, and the political stances emanating from these narratives have shaped and affected both individual and collective identities in *sengo* Japan.

The Asia-Pacific War continues to inspire a new vintage of Japanese to take up the challenge of representing it in their chosen media. Some resist turning historical representations into moral tales of the war without sufficient historical contexts. A novel by Akasaka Mari (1964–) *Tokyo Purizun* (Tokyo Prison, 2012) relates the story of a Japanese high school student in a small town in the United States in 1980. She realizes that wartime hostility runs deep in the community. Because of an assignment by her history teacher, she finds herself confronted with the challenge of studying the controversy over Emperor Hirohito's war responsibility.[7] *Periryū: rakuen no gerunika* (Peleliu: Guernica in paradise, 2016–21) by Takeda Kazuyoshi (1975–) is a fictionalized manga series based on the Battle of Peleliu fought between Japan and the United States. The protagonist, Private Tamaru, finds himself bewildered by the stark contrast between the paradise-image of the South Seas Islands and the harsh conditions of the island – exacerbated by the US attacks, hunger and disease. Tamaru's struggle for survival and his post-war life tells us of the persistence of wartime in his mind while the rest of Japan has moved on to *sengo*.[8] A novel by Takahashi Hiroki (1979–), *Yubi no hone* (Bones in Finger,

2016), presents death as a quotidian reality of war. The novel follows a Japanese soldier's gaze at sick and infirm comrades dying in a field hospital in what seems like New Guinea.[9] These new historicals in the 2010s by a new generation raises cautious optimism for stories to be told and retold, and can foster dialogues about history. Age should not hinder empathetic engagement with the past prior to our own lifetime. Even if the classroom becomes a constricted space to study history, alternatives will still exist and even thrive. The proliferation of historicals affirms the lasting power of memory, narration and history long after the end of the events. Put differently, *sengo* and the meanings of the war are far from settled, and cannot be 'cast off' so readily.

If the intersection of *sengo* and travelling memory highlights the context for historical imagination in the future, the second observation reveals subtexts that might not have been visible when analysing individual works and genres in isolation. I propose that the three subtexts of body, emotions and performance constitute the threads suturing the distinct modes of making, recording and articulating historical memory. The critical understanding of the notion of the body by Elaine Scarry is illuminating in this regard. She discusses the body as a complex reservoir of physical and mental pain that resists easy articulation and contends that war is the seminal human experience that exemplifies the pain we inflict on and receive from others.[10] Yoshikuni Igarashi applies the idea of the body further in his analysis of post-war Japan. He contends that post-war Japanese popular culture and intellectual discourse between 1945 and 1970 sanitized and erased the traumatic memories of the Japanese and the foreign others but such memories continue to linger and resurface.[11] Scarry and Igarashi acknowledge soldiers and veterans as the travelling bodies that store and move memories. They witnessed, sustained and survived mentally and physically damaging experiences of hardship, illness and harm inflicted on themselves and others.

The body as a carrier and storehouse of memory takes on particular significance when we consider the impressions of hell and the recollections of cannibalism (Chapter 2). In PNG, the soldiers found themselves confounded by the alien environment and the harsh realities marred by material and food shortages. Soldiers commonly used allusions to hell to portray their bodies as estranged from the human world, reduced to emaciated creatures. They saw themselves as increasingly remote from any prospect of a return to the 'normal' world, too distant to earn a future in paradise or heaven. The most basic need for food could not even be satisfied and hunger was so dire that they went to the extent of committing cannibalism for their survival. The misery that survivors related accentuates the victim narrative and undermines the image of the exemplary figure of the hyper-masculine soldier defending the Japanese empire. Army doctors' accounts add further layers to the significance of the body on the battleground (Chapter 3). The sights of so many physically and mentally ill and dead and soldiers overwhelmed the doctors' supposedly detached and dispassionate medical gaze. This helplessness exacerbated the sense that they were redundant bodies unable to fulfil their duties, with the significant exception of mercy killing. In this regard, we could understand Mitsukawa Motoyuki's refusal to eat and Asō Tetsuo's insistence on self-discipline as an effort to maintain their corporeal and mental integrity in the face of adverse conditions.

The chapters on audiovisual representations and travelogues during the post-war generations offer compelling arguments about the metaphorical importance of the body. The memoir-to-film adaptation of Katō Daisuke's *Minami-no-shima ni yuki ga furu* (Chapter 4) exemplifies how the passage of time affords new angles for us to look back at the past. His leading of a theatre group transformed his body from a medic to an actor and helped him identify his *ikigai*. Two film adaptations and the variations between them reflected the respective *zeitgeist* of the respective time periods when they were made. While the 1961 adaptation celebrates the acting bodies seen on screen as those building an upbeat post-war era, the 1995 adaption presents the self-focused purpose of the protagonist Sudō as inimical to the mourning of his deceased comrades. Meanwhile his body ceases to fulfil his ambitions. At the same time, the fetishized representation of the female dancer illustrates the imperial fantasy of the South Seas female body surviving well into the post-war era.

Film-makers and vicarious consumer travellers travel into memory and history (Chapters 5 and 7). The three film-makers Sekiguchi Noriko, Hara Kazuo and Ushiyama Jun'ichi followed the footsteps of others to record, imagine and assimilate war stories to create their historical accounts. These documentaries form part of what Alison Landsberg calls 'prosthetic memory' which allows viewers and readers to reach memories beyond their lifetime.[12] This 'prosthetic' function has the capacity to stimulate further curiosity and imagination in people without real-time experience, lived memory or personal connections to get to know a past beyond their reach. Vicarious consumer travel sits on this tangent. The traveller's empathetic engagement with the past can inform, reinforce, or even reverse their views on the past. On this score, one could also regard film-makers and writers as vicarious consumer travellers whose travel stimulates our further understanding of history.

The second subtext looks at how empathy can elevate the role of emotions in our understanding of history. Historians have long dismissed or overlooked claims about emotions influencing our actions and judgement as well as shaping our perceptions of the past and the present. Current historiographical trends bring emotions into the fold.[13] Feelings of despair, resentment and helplessness permeated the memoirs of soldiers and doctors as they were confronted with material struggles that provoked existential crises. Veterans' accounts of cannibalism, in particular, make a clear illustration of this point. Though not always explicitly stated, veterans write memoirs as a duty to their dead comrades. Graphic media capturing their demeanour and raw emotions can articulate feelings and thoughts that literary media cannot express. Film-makers' sequencing of scenes and use of audiovisual elements, be they documentaries or fiction, can influence the audience's reaction. For instance, the two film adaptations of Katō's memoir as a comedy and a tragedy could not be more different in the emotions each film conveyed to the viewers and attempted to elicit from them. Documentaries, too, put emotions out to the viewers, and draw the audience into empathetic engagement with the subjects' testimonies on screen.

The historicals examined in this book highlight that not all writers and creators could find the words or tap into publicly acknowledged concepts to describe their suffering. For instance, as pointed out in Chapter 2, what we know today as trauma and post-traumatic stress are relatively new in Japan. Chapters 2, 3 and 6 point to the depth of trauma the veterans attempted to express with their own words and imagery, rather than the readily usable labels of trauma and post-traumatic stress. The suffering not only blurs the binary of the victim and the aggressors, but also involves the post-war generation. Recent years have seen a growing interest in how intergenerational trauma passed down from Japanese veterans to their families and children.[14] Thus, veterans' writings can guide unearthing the mental and physical trauma they carried back home.

This book has gone back to the memories of the New Guinea campaign to uncover various manifestations of trauma in days before the concept entered the common parlance. From unspeakable sentiments to outbursts of insanity, soldiers' memories of the war persisted in their minds even while the rest of Japan moved on and forward into the *sengo* era. Documentaries capture the rawness of emotions: Okuzaki's dogged pursuit for the truth from reluctant ex-officers, ex-Captain Watanabe's apology and Papua New Guineans' accounts of sexual violence and massacre. Furthermore, Mizuki Shigeru's graphic art made a daring and effective public assertion of his pent-up anger at Emperor Hirohito. However, assuming the Japanese to be the only bearers of trauma of the war ends up reproducing the domestically focussed narratives of the Japanese as the heroes and victims. The lengths the film-makers and the travellers went to listen in to the voices of the foreign victims of Japanese aggression demonstrate a clear stance against the simple binary of hero and victim narratives. The burden of the war on the mind is evident in the victims and witnesses of sexual violence and massacre that the Papua New Guineans narrate. Even though subtle nuances can become obscured and altered in translation, these testimonies tell us that the Japanese troops did commit grievous acts of violence towards the local population. These accounts make it apparent that seeing the Japanese troops solely as victims of their circumstances is to make a whole story out of a fraction of the truth. However, more often than not, slotting the servicemen into clear-cut roles proves problematic and fails to reflect the complexity of the military as an institution and the personnel behind the orders that injure the moral fibres of the soldiers. These limitations can upset stable categories and warrant reinterpreting the extant accounts through the prism of the implicated subject. Trauma and moral injury can thus provide new lenses with which to rethink the trans-war lives of soldiers and veterans.

The third subtext is history-as-performance, an exercise of our understanding of the past in our lives. Of great significance here is Greg Dening's contention about history-as-performance being an essential human endeavour. Storytelling makes up who we are as human beings, as does the telling and making of history. What we do to make sense of the past and express our understanding of it involves the use of our bodies, senses and emotions. These actions may be conscious, unconscious, spontaneous, or premeditated. Many of these performances and dialogues occur in the everyday as one-offs that cannot be replicated; some we transcribe, translate and transfer into signs. These performances create dialogues about ways of remembering and interpreting the past and inform our visions of the present and the future.[15]

The analysis of the historicals in this book brings out the role of the narrators' performance of history. It is through their performance that they sculpt their subjectivity. The narrator probes their wartime and post-war selves and articulates the historical truth that best represents their relationship to the worlds of the past and present. Soldiers and army doctors carry the burden of moral and physical injury and assert their identities as the victims of the war. The cinematic adaptations of Katō's memoir dramatized the clashing views of a soldier's life and death. Travel to former battle sites can either confine the traveller in the safety of a tourist bubble or challenge them, resulting in the unravelling of history-as-performance in varying degrees. Veterans returning to PNG found themselves confronted with memories of the local residents and opportunities to re-examine their opinions. The return visits by Watanabe and

Mizuki prompted recognition of the Japanese as perpetrators and their public appearance and statements made their views known to the public. Watanabe presented himself as a contrite veteran seeking forgiveness from the massacre he had commanded. Mizuki's shifting impressions of New Britain and multiple recollections of the used truck tell us that story-telling is not a one-off event. Mizuki took it as an evolving exercise of interpreting and making the self even though he had exposed his fallibility as an unreliable narrator. Similarly, the impact of travel upon vicarious consumer travellers' understanding of the war feeds into the process of one's becoming. However elusive the search for the true self may be, each performance presents the self as a constant work-in-progress project and puts a human face to the public dialogue about the meanings of the war. The processes of making history can point to the coincidence in the Japanese language. The word for imagination and creation are homonyms in Japanese, albeit different in the *kanji* script (*sōzō*, 想像 and 創造). The homonyms invite us to explore how our imagining and reimagining can foster the historicals we create and recreate.

History-as-performance brings us to the third observation of the implicated subject. People who make and tell stories and histories, and people who 'consume' them form a web of community. The book has addressed the ways the veterans, film-makers, testaments and travellers are embedded in the legacy of the war. The bridging of emotional gaps by travel made such travellers realize they were, as Michael Rothberg terms it, 'implicated subjects' and their journeys implicated in the complex web of history that binds the past and the present as well as the home communities of the travellers and the people of the erstwhile war zone.[16] One example is the reactions to the Timbunke residents' recollections of the massacre, which make a telling instance of the effect travel can have on the visitors' perception of a place, history and themselves. Watanabe, Ushiyama and Miyakawa Masayo each told of how their journeys fostered vicarious imagining of the suffering the Japanese caused, which affected the visitors' perception of their position vis-à-vis the war, Japan and PNG. Conversely, this complexity can put the onus onto the travellees as performers and even managers of their history, memory and heritage.[17]

The condition of being implicated is no less different for the postmemory generation. As the author of this book, I, too, cannot turn away from my being implicated in history. In the preface I mentioned that the absence of input from my family and repeated encounters with the vestiges of the Asia-Pacific War drove me to learn more about it. For many years I was familiar with the idea of us being implicated in history, but my lack of imagination and ability to clarify it kept niggling at me. The concepts of 'travelling memory' and 'the implicated subject' gave me the idiom by which to articulate what I knew but had no concrete words for.

My formative years presented occasions when I myself was confronted about my ignorance of the war. An experience I had in 2011 taught me the same lesson but with a greater impact. Not long after I began teaching at Fiji National University, I inherited an introductory course on Pacific history from my predecessor and had to teach it with little time to prepare. Towards the end of the course was one lecture devoted to the Asia-Pacific War and its wide impact on the lives of the Pacific Islanders. It was during the preparation for this session that I learnt that Japan and Fiji were once at war with one another. As a British colony, Fiji raised and deployed 2,029 Fijian soldiers to the Solomon Islands to support the Allies' war effort. My predecessor's notes featured an episode about Colonel Sefanaia Sukanaivalu, a Fijian soldier, who served in Bougainville.[18] On 23 June 1944, the Japanese ambushed and attacked Sukanaivalu's platoon and two Fijian soldiers were wounded. Sukanaivalu crawled alone from the rear to the front and rescued his comrades. He was shot on the way back. His comrades came to his rescue amid gunfire and mortar. Sukanaivalu then stood up in a deliberate attempt to shield his comrades from further Japanese attacks, which he knew would destroy the whole platoon. His death earned him the posthumous award of the Victoria Cross, the highest military honour in the British army.[19]

Learning about Sukanaivalu's death marked yet another occasion that informed me of how little I knew about the war. My surprise turned into a naively belated realization that Japan and the Asia-Pacific War formed a chapter in Fiji's history of international military deployment. Instead of simply 'teaching the content', I wanted to share how little I knew of Sukanaivalu with the students so that I could learn from them about what his death meant to Fiji as a nation and to them personally. I discovered that most of the fifty students enrolled in the course had learnt of him at some point in their schooling. They told me that Sukanaivalu's death was a moving story of sacrifice. No one said he was a victim of foreign aggressors or saw the Japanese in a hostile light. I suspected that the students were being too diplomatic, mindful of my Japanese origins, or aware of the power differential between lecturer and student. I also wondered if Japan's post-war trade and aid diplomacy had influenced the framing of Sukanaivalu's death as a story of heroic sacrifice and camaraderie.[20] At any rate, my students 'let me off the hook' but left me with an abiding anxiety to overcome my ignorance about the past. Unlike other occasions, the impact on me was more visceral than cerebral. I began putting my past travel – physical and metaphorical – and my relationship with history against the backdrop of the journeys that Japanese made to the Pacific Islands. This interaction with the students led me to question my practice and, indeed, performance of history in both the academic and the everyday.

Around the world, war is one subject that continues to arouse intense emotions and controversies in scholarly, political, sociocultural and other realms. Many aver that war is horrible and many more aspire to end wars and the misery they cause. Paradoxically, wars have punctuated and shaped human history, as do stories about them. The circulation of experience, testimony and memory in multiple media have continually articulated historical arguments resting on narratives and interpretations. Cultural commodities that lie outside of our lifespan can foster empathy with the past. The imaginative and creative energy and capacity the authors and creators expended to tell their stories promise the continuation of mnemonic engagement with the past for subsequent generations. Hindsight may not pave smooth and straight paths for memory travellers of today and tomorrow, but it will at least help us to be mindful of the potholes along the way.

Glossary

Chikushōdō	Realm of beasts. One of the Six Realms of Existence for sinners
Gaki	Hungry demons or ghosts
Gakidō	The realm of hungry ghosts
Ikigai	That which makes life worth living
Jigoku	Hell
Kandere	(Tok Pisin, lingua franca of PNG). A member of the mother's side of the family. A term used in areas practising matrilineal descent
Kanji	Chinese ideographic writing adopted into the Japanese writing system
Nanpō-byō	South Seas syndrome. A condition manga artist Mizuki Shigeru gave to his own insatiable yearning for New Britain Island, PNG
Nanshi	Meaningless death (lit. difficult death)
Ofuda	Talisman(s) issued at Buddhist temples and Shinto shrines in Japan. Typically made of paper and wooden materials
Oni	Ogres or demons
Onnagata	Male actors designated to perform female roles
Sange	Meaningful death (lit. glorious death)
Sengo	Post-war
Shinto	A Japanese spiritual belief system incorporating the worship of ancestors and nature. Shinto recognizes sacred power in inanimate and animate objects
Travellee	People whom the traveller meets and writes about. A term coined by Mary Louise Pratt in *The Imperial Eye*
Tsuitaiken	Experience in the footsteps of someone else
Yōkai	Supernatural creatures rooted in ancient folklore and legends

Notes

Note to the Reader

1 Philip Seaton, *Japan's Contested War Memories: The 'Memory Rifts' in Historical Consciousness of World War II*. eBook (Abingdon: Routledge, 2007), 37.
2 Yoshikuni Igarashi, *Bodies of Memory: Narratives of War in Postwar Japanese Culture, 1945–1970* (Princeton: Princeton University Press, 2000), 3.

Preface

1 E. H. Carr, *What Is History: The George Macaulay Trevelyan Lectures Delivered in the University of Cambridge, January-March 1961* (2nd edn), ed. R. W. Davies, 1961 (London: Penguin, 1987), 23.
2 Ichinose Toshiya, *Kōgun heishi no nichijyō seikatsu* (Tokyo: Kōdansha, 2009), 38–42.

1 Introduction

1 Abe Shinzō, 'Remarks by Prime Minister Abe to the Australian Parliament', in Prime Minister of Japan and His Cabinet, 8 July 2014, https://japan.kantei.go.jp/96_abe/statement/201407/0708article1.html. (accessed 21 April 2022) Abe made his speech in English.
2 Sakaguchi Yukihiro, 'Shushō, Papua Nyūginia no senbotsusha ireihi in kenka', *Nihon Keizai Shinbun*, 11 July 2014, evening edn, 3; *Yomiuri Shinbun*, 'Shushō Papua senbetsuha irei', 11 July 2014, Tokyo, evening edn, 3; *Mainichi Sihinbun*, 'Abe Shushō: Papua Nyūginia 'Senbotsusha no hi' ni kenka', 11 July 2014, evening edn, 3.
3 For instance, *Nihon Keizai Shinbun*, 'Gō, Papua e shigen gaikō', 3 July 2014, morning edn, 4; *Asahi Shinbun*, 'Shushō, shigen antei o motomeru tabi', 11 July 2014, morning edn, 4.
4 Noro Kuninobu, *Ushinawareta heishi tachi*, 1977 (Tokyo: Bungei Shunjū, 2015), 79.
5 Tanaka Hiromi, *Makkāsā to tatakatta Nihon-gun: Nyūginia-sen no kiroku* (Tokyo: Yumani Shobō, 2009), 1–2, 17–20.
6 Astrid Erll, 'Travelling Memory', *Parallax*, vol. 17, no. 4 (2011): 4–18.

7 Yoshida Yutaka, *Nihon-gun heishi: Ajia-Taiheiyō Sensō no genjitsu* (Tokyo: Chūōkōronsha, 2017), 185.
8 Fujii Tadatoshi, *Heitachi no sensō: tegami, nikki, taikenki o yomitoku* (Tokyo: Asashi Shinbunsha, 2000), 182.
9 Fujiwara Akira, *Uejinishita eirei tachi* (Tokyo: Aoki Shoten, 2001), 3, 12, 29, 135.
10 Damian Fenton, 'How Many Died?' in *Remembering the War in New Guinea: The Australia-Japan Research Project*, The Australian War Memorial, 1 June 2004, http://ajrp.awm.gov.au/AJRP/remember.nsf/709e228818bdf765ca256a9a001dad4d/58ebd6d993e15ce8ca256d05002671fd (accessed 27 November 2020).
11 The Ministry of Health, Labour and Welfare (Kōsei rōdōshō), which administers veterans' affairs, shows that of the total of 2.4 million deceased soldiers, 1.276 million (53.1 per cent) have been identified and repatriated and 1.124 million (46.8 per cent) unidentified and not repatriated. The statistics group the Solomon and the Bismarck archipelagos together. Total deceased 118,700; collected 60,950 (51.3 per cent); uncollected 57,750 (48.6 per cent). Kōsei rōdō-shō (Ministry of Health, Labour and Welfare, Japan), 'Chiiki betsu senbotsusha ikotsu shūyō gaikenzu', https://www.mhlw.go.jp/content/12100000/000337565.pdf (accessed 27 January 2021).
12 Fenton, 'How many died'; Damian Fenton, 'Who fought in New Guinea?', in *Remembering the War in New Guinea, The Australia-Japan Research Project*, The Australian War Memorials (1 June 2004), http://ajrp.awm.gov.au/ajrp/remember.nsf/pages/NT0000179A (accessed 27 November, 2020).
13 Hank Nelson, 'Kokoda: And Two National Histories', *Journal of Pacific History*, vol. 42, no. 1 (2007): 74–5; Hank Nelson, 'Papua Nyūginia to Ajia-Taiheiyō Sensō ', trans. Karashima Masato, in *Dōin, teikō, yokusan: Iwanami kōza Taiheiyō Sensō*, ed. Kurasawa Aiko, et al. (Tokyo: Iwanami Shoten, 2006), 233–41.
14 Ibid., 219.
15 Nelson, 'Kokoda', 73.
16 Noah J. Riseman, *Defending Whose Country? Indigenous Soldiers in the Pacific War* (Lincoln: University of Nebraska Press, 2012); Neville Robinson, *Villagers at War: Some Papua New Guinean Experiences in World War II*, ed. E. Fisk (Canberra: Australian National University, 1981); August Ibrum Kituai, *My Gun, My Brother: The World of the Papua New Guinea Colonial Police, 1920–1960* (Honolulu: University of Hawai'i Press, 1998).
17 See, for example, Jonathan Ritchie, 'Papua New Guineans Reconstructing their Histories: The Pacific War Revisited', *Oceania* 87, no. 2 (2017): 126–7; Victoria Stead, 'Violent Histories and the Ambivalences of Recognition in Postcolonial Papua New Guinea', *Postcolonial Studies* 20, no. 1 (2017): 68–72.
18 Steven Bullard and Keiko Tamura Keiko, eds, *From a Hostile Shore: Australia and Japan at War in New Guinea*. (Canberra: Australian War Memorial, 2004); Yukio Toyoda and Hank Nelson, eds, *The Pacific War in Papua New Guinea:*

Memories and Realities (Tokyo: Rikkyō University Centre for Asian Area Studies, 2006).
19 Tessa Morris-Suzuki, *The Past within Us: Media, Memory, History* (London: Verso, 2005).
20 Michael Rothberg, *The Implicated Subject: Beyond Victims and Perpetrators* (Stanford: Stanford University Press, 2019), 1.
21 Ibid., 9, 11, 20.
22 Morris-Suzuki, *Past within Us*, 26–27. Emphasis in original.
23 Ibid., 20.
24 Ibid., 24–5; quote from Rothberg, *Implicated Subject*, 212, n. 50.
25 Morris-Suzuki, *Past within Us*, 28.
26 Jerome de Groot, *Consuming History: Historians and Heritage in Contemporary Popular Culture*, 2nd edn (London: Routledge, 2016), 1, 3, 310–11.
27 Key introductory texts to memory studies are: Anne Whitehead, *Memory* (London: Routledge, 2009); Susannah Radstone and Bill Schwarz, eds, *Memory: Histories, Theories, Debates* (New York: Fordham University Press, 2010); Trevor Hagen and Anna Lisa Tota, eds, *Routledge International Handbook of Memory Studies* (London: Routledge, 2015).
28 Geoffrey Cubitt, *History and Memory* (Manchester: Manchester University Press, 2007), 230–1.
29 Mieke Bal, *Travelling Concepts in the Humanities: A Rough Guide* (Toronto: University of Toronto Press, 2002), 24.
30 Erll, 'Travelling Memory', 11.
31 Ibid., 14.
32 Maria Elisabeth Dorr, et al., 'Introduction: Travel, Locatedness, and New Horizons in Memory Studies', *Journal of Aesthetics & Culture*, vol. 11, supplement 1 (2019): 2.
33 Marianne Hirsch, *The Generation of Postmemory: Writing and Visual Culture after the Holocaust* (New York: Columbia University Press, 2012).
34 Alison Landsberg, *Prosthetic Memory: The Transformation of American Remembrance in the Age of Mass Culture* (New York: Columbia University Press, 2004).
35 Narita Ryūichi, *Zōho 'sensō keiken' no sengoshi: katarareta taiken/shōgen/kioku*, rev. edn, (Tokyo: Iwanami Shoten, 2020), 26, 66–8.
36 Ibid., 17–21, 292–5; Narita Ryūichi, *Sengoshi nyūmon* (Tokyo: Kawade Shobō Shisha, 2015), 214. Narita seems to have conceived his model independently from Western theorists. His model shares semblance with Jan Assmann's refinement of Halbwach's collective memory. In what Assmann names communicative memory, informal face to face and oral communication can happen within sixty to eighty years that coincides with the lifespan of the first generation. What supersedes it is cultural memory. Texts, artefacts and commemorative practices are mediated and institutionalized forms of selecting, recording and remembering the events

beyond our living memory. Jan Assmann, 'Communicative and Cultural Memory', in *Cultural Memory Studies: An International and Interdisciplinary Handbook*, ed. Astrid Erll and Ansgar Nünning (Berlin: De Gruyter, 2008), 110–11.

37 Philip Seaton, *Japan's Contested War Memories: The 'Memory Rifts' in Historical Consciousness of World War II*, eBook (Abingdon: Routledge, 2007), 6.

38 Journalist Onda Shigetaka's two-volume work uses veterans' testimonies to chronicle the battles and military operations in East New Guinea. Tanaka Hiromi's military history uses archival resources in Japanese and English and provides a comprehensive account of the Japanese battles against the Australian and American forces. Onda Shigetaka, *Tōbu Nyūginia-sen: kono kiroku o tōbu Nyūginia senjō de shinde itta heishi tachi ni sasageru* (2 vols) (Tokyo: Gendaishi Shuppankai, 1977); Tanaka, *Makkāsā*; on Japanese war crimes committed in PNG, see Tanaka Toshiyuki, *Shirarezaru sensōhanzai: Nihon-gun wa Ōsutoraria-jin ni nani o shitaka* (Tokyo: Ōtsuki Shoten, 1993), chapter 4, on cannibalism committed in PNG. The English translation of this book comes with an additional chapter on a massacre of German missionaries and Allied civilians by the Japanese navy in Kavieng (New Ireland Island, part of today's PNG) in March 1944. Yuki Tanaka, *Hidden Horrors: Japanese War Crimes in World War II*, rev. edn (Lanham, MD: Rowman & Littlefield, 2018), chapters 4 and 7.

39 Morris-Suzuki, *Past within Us*.

40 Seaton, *Japan's Contested War Memories*.

41 Hayden White, *The Content of the Form: Narrative Discourse and Historical Representation* (Baltimore, MD: Johns Hopkins University Press, 1987), 42–3.

42 Akiko Hashimoto, *The Long Defeat: Cultural Trauma, Memory, and Identity in Japan* (New York: Oxford University Press, 2015), 7, 113.

43 Ibid., 7.

44 On the controversy of the Yasukuni shrine written in English, see Akiko Takenaka, *Yasukuni: History, Memory, and Japan's Unending Postwar* (Honolulu: University of Hawai'i Press, 2015).

45 Tetsuya Takahashi, 'The National Politics of the Yasukuni Shrine', trans. Philip Seaton, in *Nationalisms in Japan*, ed. Naoko Shimizu (Abingdon: Routledge, 2006), 156–7.

46 James Orr, *The Victim as Hero: Ideologies of Peace and National Identity in Postwar Japan* (Honolulu: University of Hawai'i Press, 2001), chapter 2, esp. 32–5.

47 Hashimoto, *Long Defeat*, 8; Seaton, *Japan's Contested War Memories*, 35–6.

48 Seaton, *Japan's Contested War Memories*, 34.

49 Ibid.

50 Hiro Saito, *The History Problem: The Politics of War Commemoration in East Asia* (Honolulu: University of Hawai'i Press, 2016), 5–7.

51 Seaton, *Japan's Contested War Memories*, 19–23.

52 Ibid., 2, 19, 64.

53 Saito, *History Problem*, 186–8.
54 A regrettable omission is Yūki Shōji's novel *Gunki hatameku motoni* (1970). It became a feature film of the same title (dir. Fukusaku Kinji, 1972). The plot involves a widow's quest for the facts about her husband's death in New Guinea. She discovers Japanese troops executed him for the alleged offence of desertion. For an analysis of the film adaptation, see Fukuma Yoshiaki, 'Eiga *Gunki Hatameku moto ni*: kutsugae saretsuzukeru "yoki"', in *Sengo Nihon kioku no rikigaku: 'keishō to iu danzetsu' to bunansa no seijigaku*. Fukuma Yoshiaki (Tokyo: Sakuhinsha, 2020), 149–98.
55 Samuel Hynes, *The Soldiers' Tale: Bearing Witness to Modern War* (New York: Viking, 2001), 12.
56 Ibid., xiii–xiv; Philip Dwyer, 'Making Sense of the Muddle: War Memoirs and the Culture of Remembering', in *War Stories: The War Memoir in History and Literature*, ed. Philip Dwyer (Oxford: Berghahn, 2018), 1–2.
57 Fujii, *Heitachi no sensō*; Takahashi Saburō, *Seniki mono o yomu* (Kyoto: Academia Shuppankai, 1988); Yoshimi Yoshiaki, *Kusanone no fashizumu* (Tokyo: Tokyo University Press, 1987), translated into English as *Grassroots Fascism: The War Experience of the Japanese People*, trans., ed. and annotated by Ethan Mark (New York: Columbia University Press, 2016).
58 Yuval Noah Harari, *The Ultimate Experience: Battlefield Revelations and the Making of Modern War Culture, 1450–2000* (Basingstoke: Palgrave Macmillan, 2008), 7–8.
59 Dwyer, 'Making Sense of the Muddle', 6.
60 Fukuma Yoshiaki, *'Sensō taiken' no sengoshi* (Tokyo: Chūōkōronsha, 2009), 154, 157.
61 Hiromitsu Iwamoto, 'Japanese Perceptions on the Pacific War in Papua New Guinea: Views in Publications', in *The Pacific War in Papua New Guinea: Memories and Realities*, ed. Yukio Toyoda and Hank Nelson (Tokyo: Rikkyō University Centre for Asian Area Studies, 2006), 50. Even considering that some are republications of the previous editions with new titles, the number suggests that the memoirs do constitute a vital medium. My additional search of the National Diet Library catalogue for the period between 1999 and 2020 returned twenty-one books and two magazine articles.
62 Ibid., 52.
63 Myriam Jansen-Verbeke and Wanda George, 'Reflections on the Great War Centenary: From Warscapes to Memoryscapes in 100 Years', in *Tourism and War*, ed. Richard Butler and Wantanee Suntikul (London: Routledge, 2013), 275.
64 Robert Rosenstone, *History on Film/Film on History* (New York: Pearson, 2006), 31, 163.
65 Robert Burgoyne, *The Hollywood Historical Film* (Malden, MA: Blackwell, 2008), 8–10.

66 Seaton, *Japan's Contested War Memories*, 145.
67 Kasuga Taichi, *Nihon no sensō eiga* (Tokyo: Bungei Shunjū, 2020), 3.
68 Greg Dening, *Performances* (Melbourne: Melbourne University Press, 1996); Hokari Minoru, *Radikaru ōraru hisutorī: Ōsutoraria senjūmin Aboriginī no rekishi jissen*, reprinted edn, 2004 (Tokyo: Iwanami Shoten, 2018).
69 Landsberg, *Prosthetic Memory*.
70 John Lennon and Malcolm Foley, *Dark Tourism: The Attraction of Death and Disaster* (London: Continuum, 2000).
71 Richard Sharpley and Philip R. Stone, eds, *The Darker Side of Travel: The Theory and Practice of Dark Tourism* (Bristol: Channel View Publications, 2009).
72 Robert Clarke, Jacqueline Dutton and Anna Johnston, 'Shadow Zones: Dark Travel and Postcolonial Cultures', *Postcolonial Studies*, vol. 17, no. 3 (2014): 221–35; Anthony Carrigan, 'Dark Tourism and Postcolonial Studies: Critical Intersections', Postcolonial Studies, vol. 17, no. 3 (2014): 236–50.
73 Carl Thompson, *Travel Writing* (Abingdon: Routledge, 2011), 13–17, 26; Tim Youngs, *The Cambridge Introduction to Travel Writing* (Cambridge: Cambridge University Press, 2013), 1–3, 174. Scholars spent decades delineating and defining the remit of travel writing, travel book and travelogue. This book uses travelogue for brevity and consistency, but follows the customary convention of calling travel writing studies and travel writers.
74 Mary Louise Pratt, *Imperial Eyes: Travel Writing and Transculturation*, 2nd edn (New York: Routledge, 2008), 7.
75 Carrigan, 'Dark Tourism and Postcolonial Studies', 240.

2 To hell and back: The question of cannibalism in memoirs of the New Guinea campaign

1 Majima Mitsuru, *Jigoku no senjō Nyūginia senki: sangaku mitsurin ni kieta hiun no guntai*, 1988 (Tokyo: Kōjinsha, 1996), 76.
2 Ibid., 205.
3 Toyotani Hidemitsu, *Nyūginia donpei jigoku angya* (Tokyo: Kindai Bungeisha, 1996), 192.
4 Robert Thomas Tierney, *Tropics of Savagery: The Culture of Japanese Empire in Comparative Frame* (Berkeley: University of California Press, 2010), 186.
5 Ibid., 196. The novels he analysed are Takeyama Michio's *Biruma no tategoto* (The Burmese Harp, 1948), Ōoka Shōhei's *Nobi* (Fires on the Plain, 1952) and Takeda Taijun's *Hikarigoke* (Luminous Moss, 1954).
6 David C. Stahl, *Burdens of Survival: Ōoka Shōhei's Writings on the Pacific War* (Honolulu: University of Hawai'i Press, 2003), 129.

7 Nancy Sherman, *Afterwar: Healing the Moral Wounds of Our Soldiers* (New York: Oxford University Press, 2015), 8, 174.
8 For instance, see the following works: David C. S. Sissons, 'Some Observations on Australian War Crime Trials Involving Cannibalism/Mutilation of the Dead', in *Bridging Australia and Japan. Volume 2: The Writings of David Sissons, Historian and Political Scientist*, ed. Keiko Tamura and J. A. A. Stockwin (Canberra: Australian National University Press, 2020), 155–9; Georgina Fitzpatrick, 'Cannibalism and the War Crimes Trials', in *Australia's War Crimes Trials, 1945–1951*, ed. Georgina Fitzpatrick, Tim McCormack and Narrelle Morris (Leiden: Brill, 2016), 291–325.
9 Fitzpatrick, 'Cannibalism and the War Crimes Trials', 300–4. Webb presided over the Tokyo Trials (the International Military Tribunal of the Far East at Tokyo).
10 Peter Williams, *The Kokoda Campaign 1942: Myth and Reality* (Port Melbourne: Cambridge University Press, 2012), 178–80.
11 Takahashi Saburō, *Seniki mono o yomu* (Kyoto: Akademia Shuppankai, 1988), 105–6. Reportage of veterans' testimonies follow this pattern. Senda Kakou, *Shinikuhei no kokuhaku* (Tokyo: Chōbunsha, 1980), 197; Nagao Toshihiko, *Suterareta Nihonhei no jinnikushoku jiken* (Tokyo: San'ichi Shobo, 1996), 101–2, 213–14.
12 Yuki Tanaka, *Hidden Horrors: Japanese War Crimes in World War II*, 2nd edn (Lanham, MD: Rowman & Littlefield, 2018), 139.
13 Ibid.
14 Ibid., 142. In addition to the report Tanaka found, see another document confirming the prohibition. 'Court Exh. No. 1446: Excerpt, from Exhibit for identification only No. 1438, which is an "English Translation of a captured Japanese Memorandum concerning the training of all officers for the prevention of certain criminal officers (Including cannibalism)", dated 18 November 1944, issued by 41st Infantry Group', GHQ/SCAP Records, International Prosecution Section, Entry no. 327 Court Exhibits in English and Japanese, IPS, 1945–7), December 1946, National Diet Library Digital Collection (Japan), https://dl.ndl.go.jp/info:ndljp/pid/10270955 (accessed 20 November 2021).
15 Miya Tsugio, 'Nihon no jigoku-e', in *Zukai jigoku-e o yomu*, ed. Shibusawa Tatsuhiko and Miya Tsugio (Tokyo, Kawade Shobō Shinsha, 1999), 100–9.
16 Umehara Takeshi, *The Concept of Hell*, trans. Robert Wargo, 1967 (Tokyo: Shūeisha, 1996), Part II 'Hell in Literature'.
17 Ibid., 79, 102–4. The *kanji* for *jigoku* 地獄 may express the spatial and the temporal nature of hell. The former, *ji* 地, stands for land and the latter, *goku* 獄, prison.
18 Ogawa Masatsugu, *Shi-no-shima Nyūginia: Kyokugen no naka no ningen*, 1971 (Tokyo: Kōjinsha, 1998).
19 Ibid., 226. Tanaka, *Hidden Horrors*, 125–62. Tanaka translated and quoted a previous edition published in 1983, *Kyokugen no naka no ningen: 'Shi-no-shima Nyuginia'* (Tokyo: Chikuma Shobō, 1983), 166–7. The text in three of the

publications (1971, 1983 and 1998) is identical. Here I use *Shi-no-shima* (1998 edn). The words in square brackets are Ogawa's words Tanaka omitted and my alterations to Tanaka's translation. It is customary in Japanese writing to give only the initial letter of the surname to render someone's identity anonymous.

20 Ogawa, *Shi-no-shima* 210–15, 219–20.
21 Ibid., 227.
22 Noriko T. Reider, *Japanese Demon Lore: Oni from Ancient Times to the Present* (Logan, UT: Utah State University Press, 2010), xviii.
23 John W. Dower, *War without Mercy: Race and Power in the Pacific War*, 1986 (New York: Pantheon, 1993), chapter 9 'Demonic Other', 234–61.
24 For example, a popular adolescent cartoon series, *Bōken Dankichi* (1933–9), set on a fictional Pacific Island, spread the perception that cannibals inhabited the South Seas Islands, and that cannibalism was something the Pacific Island 'others' did. Tierney, *Tropics of Savagery*, 144–6, 198; Naoto Sudo, *Nanyō-Orientalism: Japanese Representations of the Pacific* (Amherst, MA: Cambria Press, 2010), 24.
25 Yoshida Yatsuo, 'Toyō no jigoku', in *Shūkyō jigoku-e zankoku jigoku-e*, ed. Yoshida Yatsuo and Tanaka Masashi (Tokyo: Daiwa Shobō, 2006), 188.
26 Ogawa, *Shi-no-shima*, 227.
27 James K. Dubnik, 'Foreword', in *Afterwar: Healing the Moral Wounds of Our Soldiers*, Nancy Sherman (New York: Oxford University Press, 2015), xv.
28 Tierney, *Tropics of Savagery*, 186–7.
29 Donald F. Tuzin, 'Cannibalism and Arapesh Cosmology: A Wartime Incident with the Japanese', in *The Ethnography of Cannibalism*, ed. Paula Brown and Donald F. Tuzin (Washington, DC: Society for Psychological Anthropology, 1983), 70.
30 Ibid., 67.
31 Majima, *Jigoku*, 77.
32 Ibid., 78. The proverb he cited in Japanese was *Ishoku tarite reisetsu o shiru*.
33 Ibid.
34 Ibid.
35 Ibid., 79.
36 Meat consumption, however, was revived with the advent of Western influence during the Meiji reforms. Katarzyna Joanna Cwiertka, *Modern Japanese Cuisine: Food, Power and National Identity* (London: Reaktion, 2006), 24.
37 Majima, *Jigoku*, 101–2.
38 Peter Williams, *Japan's Pacific War: Personal Accounts of the Emperor's Warriors*. eBook (Barnsley: Pen and Sword, 2021), 86.
39 Charles Happell, *The Bone Man of Kokoda* (Sydney: Pan Macmillan, 2008), 78.
40 NHK (Nihon Hōsōkyōkai, Japan Broadcasting Corporation), 'Nishimura Kōkichi: "Kiga no hate ni okotta koto"', *Sensō shōgen ākaibusu* (14 September 2009),

https://www2.nhk.or.jp/archives/shogenarchives/shogen/movie.cgi?das_id=D00011 00510_00000&seg_number=001 (accessed 29 November 2020).
41 Nukuda Nobuo, 'Atogaki', in *Chichi no senki*, Nukuda Ichisuke (Tokyo: Hōwa Shuppan, 1987), 200.
42 Nukuda Ichisuke, *Chichi no senki* (Tokyo: Hōwa Shuppan, 1987), 99.
43 Yoshida, 'Toyō no jigoku', 154–5.
44 Ibid.
45 Nukuda, *Chichi no senki*, 101.
46 Ibid.
47 Yoshida, 'Toyō no jigoku', 155.
48 Nukuda, *Chichi no senki*, 103.
49 Justin Aukema's phrase in 'A Hero's Defeat: Modernization Theory and Japanese Veterans' Asia-Pacific "War Tales"', *Asia-Pacific Journal: Japan Focus*, vol. 20, issue 10, no. 4 (15 May 2022) https://apjjf.org/-Justin-Aukema/5701/article.pdf (accessed 16 May 2022).
50 Nukuda, *Chichi no senki*, 170.
51 John W. Dower, *Embracing Defeat: Japan in the Wake of World War II* (New York: W. W. Norton, 1999), 496, 637, n. 23. The translation of *ichioku sōzange* is Dower's.
52 Toyotani Hidemitsu, *Harin ware senyū o kū: tōbu Nyūginia haizannpei no kokuhaku* (Tokyo: Shinseiki Shobō, 1979), 7–8.
53 Ibid., 9, 18.
54 Ibid., 157; Toyotani Hidemitsu, *Nyūginia donpei roku: jigoku angya* (Tokyo: Kindai Bungeisha, 1996), 138.
55 Andrew Gordon, *A Modern History of Japan: From Tokugawa Times to the Present*, 3rd edn (Oxford: Oxford University Press, 2013), 108–9.
56 Toyotani, *Harin*, 157; Toyotani, *Donpei*, 138.
57 Toyotani, *Harin*, 163–4; Toyotani, *Donpei*, 145–6.
58 Toyotani, *Harin*, 163; Toyotani, *Donpei*, 145.
59 Toyotani, *Harin*, 161; Toyotani, *Donpei*, 143.
60 Toyotani, *Harin*, 162–5; Toyotani, *Donpei*, 143–7.
61 Toyotani, *Harin*, 166; Toyotani, *Donpei*, 148.
62 Toyotani, *Harin*, 166; Toyotani, *Donpei*, 148.
63 Toyotani, *Harin*, 166; Toyotani, *Donpei*, 148.
64 Toyotani, *Harin*, 168–9; Toyotani, *Donpei*, 151.
65 Toyotani, *Harin*, 172. *Hannya shingyō* reflects the principles of Mahayana Buddhism, the predominant Buddhist sect in Japan.
66 Ibid.
67 Kanaoka Shūyū, *Hannya shingyō*, 1973 (Tokyo: Kōdansha, 2001), 20–2 and 154–5.
68 Toyotani, *Harin*, 175.
69 Ibid., 176.

70 Ibid.
71 Toyotani, *Donpei*, 152.
72 Toyotani, 'Maegaki', in *Donpei*, unpaginated.
73 Toyotani, *Harin*, 180; Toyotani, *Donpei*, 157.
74 Toyotani, *Harin*, 182–3; Toyotani, *Donpei*, 161–2.
75 Stahl, *Burdens of Survival*, 90, citing Robert Jay Lifton, *The Broken Connection: On Death and the Continuity of Life* (New York: Simon and Schuster, 1979), 178.
76 Nakamura Eri, *Sensō to torauma: fukashika sareta nihonhei no sensō shinkeishō* (Tokyo: Yoshikawa Kōbunkan, 2018), 7. My recent essay looks into Ogawa's struggle with trauma. Ryōta Nishino, 'War, Trauma, and Humanity in a Japanese Memoir: Ogawa Masatsugu's *"Island of Death"* (1969)', *Asia-Pacific Journal: Japan Focus*, vol. 20, issue 10, no. 4 (15 May 2022) https://apjjf.org/-Ry--ta--Nishino/5702/article.pdf (accessed 16 May 2022).
77 Toyotani, *Harin*, 184; Toyotani, *Donpei*, 162.
78 Toyotani, *Harin*, 195; Toyotani, *Donpei*, 169.
79 Igarashi Yoshikuni, *Haisen to sengo no aida de: okurete kaerishi monotachi* (Tokyo: Chikuma Shobō, 2012), 41. The television series was remade in 1994 and the film in 2008.

3 Army doctors' struggle with medical crises and self-discipline

1 Yanagisawa Gen'ichirō, *Gunn'i senki: sei to shi no nyūgijia senki*, 1979 (Tokyo: Kōjinsha, 2003), 268–9.
2 Ibid., 5.
3 Joanna Bourke, 'Wartime', in *Medicine in the Twentieth Century*, ed. Roger Cooter and John Pickstone (Amsterdam: Hardwood Academic Publishers, 2000), 593. Ben Shepard's work on military psychiatry epitomizes this trend, *War of Nerves: Soldiers and Psychiatrists in the Twentieth Century* (Cambridge, MA: Harvard University Press, 2001).
4 Mark G. E. Kelly, *Foucault and Politics: A Critical Introduction* (Edinburgh: Edinburgh University Press, 2014), 45–6; Michel Foucault, *The Birth of the Clinic: An Archaeology of Medical Perception*, 1973 (New York: Vintage Books, 1994), 89.
5 Bourke, 'Wartime', 593.
6 Aaron William Moore, *Writing War: Soldiers Record the Japanese Empire* (Cambridge, MA: Harvard University Press, 2013), 17.
7 Lee K. Pennington, *Casualties of History: Wounded Japanese Servicemen and the Second World War* (Ithaca, NY: Cornell University Press, 2015). 56–7.

8 Ibid., 59; Hara Takeshi, 'Senshōbyōsha ni taisuru iryō engo taisei', *Gunji shigaku*, vol. 49, no. 4 (2014): 44–5; Steven Bullard, '"The Great Enemy of Humanity": Malaria and the Japanese Medical Corps in Papua, 1942–43', *Journal of Pacific History*, vol. 39, no. 2 (2004): 204–8.
9 In this context, *dono* is an honorific; it indicates respect.
10 Bullard, 'Malaria', 204–11, 213–16; Iijima Wataru, *Mararia to teikoku*, 1982 (Tokyo: Tōkyō Daigaku Shuppankai, 2005), 208–17.
11 Watanabe Susumu, *Mararia to kiga no sensen: tōbu Nyūginia-sen jūgunki* (Nagoya: Asahi Shinbun Nagoya Honsha Henshū Seisaku Sentā, 1984), 92–3.
12 Hatano Katsumi, *Rabauru dōkutsu byōin* (Tokyo: Kongō Shuppan, 1971), 160.
13 Peter Williams, *The Kokoda Campaign 1942: Myth and Reality* (Port Melbourne: Cambridge University Press, 2012), 165 and 172.
14 Yanagisawa, *Gun'i senki*, 132–3.
15 Ibid., 133.
16 Yoshikuni Igarashi, *Bodies of Memory: Narratives of War in Postwar Japanese Culture, 1945–1970* (Princeton: Princeton University Press, 2000), 51–2.
17 Yanagisawa, *Gun'i senki*, 135.
18 Ibid., 180–1.
19 Nakamura Eri, *Sensō to torauma: fukakashi sareta Nihonhei no sensō shinkeishō* (Tokyo: Yoshikawa Kōbunkan, 2018), 63.
20 Ibid.; NHK (Nihon Hōsō Kyōkai, Japan Broadcasting Corporation), 'Kakusareta torauma: seishin shōgai heishi 8,000-nin no kiroku', 25 August 2018.
21 Yoshida Yutaka, *Nihon-gun heishi: Ajia-Taiheiyō sensō no genjitsu* (Tokyo: Chūōkōronsha, 2017), 115–16.
22 Nakamura, *Torauma*, 109–10.
23 Yanagisawa, *Gun'i senki*, 131.
24 Ibid.
25 Ibid., 134.
26 Watanabe, *Mararia*, 132.
27 Ibid., 235.
28 Hirao Masaharu, *Soromon gun'i senki: gun'i tai'i ga mita kaigun rikusentai no shitō*, 1980 (Tokyo: Kōjinsha, 2007), 172.
29 Mitsukawa Motoyuki, *Senki shio: tōbu Nyūginia sensen, aru taitsuki gun'i no kaisō* (Tokyo: Seiunsha, 1984), 292–3. Misukawa and Watanabe served in the same unit. Watanabe notes working with Mitsukawa from time to time, although Mitsukawa does not mention Watanabe.
30 Hatano, *Rabauru*, 15.
31 Ibid., 113.
32 Imai Kazuo, 'Atogaki', in *Rabauru dōkutsu byōin*, Hatano Katsumi (Tokyo: Kongō Shuppan, 1971), 280.

33 Suzuki Masami, *Nyūginia gun'i senki: jigoku no senjō o ikita ichigun'i no kiroku* (1982: Tokyo: Kōjinsha, 2001), 145.
34 Asō Tetsuo, *Rabauru nikki: ichi gun'i no gokuhi shiki* (Fukuoka: Sekufūsha, 1999), 66.
35 Ibid., 160.
36 Ibid.
37 Ibid.
38 Ibid., 161.
39 Ibid., 166–7.
40 Ibid.
41 Sabine Frühstück, *Colonizing Sex: Sexology and Social Control in Modern Japan* (Berkeley: University of California Press, 2003), 36–9.
42 Asō Tetsuo, 'Positive Method for the Prevention of Venereal Diseases' in Asō Tetsuo, *From Shanghai to Shanghai*, trans. Hal Gold (Norwalk, CT: East Bridge, 2004), 179.
43 Mark McLelland, *Queer Japan: From the Pacific War to the Internet Age* (Lanham, MD: Rowman & Littlefield, 2005), 38.
44 Asō, 'Positive Method', 179.
45 Asō, *Rabauru nikki*, 382.
46 Ibid., 457.
47 Ibid., 62–3 and 92–3.
48 Mitsukawa, *Senki shio*, 28.
49 Upon graduation from medical school, he underwent a physical test. Mitsukawa received the third highest grade out of the four passing grades that qualified him for conscription. He suspected that he would not have passed had there been less demand for more manpower at the time of his test. Ibid., 27.
50 Ibid., 400–1.
51 He submitted a handful of articles to medical journals. The editors rejected them, stating various reasons such as complications with printing and other infelicities. He found these reasons unconvincing and kept the manuscripts in his drawers even while he was writing his memoir. Ibid., 25–6.
52 Ibid., 35–6.
53 Yoshida, *Nihon-gun heishi*, 98.
54 G. R. Goldberg, 'Intake and Energy Requirements', in *Encyclopedia of Food Sciences and Nutrition vol. 4*, 2nd edn, ed. Benjamin Caballero (London: Academic Press, 2003), 2096.
55 Mitsukawa, *Senki shio*, 37.
56 Ibid., 27, 127 and 269. Based on the information Mitsukawa has given, his body mass index comes to 17.5. This puts him in the underweight category (< 18.5). In 1943, the average height of twenty-year-old males was 161.3 centimetres and

average weight 60 kilograms. Towards the end of the war the average weight decreased to 54 kilograms. Yoshida, *Nihon-gun heishi,* 186.

57 Noda Masaaki, *Senso to zaiseki* (Tokyo: Iwanami Shoten, 1988), 73; Yoshida, *Nihon-gun heishi,* 40–1. Ogawa was not related to Ogawa Masatsugu, whose memoir appeared in the previous chapter.

58 Ibid. Aoki Tōru, *Hiroku: sensō eiyōshicchōshō* (Tokyo: Korube, 1979), 110, 172–3, 212–15, 259–67, 292–3, 299, 310.

59 Yoshida, *Nihon-jin heishi,* 67–71; Nakamura, *Torauma,* 115; Ogawa Masatsugu, *Tōbu Nyūginia sensen: suterareta butai* (Tokyo: Kōjinsha, 2002), 187.

60 Miyoshi Masayuki, *Kyokugen no Nyūginia-sen o ikiru* (Ajisu-chō, Yamaguchi Prefecture: Self-published, 2004), 35. Unlike many privately published memoirs, Miyoshi's memoir is held at the National Diet Library, Tokyo.

61 NHK, 'Miyoshi Masayuki: "Moruhine o tsukau"', *Sensō shōgen ākaibusu,* (2 and 3 November 2010), https://www2.nhk.or.jp/archives/shogenarchives/shogen/movie.cgi?das_id=D0001100755_00000&seg_number=001 (accessed 30 November 2020).

62 Ibid.

63 Hosaka Masayasu, *Senjō taikensha: chinmoku no kiroku* (Tokyo: Chikuma Shobō, 2015), 137.

4 Finding reasons for living and dying in a war zone: Cinematic adaptations of Katō Daisuke's *Minami-no-shima ni yuki ga furu*

1 *Asahi Shinbun,* 'Chosha to ichijikan', 1 October 1961, morning edn, 14.

2 Ibid.

3 Katō Daisuke, *Minami-no-shima ni yuki ga furu,* 1961 (Tokyo: Kōbunsha, 2005), 283. A veteran of the Manokwari campaign, aged eighty-three, wrote a letter about seeing the performances by Katō's theatre group and expressed the same sentiment. *Asahi Shinbun,* 'Katari tsugu senso: *Minami-no-shima ni yuki ga furu*', 6 August 2007, morning Osaka edn, 21.

4 *Minami-no-shima* became a TV drama in April 1961, airing on NHK (single episode, one hour) and Fuji TV in January 1964 (four parts, 30 min. per episode). The last professional theatre production was held in 2015. Hamada Kengo, *Wakiyakubon zōho bunkoban* (Tokyo: Chkuma Shobō, 2018), 39. The 1961 film adaptation was rereleased on DVD. The 1995 adaptation was re-released on VHS video; the director has since placed the film on YouTube, see note 37 below.

5 For instance, *Saraba Rabauru* (Farewell Rabaul, 1954) gained modest mainstream recognition for its depiction of Japanese soldiers in Rabaul struggling to withstand the Allies' air raids with a romantic subplot. A novel by Yūki Shōji, *Gunki hatameku*

motoni (1970) and its cinematic adaptation of the same title became cult classics upon release in 1972.

6 Kasuga Taichi, *Nihon no sensō eiga* (Tokyo: Bungei Shunjū, 2020), 77–9.
7 Isolde Standish, *A New History of Japanese Cinema: A Century of Narrative Film.* (New York: Continuum, 2005), 187.
8 Robert Burgoyne, *The Hollywood Historical Film* (Malden, MA: Blackwell, 2008), 10–11.
9 Jennifer Coates, 'Victims and Bystanders: Women in the Japanese War-Retro Film', *Media, War & Conflict*, vol. 6, no. 3 (2013): 236.
10 Sandra Wilson, 'Film and Soldier: Japanese War Movies in the 1950s', *Journal of Contemporary History*, vol. 48, no. 3 (2013): 554.
11 Yomota Inuhiko, *What is Japanese Cinema? A History*, trans. Philip Kaffen (New York: Columbia University Press, 2019), 112.
12 Fukuma Yoshiaki, *Sengo Nihon, kioku no rikigaku: 'keishō to iu danzetsu' to bunan sa no seijigaku* (Tokyo: Sakuhinsha, 2020), 270–1.
13 Oda Makoto, *Nanshi no shisō*, 1969 (Tokyo: Iwanami Shoten, 2008), 3–9 and 305. The *kanji* writing for *nanshi* read as 'difficult death'. However, the English translation is 'meaningless death'. Both renditions are context dependent and appropriate.
14 Ibid., 222.
15 Gordon Mathews, 'Can "A Real Man" Live for His Family? *Ikigai* and Masculinity in Today's Japan', in *Men and Masculinities in Contemporary Japan: Dislocating the Salaryman Doxa*, ed. James E. Roberson and Nobue Suzuki (London: Routledge Curzon, 2003), 121.
16 Katō, *Minami-no-shima*, 281–2.
17 Tanaka Hiromi, *Makkāsā to tatakatta Nihon-gun: Nyūginia-sen no kiroku* (Tokyo: Yumani Shobō, 2009), 603.
18 The origin of *onnagata* goes back to the prohibition of females in public performance by the Edo government in 1629. Katherine Mezur, *Beautiful Boys/Outlaw Bodies: Devising Kabuki Female-Likeness* (New York: Palgrave Macmillan, 2005), 1.
19 Katō, *Minami-no-shima*, 153.
20 Ibid., 205.
21 Ibid., 280.
22 Ibid., 98.
23 Hosaka Masayasu, 'Kaisetsu', *Minami-no-shima ni yuki ga furu,* Katō Daisuke (Tokyo: Kōbunsha, 2005), 289, 292; Yano Kanji, *Hansen eiga kara no koe: ano jidai ni modoranai tameni* (Fukuoka: Gen Shobō, 2017), 55–7.
24 Hamada, *Wakiyakubon*, 38.
25 For example, Kimura Tadashi, 'Fūgawari na heitai mono', *Mainichi Shinbun*, 30 September 1961, evening edn, 8.

26 Best-known series in the genre are: *Nitōhei monogatari* (1955–61) and *Haikei Tennōheika-sama* (1963–4). Michael Baskett, 'Dying for a Laugh: Post-1945 Japanese Service Comedies', *Historical Journal of Film, Radio and Television*, vol. 23, no. 4 (2003): 291–310; Kasuga, *Sensō eiga*, 65.
27 Satō Tadao, *Nihon eigashi: zōho-ban 3, 1960–2005* (Tokyo: Iwanami Shoten, 2006), 29–30, 35; Baskett, 'Dying for a Laugh', 308, n. 24.
28 Katō, *Minami-no-shima*, 76.
29 The song featured prominently in *Saraba Rabauru*.
30 The lyrics here are quoted as performed in the film. The English translation is a modification of Greg Dvorak's translation. Greg Dvorak, *Coral and Concrete: Remembering Kwajalein Atoll between Japan, America, and the Marshall Islands* (Honolulu: University of Hawai'i Press, 2018), 68.
31 A prototype of the song goes back to the 1920s. Ibid., 62 and 72.
32 Tanaka, *Makkāsā* 601–3 and Teshima Fusatarō, 'Jobun' in *Chi no hate ni shisu*, Uematsu Jinsaku (Tokyo: Tosho Shuppansha, 1976), 3.
33 Katō, *Minami-no-shima*, 48.
34 Masubuchi Tsuyoshi, '*Minami-no-shima ni yuki ga furu*', *Kinema Junpō*, no. 1183, 1 February 1996, 171–2.
35 Mizushima Satoru, 'Masubuchi Tsuyoshi shi *Minami-no-shima ni yuki ga furu* hyō ni taisuru hanron', *Kinema Junpō*, no. 1188, 15 April 1996, 169.
36 Ibid., 170. The articles he cites are: Yamamoto (Anon), 'Sengo 50-nen no Nihon o tou', *Kobe Shinbun*, 13 January 1996, 15; Hisada Megumi, '*Minami-no-shima ni yuki ga furu*', *Tokyo Shinbun*, 7 December 1995, 15.
37 Mizushima put the entire film on YouTube on two occasions with pre-feature commentaries. 'Tokubetsu kōkai eiga *Minami-no-shima ni yuki ga furu*', YouTube (initially screened in December 1995), (10 August 2013) https://www.youtube.com/watch?v=O2_izEaxxVw and 'Ch Hokkaidō eiga *Minami-no-shima ni yuki ga furu*', YouTube (uploaded 30 April 2019) https://www.youtube.com/watch?v=NifRizUC2Yw (both last accessed 23 September 2021).
38 Yoshikuni Igarashi, *Bodies of Memory: Narratives of War in Postwar Japanese Culture, 1945–1970* (Princeton: Princeton University Press, 2000), 195.
39 Ibid., 196–7; Oda, *Nanshi no shisō*, 189–96.
40 Mizushima, 'Eiga', pre-feature commentary, 10 August 2013.
41 Isolde Standish, *Myth and Masculinity in the Japanese Cinema: Towards a Political Reading of the 'Tragic Hero'* (London: Routledge, 2000), 58–9, 69 and 209–10, n. 18.
42 This is a point film critic Satō Tadao makes in his observation of fatherless families portrayed in the six-part film *Ningen no jōken* (Human Conditions, 1959–61). James Orr, *The Victim as Hero: Ideologies of Peace and National Identity in Postwar Japan* (Honolulu: University of Hawai'i Press, 2001), 127, citing Satō Tadao, *Currents in Japanese Cinema: Essays by Satō Tadao*, trans. Gregory Barrett (Tokyo: Kōdansha International, 1982), 113.

43 Kawamura Minato, 'Popular Orientalism and Japanese Views of Asia', trans. Kota Inoue and Helen J. S. Lee, in *Reading Colonial Japan: Text, Context, and Critique*, ed. Michele M. Mason and Helen J. S. Lee (Stanford: Stanford University Press, 2012), 272–4. For a translation of *Bōken Dankichi* in English, see Shimada Keizō, 'The Adventure of Dankichi', trans. Helen J. S. Lee, in *Reading Colonial Japan: Text, Context, and Critique*, ed. Michele M. Mason and Helen J. S. Lee (Stanford: Stanford University Press, 2012), 245–70.

44 Ivan Morris, *The Nobility of Failure: Tragic Heroes in the History of Japan*, eBook (New York: Holt, Rinehart and Winston, 1975), 127.

45 John W. Dower, *War without Mercy: Race and Power in the Pacific War* (1986; New York: Pantheon, 1993), 67–9.

46 For a critical survey of the plot and audience reception, see Philip Seaton, *Japan's Contested War Memories: The 'Memory Rifts' in Historical Consciousness of World War II* (Abingdon: Routledge, 2007), 141; Robert Thomas Tierney, *Tropics of Savagery: The Culture of Japanese Empire in Comparative Frame.* (Berkeley: University of California Press, 2010), 188–9.

5 Documentaries as co-performative partnership: Framing and presenting testimonies of painful memories

1 The documentary is held at Hōsō Library (Broadcasting Library) in Yokohama, Kawasaki Shimin Myūjiamu (Kawasaki City Museum) and Ryūgasaki Shiritsu Chūō Toshokan (Ryūgasaki Public Library).

2 Stella Bruzzi, *New Documentary*, 2nd edn (London: Routledge, 2006), 186.

3 John Ellis, *Documentary: Witness and Self-Revelation* (Abingdon: Routledge, 2012), 53. Italics mine.

4 Belinda Smaill, *The Documentary: Politics, Emotion, Culture* (Basingstoke: Palgrave Macmillan, 2015), 6–7, 19–21, 54, 62.

5 The official English translation of the title is 'The Emperor's Naked Army Marches On'. The literal translation is 'Onwards the Divine Army'.

6 Yuki Tanaka, '"Yamazaki, Shoot Emperor Hirohito!" Okuzaki Kenzo's Legal Action to Abolish Chapter One (the Emperor) of Japan's Constitution', *Asia–Pacific Journal: Japan Focus*, vol. 17, issue 20, no. 1 (15 October 2019): 16 and n.17, https://apjjf.org/-Yuki-Tanaka/5318/article.pdf (accessed 24 October 2019).

7 An anthology published ten years after the original theatrical release contains fifty-one previously published and new essays. Matsuda Masao and Takahashi Taketomo, eds, *Gunron Yukiyukite Shingun* (Tokyo: Tōgosha, 1998).

8 Yoshimoto Takaaki, '"Hakuriki" ko to "kyōryoku" eiga', in *Gunron Yukiyukite Shingun*, ed. Matsuda Masao and Takahashi Taketomo (Tokyo: Tōgosha, 1998), 273.

9 Karatani Kōjin, Itō Seikō and Nakamori Akio, '*Yukiyukite Shingun*: Okuzaki Kenzō o tanken suru', *Shokun*, vol. 19, no. 11 (1987): 186.
10 Jeffrey Ruoff and Kenneth Ruoff, *The Emperor's Naked Army Marches On: Yukiyukite shingun* (Trowbridge: Flicks Books, 1998), 24.
11 Bill Nichols, *Introduction to Documentary*, 3rd edn (Bloomington: Indiana University Press, 2017), 132–3.
12 Hara Kazuo, '*Yukiyukite Shingun* no kakushin o kataru', *Shinario*, vol. 44, no. 3 (1988), 18–19; Hara Kazuo and Shissō Purodakushon, *Dokyumento* Yukiyukite shingun *zōhoban*, 1994, reprinted with additional material (Tokyo: Kōseisha, 2018), 2–3, 28, 47–8.
13 Hara Kazuo, Ishizaka Kenji and Ido Kishū, *Fumikoeru kyamera: waga hōhō akushon dokyumentarī* (Tokyo: Firumuāto-sha, 1995), 20.
14 Hara and Shissō Purodakushon, *Dokyumento*, 47.
15 John Breen, 'Voices of Rage: Six Paths to the Problem of Yasukuni', in *Politics and Religion in Modern Japan: Red Sun, White Lotus*, ed. Roy Starrs (London: Palgrave Macmillan, 2011), 289–90.
16 Akira Iriye, 'Review of *The Emperor's Naked Army Marches On*, Kazuo Hara', *American Historical Review*, vol. 94, no. 4 (1989): 1037.
17 Okuzaki Kenzō, *Yamazaki, Tennō o ute! 'Kōkyo pachinko jiken' chinjutsusho*, 1974 (Tokyo: Shinsensha, 1987), 6–9.
18 Okuzaki was one of the six survivors of the entire 1,200-member Regiment. See Okuzaki's own account of his survival, ibid., 73–4, 77–8, in addition to Tanaka's summary, 'Legal Action', 5–6.
19 Hara and Shissō Purodakushon, *Dokyumento*, 206.
20 Tanaka, 'Legal Action', 8–9. As a child, Okuzaki read the Bible, but was not a practising Christian.
21 Satō Tadao, 'Sensō hanzai no mondai', in *Nihon no dokyumentarī 2: Seiji Shakai hen*, ed. Satō Tadao (Tokyo: Iwanami Shoten, 2010), 74. The documentary is possibly better known in Australia where Sekiguchi received funding from the Australian government. The screening of *Daughters* at the 2019 Yamagata International Documentary Film Festival brought it to the attention of a Japanese audience nearly thirty years after its original screening in Japan.
22 The Australians knew of the Japanese operations of comfort stations and sexual violence as early as 1942. Hank Nelson, 'The Consolation Unit: Comfort Women in Rabaul', *Journal of Pacific History*, vol. 43, no. 1 (2008): 1–20. Sekiguchi's films feature testimonies of Rabaul residents and Dr Asō Tetsuo (Chapter 3) to this effect.
23 Sekiguchi Noriko, *Senjō no onna tachi* (Tokyo: Ritorumoa, 1990), 46. Pike is a historian and documentary film-maker. Nelson and Daws are historians. All three are born in Australia. Waiko is a PNG-born historian. Sekiguchi was a student in a class Pike taught. For the impact *Angels of War* made on the Australian and

the Pacific academies and societies, see Johnathan Ritchie, 'Papua New Guineans Reconstructing their Histories: The Pacific War Revisited', *Oceania*, vol. 87, no. 2 (2017): 127–33.
24 Sekiguchi, *Senjō no onna tachi*, 104.
25 Ibid., 87.
26 When quoting the English subtitles, I use them as they appear in *Sensō Daughters*. The translation of the Japanese subtitles into English is mine.
27 Subtitles as appeared in the English version.
28 Sekiguchi suspects that the government did not want New Guinea Island to be associated with a history of violence and exploitation. Sekiguchi, *Senjō*, 114.
29 A small number of veterans admit to inflicting damage on local residents across PNG and supporting compensation. However, these comments are in a sheer minority. Hiromitsu Iwamoto, 'Japanese Perceptions on the Pacific War in Papua New Guinea: Views in Publications,' in *The Pacific War in Papua New Guinea: Memories and Realities*, ed. Yukio Toyoda and Hank Nelson (Tokyo: Rikkyō University Centre for Asian Area Studies, 2006), 53.
30 Caroline Norma, 'Australian Military Sexual Adventurism in the New Guinean Campaign, 1942–1945', in *Transpacific Visions: Connected Histories of the Pacific across North and South*, ed. Yasuko Hassall Kobayashi and Shinnosuke Takahashi (Lanham, MD: Rowman & Littlefield, 2021), 81–110.
31 See Chapter 1 for an outline of each. A website 'Voices from the War' established in 2018 by teams in PNG and Australia holds a rich collection of oral testimonies of the Asia–Pacific War by Papua New Guineans recalling many aspects of the war: http://pngvoices.deakin.edu.au.
32 Suzuki Yoshikazu, *Terebi wa danshi isshō no shigoto: dokyumentaristo Ushiyama Jun'ichi* (Tokyo: Heibonsha, 2016), 47; Niwa Yoshiyuki, *Nihon no terebi dokyumentarī* (Tokyo: Tokyo Daigaku Shuppankai, 2020), 52, 67.
33 Hamazaki Kōji and Higashino Makoto, 'Ushiyama Jun'ichi: eizō no doramaturugī', *Hōsō kenkyū to chōsa*, vol. 62, no. 5 (2012): 84–94; Niwa, *Dokyumentarī*, 59–62, 67–9; Suzuki, *Terebi*, 310–11.
34 The first documentary, *Ano namida o wasurenai!* broadcast in August 1989, pieced together testimonies of the Korean people who lived through the brutal regime of Japanese imperialism. The second documentary, *Kieta onna tachi no mura*, aired in August 1990, reported the killing of Japanese immigrants in Manchuria by the Manchurian people. The Manchurians spoke of deep-seated resentment against the Japanese as the pressure of Japanese imperialism descended more heavily. Suzuki, *Terebi*, 307–11.
35 Hata Ikuhiko, 'Timbunke Jiken (Nyūginia)' in *Sekai sensō hanzai jiten*, ed. Hata Ikuhiko, Sase Masamori and Tsuneishi Keiichi (Tokyo: Bungei Shunjū, 2002), 181–2; Alan Powell, *Third Force: ANGAU's New Guinea War, 1942–46*

(Melbourne: Oxford University Press, 2003), 210–11, 274, n. 64. In August 1994, a delegation from Timbunke visited Japan to attend an international forum for war compensation. The delegation demanded the PNG government reject foreign aid from the Japanese government and it compensate the victims of the massacre and other atrocities during the war. The Japanese rejected the demand, citing the matter was settled in the San Francisco Peace Treaty signed between Japan and Australia – which ruled PNG then. Ron Crocombe, *Asia in the Pacific Islands: Replacing the West* (Suva, Fiji: IPS Publications: The University of the South Pacific, 2007), 245–6.

36 Watanabe Masaichi, 'Papua-jin daigyakusatsu o meirei shitano wa watashi datta', *Maru*, vol. 25, no. 3, March (1972): 88–9.
37 *Seishun* translates the residents' words into Japanese subtitles.
38 Ienaga Saburō, *Sensō sekinin* (Tokyo: Iwanami Shoten, 1985), 307.
39 Michael Rothberg, *The Implicated Subject: Beyond Victims and Perpetrators* (Stanford: Stanford University Press, 2019), 1–2, 8–9, 14–15.
40 Watanabe, 'Daigyakusatsu', 88–9.

6 From a soldier to a best friend forever? Manga artist Mizuki Shigeru and the villagers of New Britain Island

1 Mizuki was his pen name; his birth name was Mura Shigeru. He always wrote and made public appearances as Mizuki Shigeru.
2 Mura Nunoe, *Gegege no nyōbō* (Tokyo: Jitsugyō no Nihonsha, 2008), 185–6; Mizuki Shigeru, *Shōwa-shi 8: kōdo seichō ikō*, 1989 (Tokyo: Kōdansha, 1994), 162–5; Mizuki Shigeru, *Kanzenban Mizuki Shigeru den: ge* (vol. 3) (Tokyo: Kōdansha, 2004), 240–9.
3 For an overview of Mizuki's war-themed manga, see Akiko Hashimoto, *The Long Defeat: Cultural Trauma, Memory, and Identity in Japan* (New York: Oxford University Press, 2015), 109–11.
4 In the English language see, Roman Rosenbaum, 'Mizuki Shigeru's Pacific War', *International Journal of Comic Arts*, vol. 10, no. 2 (2008): 354–79; Michael Dylan Foster, 'The Otherworlds of Mizuki Shigeru', *Mechademia*, vol. 3 (2008): 8–28; C. J. (Shige) Suzuki, 'Learning from Monsters: Mizuki Shigeru's Yōkai and War Manga', *Image & Narrative*, vol. 12, no. 1 (2011): 229–44; Matthew Penney, 'War and Japan: The Non-Fiction Manga of Mizuki Shigeru', *Asia–Pacific Journal: Japan Focus*, vol. 6, no. 9 (1 September 2008), https://apjjf.org/-Matthew-Penney/2905/article.pdf. (accessed 21 August 2017).
5 Sabine Marschall, 'Tourism and Remembrance: The Journey into the Self and Its Past', *Journal of Tourism and Cultural Change*, vol. 12, no. 4 (2014): 336.
6 Ibid., 337.

7 Beatrice Trefalt, 'Finding the Remains of the Dead: Photographs from a Japanese Mission to New Guinea, 1969–1970', *Asia–Pacific Journal: Japan Focus*, vol. 20, issue 10, no. 4 (15 May 2022) *Japan Focus* 20, issue 10, no. 4 (15 May 2022) https://apjjf.org/-Beatrice-Trefalt/5700/article.pdf (accessed 16 May 2022).
8 Rosenbaum, 'Mizuki's Pacific War', 366.
9 Naoto Sudō, *Nanyō-Orientalism: Japanese Representations of the Pacific* (Amherst, MA: Cambria Press, 2010), 2.
10 Mary Louise Pratt, *The Imperial Eyes: Travel Writing and Transculturation*, 2nd edn (London: Routledge, 2008), 258, n. 42.
11 Mizuki Shigeru, *Mizuki Shigeru no Rabauru senki* (Tokyo: Chikuma Shobō, 1994), 4; Mizuki Shigeru, *Karankoron hyōhakuki* (Tokyo: Shōgakukan, 2000), 56; Mizuki Shigeru, *Kanzenban Mizuki Shigeru den: jō* (vol. 1) (Tokyo: Kōdansha, 2004), 201–2, 318–19.
12 Mizuki Shigeru and Mizuki Purodakushon, *Gegege no Gēte* (Tokyo: Futabasha, 2015), 39.
13 Johann Wolfgang Von Goethe, *Conversations of Goethe, with Eckermann and Soret*, trans. John Oxenford, new edn (London: G. Bell, 1874), 315.
14 He passed the physical examination in 1942 but his poor eyesight led him to be placed low on the conscription list. Where Mizuki does not state the dates and his works provide different dates, I use the most up-to-date chronology. Mizuki Shigeru manga daizenshū henshū iinkai, ed., *Mizuki Shigeru manga daizenshū 000: sōsakuin/nenpu hōka* (Tokyo: Kōdansha, 2019).
15 Mizuki Shigeru, *Komikku Shōwa-shi 3: Nicchū zenmen sensō Taiheiyō Sensō kaishi*, 1989 (Tokyo: Kōdansha, 1994), 271; Mizuki Shigeru, *Mizuki Shigeru no musume ni kataru otōsan no senki*, 1985 (Tokyo: Kawade Shobō, 1995), 36; Mizuki Shigeru, *Neboke jinsei (shinsōban)*, 1982 (Tokyo: Chikuma Shobō, 1999), 82.
16 Mizuki claimed that 90 per cent of *Sōin gyokusai seyo* was true to his experience with the Zungen operation. Mizuki Shigeru, 'Afterword' (August 1991), in *Onward Towards Our Noble Deaths*, Mizuki Shigeru, trans. Jocelyne Allen (Montreal: Drawn & Quarterly, 2011), 368–9.
17 Australian troops and residents evacuated Rabaul following the Japanese occupation in January 1942. In February, the Japanese massacred about 160 Australian soldiers and civilians near Zungen Point. Lionel Wigmore, *The Japanese Thrust: Australia in the War of 1939–1945, IV*. 1st edn (Canberra: Australian War Memorial, 1957), 410, 665–9. The Japanese official record of the campaign, *Senshi sōsho*, does not mention the massacre. Steven Bullard, 'Translator's Introduction' in *Japanese Army Operations in the South Pacific Area: New Britain and Papua Campaigns, 1942–43*, trans. Steven Bullard (Canberra: Australian War Memorial, 2007), v. (Bōeichō bōei kenshūjo senshishitsu, ed., *Senshi sōsho: Minami Taiheiyō rikugun sakusen 2, Gadarukanaru–Buna sakusen* (Tokyo: Asagumo Shinbunsha, 1969)).

18 Mizuki Shigeru, *Kanzenban Mizuki Shigeru den: chū* (vol. 2) (Tokyo: Kōdansha, 2004), 54; Mizuki Shigeru, *Shōwa-shi 4: Taiheiyō Sensō zenhan*, 1989 (Tokyo: Kōdansha, 1994), 213-14.
19 Mizuki, *Kanzenban 2*, 54; Mizuki, *Shōwa-shi 4*, 217.
20 Mizuki recalls that on the way back he stumbled into a shack occupied by Japanese navy officers. They were impressed that he had survived and gave him a drink of sugar water. Mizuki, *Kanzenban 2*, 140; Mizuki, *Shōwa-shi 5: Taiheiyō Sensō kōhan*, 1989 (Tokyo: Kōdansha, 1994), 53; Mizuki, *Neboke jinsei*, 104; Mizuki, *Musume*, 130.
21 For instance, Mizuki, *Rabauru senki*, 154. In an interview recorded in April 2010, he repeatedly emphasized the officers telling him to die. Mizuki's repetition, facial expression and posture conveys the depth of his resentment. NHK (Nihon hōsōkyōkai, Japan Broadcasting Corporation), 'Mizuki Shigeru: "Tatta hitori ikinokotta Mizuki-san"', *Sensō shōgen ākaibusu* (recorded, 28 April 2010), http://cgi2.nhk.or.jp/shogenarchives/shogen/movie.cgi?das_id=D0001130006_00000 (accessed 15 April 2020).
22 Mizuki, *Shōwa-shi 6: shūsen kara Chōsen Sensō*, 1989 (Tokyo: Kōdansha, 1994), 27; Mizuki, *Kanzenban 2*, 284.
23 Mizuki, *Shōwa-shi 4*, 217.
24 Mizuki, *Shōwa-shi 6*, 53; Mizuki, *Kanzenban 2*, 303.
25 Foster, 'Otherworlds', 21.
26 Mizuki Shigeru, *Neboke jinsei*, 118.
27 Iwamoto Hiromitsu, 'Taiheiyō Sensō-ki ni okeru Nihon-gun no Rabauru senryō tōchi: Nihon gawa no ninshiki to sono jittai', *Shien*, vol. 63, no. 1 (2011): 14, 22-3.
28 Mizuki, *Shōwa-shi 6*, 94; Mizuki, *Kanzenban 2*, 338-40, 346; Mizuki, *Neboke jinsei*, 120.
29 Ibid., 118.
30 Mizuki, *Kanzenban 2*, 342; Mizuki, *Karankoron*, 133, 139.
31 The Japanese government lifted restrictions on foreign travel in 1964.
32 Mizuki, *Shōwa-shi 8*, 156; Mizuki, *Neboke jinsei*, 243; Mizuki, *Kanzenban 3*, 167, 240-2.
33 Mizuki, *Shōwa-shi 8*, 112-13 and 138; Mizuki, *Musume*, 222-3; Mizuki, *Neboke jinsei*, 233-5.
34 Mizuki, *Neboke jinsei*, 241.
35 'Mune shimeageru tsūkon no onnen', *Asahi Shinbun*, 10 September 1973, morning edn, 13.
36 Ibid.
37 Mizuki, *Musume*, 148-9, 193; Mizuki, *Neboke jinsei*, 111-12 and 240; Mizuki, *Karan-koron*, 192; Mizuki Shigeru, *Rabauru jūgunkōki: Topetoro tono gojū-nen*, 1995 (Tokyo: Chūōkōron Shinsha, 2002), 30 and 44.

38 Marshall Sahlins, *Stone Age Economics* (London: Aldine-Athlone, 1972), 32–9.
39 Patrick Holland and Graham Huggan, *Tourists with Typewriters: Critical Reflections on Contemporary Travel Writing* (Ann Arbor: University of Michigan Press, 2000), 22–3, 95–6.
40 Mizuki, *Neboke jinsei*, 233.
41 Mizuki, *Musume*, 223.
42 Mizuki, *Karankoron*, 239; Mizuki, *Kanzenban 3*, 152.
43 Ibid., 151, 154; Mizuki, *Musume*, 234, 239; Mizuki, *Karankoron*, 238.
44 Mizuki, *Musume*, 236–7, 244.
45 Mizuki, *Neboke jinsei*, 245–6. Ethnographic accounts by academic anthropologists testify to the spread of commercial farming in the Gazelle Peninsula, which triggered changes to lifestyle and underlying values. A. L. Epstein, *Matupit: Land, Politics, and Change among the Tolai of New Britain* (Canberra: Australian National University Press, 1969), 308.
46 Mizuki Shigeru, *Watashi wa gegege: shinpika Mizuki Shigeru den* (Tokyo: Kadokawa, 2008), 240–1.
47 Mizuki, *Neboke jinsei*, 245–6.
48 Ibid., 246.
49 Ibid., 247–8; Mizuki, *Musume*, 248–50.
50 Debbie Lisle, *The Global Politics of Contemporary Travel Writing* (Cambridge: Cambridge University Press, 2006), 15, 256–66.
51 Chris Hann, 'The Gift and Reciprocity: Perspectives from Economic Anthropology', in *The Handbook of the Economics of Giving, Altruism and Reciprocity*, ed. Serge-Christophe Kolm and Jean Mercier Ythier (Amsterdam: Elsevier, 2006), 207–23; Chris Gregory, 'Exchange', in *Handbook of Sociocultural Anthropology*, ed. James G. Carrier and Deborah B. Gewertz (London: Bloomsbury Academic, 2013), 209–26.
52 Mizuki, *Showa-shi 8*, 246.
53 Ibid.
54 Mizuki, *Shōwa-shi 8*, 248–9; also reproduced in Mizuki, *Kanzenban 3*, 277–8. See also Zack Davisson's translation in *Shōwa 1953–1989: A History of Japan* (Montreal: Drawn & Quarterly, 2015), 510–11.
55 Ian Buruma, *The Wages of Guilt: Memories of War in Germany and Japan*, 1994 (New York: New York Review of Books, 2015), 249–50.
56 Mizuki, *Shōwa-shi 8*, 254; Mizuki, *Rabauru senki*, 227–8; Mizuki, *Musume*, 255; Mizuki, *Jūgunkōki*, 162.
57 Mizuki, *Shōwa-shi 8*, 255; Mizuki, *Kanzenban 3*, 284; Mizuki, *Jūgunkōki*, 228.
58 Mizuki, *Shōwa-shi 8*, 255; Mizuki, *Kanzenban 3*, 285.
59 Mizuki, *Shōwa-shi 8*, 256; Mizuki, *Kanzenban 3*, 285.
60 Hann, 'Gift and Reciprocity', 214; David Graeber, *Toward an Anthropological Theory of Values: The False Coin of Our Own Dreams* (New York: Palgrave, 2001), 218–19.

61 Ibid., 38–9, 219–21. Graeber thinks of open and closed reciprocity on a spectrum, not a clear-cut binary.
62 A full English translation of this manga appears in Penney, 'War and Japan'.
63 Mizuki Shigeru, 'Sensō to Nihon', in *Ā gyokusai: Mizuki Shigeru senki senshū*, Mizuki Shigeru, 1991 (Tokyo: Ōzora Shuppan 2007), 397.
64 Ibid., 402.
65 Ibid.
66 Ibid., 403.
67 Ibid.
68 Ibid., 259; Mizuki, *Rabauru senki*, 227.
69 Mizuki, *Musume*, 258.
70 Mizuki, *Shōwa-shi 8*, 246. Here Mizuki makes a brief mention of the villagers building a house for him. Mizuki merely says he will return eventually and does not make connection to the truck.
71 Mizuki, *Jūgunkōki*, 157–8.
72 Ibid., 159.
73 Mizuki, *Rabauru senki*, 166–7.
74 Mizuki, *Jūgunkōki*, 163.
75 Ibid., 234.
76 Ibid., 162–3; Mizuki, *Musume*, 260–1; Mizuki, *Rabauru senki*, 228.
77 James G. Carrier, 'People Who Can Be Friends', in *Anthropology of Friendship*, ed. Sandra Bell and Simon Coleman (Oxford: Berg, 1999), 28–31, quote 30. Carrier is well aware of the cultural diversity within Melanesia. He qualifies that his comparison is of a theoretical nature and not a fixed generality.
78 Mizuki, *Kanzenban 3*, 395–6.
79 Ibid., 396.
80 Ibid., 397.
81 Ibid.
82 Ibid., 397–403; Mizuki, *Jūgunkōki*, 184–6.
83 Ibid., 190–1.
84 Ibid., 193; Mizuki, *Musume*, 270; Mizuki Shigeru, *Watashi wa gegege*, 299.

7 Vicarious consumer travel and the performance of emotional awakening in travelogues

1 Nishimura Akira, *Sengo Nihon to sensō shisha irei: shizume to furui no dainamizumu* (Tokyo: Yūshisha, 2006).
2 Sabine Marschall, 'Tourism and Remembrance: The Journey into the Self and Its Past', *Journal of Tourism and Cultural Change*, vol. 12, no. 4 (2014): 336.

3 John Urry, *Consuming Places* (London: Routledge, 2000).
4 Peter Hulme, 'Travelling to Write (1940–2000)', in *The Cambridge Companion to Travel Writing*, ed. Peter Hulme and Tim Youngs (Cambridge: Cambridge University Press, 2002), 98.
5 Hokari Minoru, *Radikaru ōraru hisutorī: Ōsutoraria senjūmin abriginī no rekishi jissen*, 2004 (Tokyo: Iwanami Shoten, 2018); Jerome de Groot, *Consuming History: Historians and Heritage in Contemporary Popular Culture*. 2nd edn (London: Routledge, 2016).
6 I have excluded self-published books, essays and magazine articles in order to limit the scope of analysis to travelogues within relatively easy reach of ordinary readers.
7 Debbie Lisle, *The Global Politics of Contemporary Travel Writing* (Cambridge: Cambridge University Press, 2006), 265.
8 Geoffrey White and Eveline Buchheim, 'Traveling War: Memory Practices in Motion', *History and Memory*, vol. 27, no. 2 (2015): 9–11.
9 Hiro Saito, *The History Problem: The Politics of War Commemoration in East Asia* (Honolulu: University of Hawai'i Press, 2016).
10 'Gendai no kataribe: Kanetaka Kaoru', *Asahi Shinbun*, 17 November 1963, evening edn, 9.
11 Yamaguchi Makoto, *Nippon no kaigai ryokō: wakamono to kankō media no 50 nenshi* (Tokyo: Chikuma Shobō, 2010), 50–1.
12 Kanetaka Kaoru, *Sekai no tabi: Oseania* (Tokyo: Jitsugyō no Nihonsha, 1962), 224.
13 Ibid., 224–6.
14 Kanetaka recorded the name of the ship as *Miyako-maru*.
15 Kanetaka, *Oseania*, 226–7.
16 Ibid., 227.
17 Kanetaka Kaoru, *Watakushi ga tabikara mananda koto: 80 sugitemo 'Sekai no tabi' wa keizokuchū desu noyo!* (Tokyo: Shōgakukan, 2010), 21–4.
18 Ibid, 36–8.
19 James Orr, *The Victim as Hero: Ideologies of Peace and National Identity in Postwar Japan* (Honolulu: University of Hawai'i Press, 2001), 3–4.
20 Kanetaka, *Oseania*, 227.
21 Ibid., 228.
22 Ibid., 251.
23 Tsumori Takudō, *Hotoke no namida: nanpō ireiki* (Sapporo: Hokkai Taimususha, 1981), 12, 21.
24 Fujiwara Akira, *Uejinishita eirei tachi* (Tokyo: Aoki Shoten, 2001), 55–64.
25 Tsumori, *Hotoke*, 77. Tsumori was counting thirty-three years since the New Guinea campaign began in 1943.
26 Namihira Emiko, *Nihon-jin no shi no katachi: dentō gishiki kara yasukuni made* (Tokyo: Asahi Shinbunsha, 2004), 177–8.

27 Ibid., 172.
28 Tsumori, *Hotoke*, 116.
29 Ibid., 70.
30 Nakayama Kaoru, 'Senbotsusha irei jumpai oboegaki: Chiba-ken Tochigi-ken Gokokujinja shusai senbotsusha irei jumpai no jireikara', *Kokugakiin Daigaku kenkyū kaihatsu suishinsentā: rekishi kiyō*, vol. 2 (2008): 206, 214, n. 49.
31 Tsumori, *Hotoke*, 67–8.
32 Ibid.
33 Ibid., 68.
34 Orr, *The Victim as Hero*, 3–6; Franziska Seraphim, *War Memory and Social Politics in Japan, 1945–2005* (Cambridge, MA: Harvard University Asia Center, 2006), 222–3.
35 He credits historian Yoshida Yutaka as the historical advisor.
36 Yasujima Takayoshi, *Aruite mita Taiheiyō sensō no shimajima* (Tokyo: Iwanami Shoten, 2010), 99.
37 Ibid., 114.
38 The Ministry of Health, Labour and Welfare (Kōsei rōdō-shō) administers veterans' affairs and records of the 53,000 soldiers who died in today's West Iryan region, located where Biak is today. As of December 2020, the remains of 19,570 (36 per cent) soldiers have yet to be identified and repatriated. 'Chiiki betsu senbotsusha ikotsu shūyō gaikenzu', https://www.mhlw.go.jp/content/12100000/000337565.pdf (accessed 27 January 2021).
39 Yasujima, *Aruite mita*, 117.
40 Ibid., 116.
41 Yasujima Takayoshi, 'Wakai sedai ni katarutsugu sensō no kioku', *Shūkan kinyōbi*, no. 810 (6 August 2010), 39.
42 Miyakawa, *Rekuiemu*, 31–2.
43 Marianne Hirsch, *The Generation of Postmemory: Writing and Visual Culture After the Holocaust* (New York: Columbia University Press, 2012), 3–5.
44 Mutsumi Hirano, *History Education and International Relations: A Case Study of Diplomatic Disputes over Japanese Textbooks* (Folkestone: Global Oriental, 2009), 118–30.
45 Miyakawa Masayo, *Papua Nyūginia rekuiemu* (Tokyo: Ushio Shuppansha, 1985), 159.
46 Ibid., 177.
47 Ibid., 184.
48 Ibid., 192–3.
49 Ibid., 193–4.
50 Ibid., 199.
51 Ibid., 197.

52 Ibid.
53 Ibid., 198. Miyakawa notes that Father Dambui was Annamarie's uncle.
54 This was the cross at which Watanabe and Ushiyama's television crew paid their respects to the victims of the massacre. See Chapter 5.
55 Miyakawa, *Rekuiemu*, 200.
56 Ibid.
57 Ibid.
58 *Rekuiemu* is the only book she published about her travels to PNG.
59 Kawaguchi Kizuki, *Papua Nyūginia tanbōki: tabō na bijinesuman no jikokeihatsu ryokō* (Tokyo: Kadensha, 1996), 125.
60 Ibid., 134.
61 The text that Kawaguchi quotes is accurate. The Japanese Ministry of Health, Labour and Welfare, who funded the memorial, publishes the entire text on its website. Kōsei rōdō-shō, 'Senbotsusha irei jigyō: Minami Taiheiyō senbotsuha no hi', http://www.mhlw.go.jp/bunya/engo/seido01/ireihi04.html (accessed 6 August 2019). Kawaguchi notes that the inscription also appears in English and Pidgin but does not quote these translations. Kawaguchi, *Tanbōki*, 133.
62 Ibid., 133–4.
63 Ibid., 200.
64 His commitment to research into war history is evident throughout the chapter. The bibliography lists fifty-nine books related to PNG, thirty-seven of which are about the Asia–Pacific War. Among the books are Miyakawa's *Rekuiemu*, memoirs by Ogawa Masatsugu and Majima Mitsuru and the Japanese edition of Yuki Tanaka's *Hidden Horrors*.
65 Kawaguchi, *Tanbōki*, 291.
66 John W. Dower, 'An Aptitude for Being Unloved: War and Memory in Japan', in *Ways of Forgetting, Ways of Remembering: Japan in the Modern World*, John W. Dower (New York: New Press, 2012), 114–18.
67 See, for instance, Hank Nelson, 'The Swinging Index: Capital Punishment and British and Australian Administrations in Papua and New Guinea, 1888–1945', *Journal of Pacific History*, vol. 13, no.3 (1978): 149–51, n. 78. Hiromitsu Iwamoto, 'Memories and Realities of the Japanese Occupation of Mainland New Guinea', in *The Pacific War in Papua New Guinea: Memories and Realities*, ed. Yukio Toyoda and Hank Nelson (Tokyo: Rikkyō University Centre for Asian Area Studies, 2006), 285–92.
68 Kawaguchi, *Tanbōki*, 201.
69 Kawaguchi Kizuki, *Papua Nyūginia: seirei no ie, NGO, sensō, ningen moyō ni deau tabi* (Tokyo: Kadensha, 2000).
70 He visited Lyete seven times between February 1999 and March 2006. These visits fall under Marschall's personal memory tourism for his direct family tie to his father. His travel to other destinations makes him an outsider to the mnemonic

community of the grieving families of dead soldiers. For an account of his trips to Lyete, see Makino Hiromichi, *Senseki ni inoru* (Tokyo: Sankei Shinbun Shuppan 2007), 282–319.
71 Ibid., 103.
72 Ibid., 104.
73 The airfield functioned as an airport until September 1994 when volcanic eruption forced its relocation. At the time of Makino and his group's travel, the airfield was covered in ash; it was no longer operational. Makino Hiromichi, *Senseki o aruku* (Tokyo: Shūeisha 2002), 148.
74 Ibid.
75 Ibid., 150. Kina is the currency of PNG. The Japanese yen equivalent presumably comes from the time of Makino's travel.
76 Mary Louise Pratt, *The Imperial Eyes: Travel Writing and Transculturation*, 2nd edn (New York: Routledge, 2008), 52, 132.
77 Makino, *Senseki o aruku*, 151.

8 Conclusion: The road behind and ahead

1 Ryu Yongwook, 'Departing from the Postwar Regime: The Revision of the 'Peace Constitution' and Japan's National Identity', in *Routledge Handbook of Japanese Foreign Policy*, ed. Mary McCarthy (Abingdon: Routledge, 2018), 51.
2 Akiko Takenaka, 'Japanese Memories of the Asia–Pacific War: Analyzing the Revisionist Turn Post-1995', *Asia–Pacific Journal: Japan Focus*, vol. 14, issue 20, no. 8 (15 October, 2016), https://apjjf.org/-Akiko-Takenaka/4967/article.pdf (accessed 26 November, 2020).
3 Tawara Yoshifumi, 'The Abe Government and the 2014 Screening of Japanese Junior High School History Textbooks', trans. Sven Saaler with introduction by the Asia–Pacific Journal, *Asia–Pacific Journal: Japan Focus*, vol. 13, issue 17, no. 2 (27 April 2015), https://apjjf.org/-Tawara-Yoshifumi/4312/article.pdf (accessed 28 October, 2021).
4 Felix Spremberg, 'The Asia–Pacific War in Japan's New Moral Education Textbooks', *Asia–Pacific Journal: Japan Focus*, vol. 19, issue 18, no. 2 (15 September, 2021) https://apjjf.org/-Felix-Spremberg/5632/article.pdf (accessed 28 October, 2021).
5 Fukuma Yoshiaki, *Sengo Nihon, kioku no rikigaku: 'keishō to iu danzetsu' to bunan sa no seijigaku* (Tokyo: Sakuhinsha, 2020).
6 Amamiya Karin and Furuichi Noritoshi, '"Sensō" o shiranaitte sonna ni warui koto desuka?', *Shūkan kinyōbi*, no. 989 (25 April 2014): 24.
7 Akasaka Mari, *Tokyo Purizun* (Tokyo: Kawade Shobō Shinsha, 2012).

8 Takeda Kazuyoshi, *Periryū: rakuen no gerunika*, 11 volumes (Tokyo: Hakusensha 2016–21).
9 Takahashi Hiroki, *Yubi no hone* (Tokyo: Shinchōsha, 2016).
10 Elaine Scarry, *The Body in Pain: The Making and Unmaking of the World* (New York: Oxford University Press, 1985), 63 and 109.
11 Yoshikuni Igarashi, *Bodies of Memory: Narratives of War in Postwar Japanese Culture, 1945-1970* (Princeton: Princeton University Press, 2000).
12 Alison Landsberg, *Prosthetic Memory: The Transformation of American Remembrance in the Age of Mass Culture* (New York: Columbia University Press, 2004).
13 Lynn Hunt, *Gurōbaru jidai no rekishigaku,* trans. Hasegawa Takahiko (Tokyo: Iwanami Shoten, 2016), 80–1, 108–10.
14 NHK (Nihon Hōsō Kyōkai), 'Kakusareta torauma: seishin shōgai heishi 8,000-nin no kiroku', 25 August 2018.
15 Greg Dening, *Performances* (Melbourne: Melbourne University Press, 1996), xv–xvi.
16 Michael Rothberg, *The Implicated Subject: Beyond Victims and Perpetrators* (Stanford: Stanford University Press, 2019).
17 See, for example, Victoria Stead, 'History as Resource: Moral Reckonings with Place and with the Wartime Past in Oro Province, Papua New Guinea', *Anthropological Forum*, vol. 28, no. 1 (2018): 16–31.
18 The island belongs to the Solomon Islands group. Following German colonization, Bougainville became part of New Guinea.
19 Robert Lowry, *Fortress Fiji: Holding the Line in the Pacific War, 1939-45* (Sutton, NSW: Self-published, 2006), 81, quoting Robert A. Howlett, *History of the Fijian Military Forces, 1939-1945* (London: Crown Agents for the Colonies, 1948), 130–1.
20 The narrative angle of heroic sacrifice is a common one circulated in Fiji's media to this day. RFMF Archives, 'The Fiji Infantry Regiment Operations in World War', *Fiji Sun*, 23 June 2020, https://fijisun.com.fj/2020/06/23/the-fiji-infantry-regiment-operations-in-world-war-ii (accessed 27 January 2021).

Select Bibliography

Newspapers

Asahi Shinbun
The Fiji Sun
Mainichi Shinbun
Nihon Keizai Shinbun
Yomiuri Shinbun

Internet-Based Archive

Abe Shinzō, 'Remarks by Prime Minister Abe to the Australian Parliament', in Prime Minister of Japan and His Cabinet, 8 July 2014, https://japan.kantei.go.jp/96_abe/statement/201407/0708article1.html (accessed 21 April 2022).

Australia-Japan Research Project. *Remembering the War in New Guinea*, created 1 June 2003, http://ajrp.awm.gov.au/ (accessed 28 October 2020).

National Diet Library Digital Collection (Japan).

NHK. (Nihon hōsōkyōkai, Japan Broadcasting Corporation). 'Mizuki Shigeru: "Tatta hitori ikinokotta Mizuki-san"'. *Sensō shōgen ākaibusu* (28 April 2010), http://cgi2.nhk.or.jp/shogenarchives/shogen/movie.cgi?das_id=D0001130006_00000 (accessed 15 April 2020).

NHK. 'Miyoshi Masayuki: "Moruhine o tsukau"'. *Sensō shōgen ākaibusu* (2 and 3 November 2010), https://www2.nhk.or.jp/archives/shogenarchives/shogen/movie.cgi?das_id=D0001100755_00000&seg_number=001 (accessed 30 November 2020).

NHK. 'Nishimura Kōkichi: "Kiga no hate ni okotta koto"'. *Sensō shōgen ākaibusu* (14 September 2009), https://www2.nhk.or.jp/archives/shogenarchives/shogen/movie.cgi?das_id=D0001100510_00000&seg_number=001 (accessed 29 November 2020).

Memoirs

Asō Tetsuo. *Rabauru nikki: ichi gun'i no gokuhi shiki*. Fukuoka: Sekufūsha, 1999.
Hatano Katsumi. *Rabauru dōkutsu byōin*. Tokyo: Kongō Shuppan, 1971.

Hirao Masaharu. *Soromon gun'i senki: gun'i tai'i ga mita kaigun rikusentai no shitō*. 1980. Reprinted with a new title. Tokyo: Kōjinsha, 2007.
Katō Daisuke. *Minami-no-shima ni yuki ga furu*. 1961. Reprint. Tokyo: Kōbunsha. 2005.
Majima Mitsuru. *Jigoku no senjō Nyūginia senki: sangaku mitsurin ni kieta hiun no guntai*. 1988. Reprint. Tokyo: Kōjinsha, 1996.
Mitsukawa Motoyuki. *Senki shio: tōbu Nyūginia sensen, aru taitsuki gun'i no kaisō*. Tokyo: Seiunsha, 1984.
Miyoshi Masayuki. *Kyokugen no Nyūginia-sen o ikiru*. Ajisu-chō, Yamaguchi Prefecture: Self-published, 2004.
Mizuki Shigeru. 'Afterword'. In *Onward Towards Our Noble Deaths*. Translated by Jocelyne Allen, August 1991, 368–9. Montreal: Drawn & Quarterly, 2011.
Mizuki Shigeru. *Kanzenban Mizuki Shigeru den* (3 vols.). Tokyo: Kōdansha, 2004.
Mizuki Shigeru. *Karankoron hyōhakuki*. Tokyo: Shōgakukan, 2000.
Mizuki Shigeru. *Komikku Shōwa-shi* (8 vols.). 1988–9. Reprint. Tokyo: Kōdansha, 1994.
Mizuki Shigeru. *Mizuki Shigeru no musume ni kataru otōsan no senki*. 1985. Reprint. Tokyo: Kawade Shobō, 1995.
Mizuki Shigeru. *Mizuki Shigeru no Rabauru senki*. Tokyo: Chikuma Shobō, 1994.
Mizuki Shigeru. *Neboke jinsei (shinsōban)*. 1982. Reprint. Tokyo: Chikuma Shobō, 1999.
Mizuki Shigeru. *Rabauru jūgunkōki: Topetoro tono gojū-nen*. 1995. Reprint. Tokyo: Chūōkōron Shinsha, 2002.
Mizuki Shigeru. 'Sensō to Nihon'. In *Ā gyokusai: Mizuki Shigeru senki senshū*. Edited by Mizuki Shigeru, 381–403. 1991. Reprint. Tokyo: Ōzora Shuppan, 2007.
Mizuki Shigeru. *Showa 1953–1989: A History of Japan*. Translated by Zack Davisson. Montreal: Drawn & Quarterly, 2015.
Mizuki Shigeru. *Watashi wa gegege: shinpika Mizuki Shigeru den*. Tokyo: Kadokawa, 2008.
Mizuki Shigeru and Mizuki Purodakushon. *Gegege no Gēte*. Tokyo: Futabasha, 2015.
Nukuda Nobuo. 'Atogaki'. In *Chichi no senki*. Nukuda Ichisuke, 198–201. Tokyo: Hōwa Shuppan, 1987.
Nukuda Ichisuke. *Chichi no senki*. Tokyo: Hōwa Shuppan, 1987.
Ogawa Masatsugu. *Shi-no-shima Nyūginia: Kyokugen no naka no ningen*. 1971. Reprinted with a new title. Tokyo: Kōjinsha, 1998.
Ogawa Masatsugu. *Tōbu Nyūginia sensen: suterareta butai*. Tokyo: Kōjinsha, 2002.
Okuzaki Kenzō. *Yamazaki, Tennō o ute! 'Kōkyo pachinko jiken' chinjutsusho*. 1974. Reprint. Tokyo: Shinsensha, 1987.
Suzuki Masami. *Nyūginia gun'i senki: jigoku no senjō o ikita ichigun'i no kiroku*. 1982. Reprinted with a new title. Tokyo: Kōjinsha, 2001.
Toyotani Hidemitsu. *Harin ware senyū o kū: tōbu Nyūginia haizannpei no kokuhaku*. Tokyo: Shinseiki Shobō, 1979.
Toyotani Hidemitsu. *Nyūginia donpei roku: jigoku angya*. Tokyo: Kindai Bungeisha, 1996.

Watanabe Susumu. *Mararia to kiga no sensen: tōbu Nyūginia senjūgunki*. Nagoya: Asahi Shinbun Nagoya Honsha Henshū Seisaku Sentā, 1984.

Yanagisawa Gen'ichirō. *Gun'i senki: sei to shi no nyūgijia senki*. 1979. Reprinted with a new title. Tokyo: Kōjinsha, 2003.

Travelogues

Kanetaka Kaoru. *Sekai no tabi: Oseania*. Tokyo: Jitsugyō no Nihonsha, 1962.

Kawaguchi Kizuki. *Papua Nyūginia tanbōki: tabō na bijinesuman no jikokeihatsu ryokō*. Tokyo: Kadensha, 1996.

Makino Hiromichi. *Senseki ni inoru*. Tokyo: Sankei Shinbun Shuppan, 2007.

Makino Hiromichi. *Senseki o aruku*. Tokyo: Shūeisha, 2002.

Miyakawa Masayo. *Papua Nyūginia rekuiemu*. Tokyo: Ushio Shuppansha, 1985.

Tsumori Takudō. *Hotoke no namida: nanpō ireiki*. Sapporo: Hokkai Taimususha, 1981.

Yasujima Takayoshi. *Aruite mita Taiheiyō sensō no shimajima*. Tokyo: Iwanami Shoten, 2010.

Films and Documentaries

Hara Kazuo, dir. *Yukiyukite shingun*. 1987. DVD. Tokyo: Shissō Purodakushon, 2007.

Hisamatsu Seiji, dir. *Minami-no-shima ni yuki ga furu*. 1961. VHS. Tokyo: Tōhō, 19–.

Mizushima Satoru dir. *Minami-no-shima ni yuki ga furu*. 1995. VHS. Tokyo: Ribāsu. 1996.

Mizushima Satoru. 'Tokubetsu kōkai eiga *Minamino-shima-ni yuki ga furu*', (film, with a pre-feature commentary), 10 August 2013, https://www.youtube.com/watch?v=O2_izEaxxVw (accessed 29 January 2021).

Mizushima Satoshi. Prescreening commentary. 'Ch. Hokkaidō, eiga *Minamino-shima-ni yuki ga furu*', (film, with a pre-feature commentary), 30 April 2019, https://www.youtube.com/watch?v=NifRizUC2Yw (accessed 29 January 2021).

Sekiguchi Noriko, dir. *Senjō no onnatachi*. 1989. DVD. Tokyo: Siglo, 2005.

Sekiguchi Noriko, dir. *Sensō Daughters*. 1990. DVD. Tokyo: Siglo, 2005.

Ushiyama Jun'ichi, dir. *New Guinea ni chitta 16-man no seishun*. Terebi Asashi. Aired 14 August 1991.

Secondary Materials

Akasaka Mari. *Tokyo Purizun*. Tokyo: Kawade Shobō Shinsha, 2012.

Amamiya Karin and Furuichi Noritoshi. '"Sensō" o shiranaitte sonna ni warui koto desuka?' *Shūkan kinyōbi*, no. 989 (25 April 2014): 24–7.

Aoki Tōru. *Hiroku: sensō eiyōshicchōshō*. Tokyo: Korube, 1979.

Asō Tetsuo. 'Positive Method for the Prevention of Venereal Diseases'. In *From Shanghai to Shanghai*. Asō Tetsuo. Translated by Hal Gold, 172–85. Norwalk, CT: East Bridge, 2004.

Assmann, Jan. 'Communicative and Cultural Memory'. In *Cultural Memory Studies: An International and Interdisciplinary Handbook*. Edited by Astrid Erll and Ansgar Nünning, 109–88. Berlin: De Gruyter, 2008.

Aukema, Justin. 'A Hero's Defeat: Modernization Theory and Japanese Veterans' Asia-Pacific "War Tales"'. *Asia-Pacific Journal: Japan Focus* 20, issue 10, no. 4 (15 May 2022) https://apjjf.org/-Justin-Aukema/5701/article.pdf (accessed 16 May 2022).

Bal, Mieke. *Travelling Concepts in the Humanities: A Rough Guide*. Toronto: University of Toronto Press, 2002.

Baskett, Michael. 'Dying for a Laugh: Post-1945 Japanese Service Comedies'. *Historical Journal of Film, Radio and Television* 23, no. 4 (2003): 291–310.

Bōeichō bōei kenshūjo senshishitsu, ed. *Senshi sōsho: Minami Taiheiyō rikugun sakusen 2, Gadarukanaru–Buna sakusen*. Tokyo: Asagumo Shinbunsha, 1969.

Bourke, Joanna. 'Wartime'. In *Medicine in the Twentieth Century*. Edited by Roger Cooter and John Pickstone, 589–600. Amsterdam: Hardwood Academic Publishers, 2000.

Breen, John. 'Voices of Rage: Six Paths to the Problem of Yasukuni'. In *Politics and Religion in Modern Japan: Red Sun, White Lotus*. Edited by Roy Starrs, 278–304. London: Palgrave Macmillan, 2011.

Bruzzi, Stella. *New Documentary* (2nd edn). London: Routledge, 2006.

Bullard, Steven. '"The Great Enemy of Humanity": Malaria and the Japanese Medical Corps in Papua, 1942–43'. *Journal of Pacific History* 39, no. 2 (2004): 203–20.

Bullard, Steven. 'Translator's Introduction'. In *Japanese Army Operations in the South Pacific Area: New Britain and Papua Campaigns, 1942–43*. Translated by Steven Bullard, ii–vi. Canberra: Australian War Memorial, 2007.

Bullard, Steven, and Keiko Tamura, eds. *From a Hostile Shore: Australia and Japan at War in New Guinea*. Canberra: Australian War Memorial, 2004.

Burgoyne, Robert. *The Hollywood Historical Film*. Malden, MA: Blackwell, 2008.

Buruma, Ian. *The Wages of Guilt: Memories of War in Germany and Japan*. 1994. Reprint. New York: New York Review of Books, 2015.

Carr, E. H. *What Is History: The George Macaulay Trevelyan Lectures Delivered in the University of Cambridge, January–March 1961* (2nd edn). Edited by R. W. Davies. London: Penguin, 1987.

Carrier, James G. 'People Who Can Be Friends'. In *Anthropology of Friendship*. Edited by Sandra Bell and Simon Coleman, 21–38. Oxford: Berg, 1999.

Carrigan, Anthony. 'Dark Tourism and Postcolonial Studies: Critical Intersections'. *Postcolonial Studies* 17, no. 3 (2014): 236–50.
Clarke, Robert, Jacqueline Dutton and Anna Johnston. 'Shadow Zones: Dark Travel and Postcolonial Cultures'. *Postcolonial Studies* 17, no. 3 (2014): 221–35.
Coates, Jennifer. 'Victims and Bystanders: Women in the Japanese War-Retro Film'. *Media, War & Conflict* 6, no. 3 (2013): 233–48.
Crocombe, Ron. *Asia in the Pacific Islands: Replacing the West*. Suva, Fiji: IPS Publications, University of the South Pacific, 2007.
Cubitt, Geoffrey. *History and Memory*. Manchester: Manchester University Press, 2007.
Cwiertka, Katarzyna Joanna. *Modern Japanese Cuisine: Food, Power and National Identity*. London: Reaktion, 2006.
De Groot, Jerome. *Consuming History: Historians and Heritage in Contemporary Popular Culture* (2nd edn). London: Routledge, 2016.
Dening, Greg. *Performances*. Chicago: University of Chicago Press, 1996.
Dorr, Maria Elisabeth, Astrid Erll, Erin Högerle, Paul Vickers and Jarula M. I. Wegner. 'Introduction: Travel, Locatedness, and New Horizons in Memory Studies'. *Journal of Aesthetics & Culture* 11, supplement 1 (2019): 1–5.
Dower, John W. 'An Aptitude for Being Unloved: War and Memory in Japan'. In *Ways of Forgetting, Ways of Remembering: Japan in the Modern World*. John W. Dower, 105–35. New York: New Press, 2012.
Dower, John W. *Embracing Defeat: Japan in the Wake of World War II*. New York: W. W. Norton, 1999.
Dower, John W. *War without Mercy: Race and Power in the Pacific War*. 1986. Corr. by author. New York: Pantheon, 1993.
Dubnik, James K. 'Foreword'. In *Afterwar: Healing the Moral Wounds of Our Soldiers*. Nancy Sherman, vi–xvii. New York: Oxford University Press, 2015.
Dvorak, Greg. *Coral and Concrete: Remembering Kwajalein Atoll between Japan, America, and the Marshall Islands*. Honolulu: University of Hawai'i Press, 2018.
Dwyer, Philip. 'Making Sense of the Muddle: War Memoirs and the Culture of Remembering'. In *War Stories: The War Memoir in History and Literature*. Edited by Philip Dwyer, 1–26. Oxford: Berghahn, 2018.
Ellis, John. *Documentary: Witness and Self-Revelation*. Abingdon: Routledge, 2012.
Epstein, A. L. *Matupit: Land, Politics, and Change among the Tolai of New Britain*. Canberra: Australian National University Press, 1969.
Erll, Astrid. 'Travelling Memory'. *Parallax* 17, no. 4 (2011): 4–18.
Fenton, Damian. 'How Many Died?' In *Remembering the War in New Guinea: The Australia-Japan Research Project*. The Australian War Memorial (1 June 2004), http://ajrp.awm.gov.au/AJRP/remember.nsf/709e228818bdf765ca256a9a001dad4d/58ebd6d993e15ce8ca256d05002671fd (accessed 27 November 2020).
Fenton, Damian. 'Who Fought in New Guinea?' In *Remembering the War in New Guinea: The Australia-Japan Research Project*. The Australian War Memorial (1 June

2004), http://ajrp.awm.gov.au/ajrp/remember.nsf/pages/NT0000179A (accessed 27 November, 2020).

Fitzpatrick, Georgina. 'Cannibalism and the War Crimes Trials'. In *Australia's War Crimes Trials, 1945–1951*. Edited by Georgina Fitzpatrick, Tim McCormack and Narrelle Morris, 291–325. Leiden: Brill, 2016.

Foster, Michael Dylan. 'The Otherworlds of Mizuki Shigeru'. *Mechademia* 3 (2008): 8–28.

Foucault, Michel. *The Birth of the Clinic: An Archaeology of Medical Perception*. 1973. Reprint. New York: Vintage Books, 1994.

Frühstück, Sabine. *Colonizing Sex: Sexology and Social Control in Modern Japan*. Berkeley: University of California Press, 2003.

Fujii Tadatoshi. *Heitachi no sensō: tegami, nikki, taikenki o yomitoku*. Tokyo: Asashi Shinbunsha, 2000.

Fujiwara Akira. *Uejinishita eirei tachi*. Tokyo: Aoki Shoten, 2001.

Fukuma Yoshiaki. *Sengo Nihon, kioku no rikigaku: 'keishō to iu danzetsu' to bunansa no seijigaku*. Tokyo: Sakuhinsha, 2020.

Fukuma Yoshiaki. *'Sensō taiken' no sengoshi*. Tokyo: Chūōkōronsha, 2009.

Goldberg, G. R. 'Intake and Energy Requirements'. In *Encyclopedia of Food Sciences and Nutrition, Vol. 4* (2nd edn). Edited by Benjamin Caballero, 2091–8. Oxford: Academic Press, 2003.

Gordon, Andrew. *A Modern History of Japan: From Tokugawa Times to the Present* (3rd edn). New York: Oxford University Press, 2013.

Graeber, David. *Toward an Anthropological Theory of Values: The False Coin of Our Own Dreams*. New York: Palgrave, 2001.

Gregory, Chris. 'Exchange'. In *Handbook of Sociocultural Anthropology*. Edited by James G. Carrier and Deborah B. Gewertz, 209–26. London: Bloomsbury Academic, 2013.

Hagen, Trevor, and Anna Lisa Tota, eds. *Routledge International Handbook of Memory Studies*. London: Routledge, 2015.

Hamada Kengo. *Wakiyakubon zōho bunkoban*. Tokyo: Chikuma Shobō, 2018.

Hamazaki Kōji and Higashino Makoto. 'Ushiyama Jun'ichi: eizō no doramaturgī'. *Hōsō kenkyū to chōsa* 62, no. 5 (2012): 84–102.

Hann, Chris. 'The Gift and Reciprocity: Perspectives from Economic Anthropology'. In *The Handbook of the Economics of Giving, Altruism and Reciprocity*. Edited by Serge-Christophe Kolm and Jean Mercier Ythier, 207–23. Amsterdam: Elsevier, 2006.

Happell, Charles. *The Bone Man of Kokoda*. Sydney: Pan Macmillan, 2008.

Hara Kazuo. '*Yukiyukite Shingun* no kakushin o kataru'. *Shinario* 44, no. 3 (1988): 16–37.

Hara Kazuo and Shissō Purodakushon. *Dokyumento* Yukiyukite shingun *zōhoban*. 1994. Reprinted with additional material. Tokyo: Kōseisha, 2018.

Hara Kazuo, Ishizaka Kenji and Ido Kishū. *Fumikoeru kyamera: waga hōhō akushon dokyumentarī*. Tokyo: Firumuātosha, 1995.

Hara Takeshi. 'Senshōbyōsha ni taisuru iryō engo taisei'. *Gunji shigaku* 49, no. 4 (2014): 38–49.
Harari, Yuval Noah. *The Ultimate Experience: Battlefield Revelations and the Making of Modern War Culture, 1450–2000*. Basingstoke: Palgrave Macmillan, 2008.
Hashimoto, Akiko. *The Long Defeat: Cultural Trauma, Memory, and Identity in Japan*. New York: Oxford University Press, 2015.
Hata Ikuhiko. 'Timbunke jiken (Nyūginia)'. In *Sekai sensō hanzai jiten*. Edited by Hata Ikuhiko, Sase Masamori and Tsuneishi Keiichi, 181–2. Tokyo: Bungei Shunjū, 2002.
Hirano, Mutsumi. *History Education and International Relations: A Case Study of Diplomatic Disputes over Japanese Textbooks*. Folkestone: Global Oriental, 2009.
Hirsch, Marianne. *The Generation of Postmemory: Writing and Visual Culture After the Holocaust*. New York: Columbia University Press, 2012.
Hokari Minoru. *Radikaru ōraru hisutorī: Ōsutoraria senjūmin Aboriginī no rekishi jissen*. 2004. Reprint. Tokyo: Iwanami Shoten, 2018.
Holland, Patrick, and Graham Huggan. *Tourists with Typewriters: Critical Reflections on Contemporary Travel Writing*. Ann Arbor: Michigan University Press, 2000.
Hosaka Masayasu. 'Kaisetsu'. In *Minami-no-shima ni yuki ga furu*, Katō Daisuke, 289–95. Tokyo: Kōbunsha, 2005.
Hosaka Masayasu. *Senjō taikensha: chinmoku no kiroku*. Tokyo: Chikuma Shobō, 2015.
Hulme, Peter. 'Travelling to Write (1940–2000)'. In *The Cambridge Companion to Travel Writing*. Edited by Peter Hulme and Tim Youngs, 87–101. Cambridge: Cambridge University Press, 2002.
Hunt, Lynn. *Gurōbaru jidai no rekishigaku*. Translated by Hasegawa Takahiko. Tokyo: Iwanami Shoten, 2016.
Hynes, Samuel. *The Soldiers' Tale: Bearing Witness to Modern War*. New York: Viking Books, 2001.
Ichinose Toshiya. *Kōgun heishi no nichijōseikatsu*. Tokyo: Kōdansha, 2009.
Ienaga Saburō. *Sensō sekinin*. Tokyo: Iwanami Shoten, 1985.
Igarashi, Yoshikuni. *Bodies of Memory: Narratives of War in Postwar Japanese Culture, 1945–1970*. Princeton: Princeton University Press, 2000.
Igarashi Yoshikuni. *Haisen to sengo no aida de: okurete kaerishi monotachi*. Tokyo: Chikuma Shobō, 2012.
Iijima Wataru. *Mararia to teikoku*. Tokyo: Tokyō Daigaku Shuppankai, 2005.
Iriye, Akira. 'Review of *The Emperor's Naked Army Marches On*, Kazuo Hara'. *American Historical Review* 94, no. 4 (1989): 1036–7.
Iwamoto, Hiromitsu. 'Japanese Perceptions on the Pacific War in Papua New Guinea: Views in Publications'. In *The Pacific War in Papua New Guinea: Memories and Realities*. Edited by Yukio Toyoda and Hank Nelson, 49–57. Tokyo: Rikkyō University Centre for Asian Area Studies, 2006.
Iwamoto, Hiromitsu. 'Memories and Realities of the Japanese Occupation of Mainland New Guinea'. In *The Pacific War in Papua New Guinea: Memories and Realities*.

Edited by Yukio Toyoda and Hank Nelson, 279–96. Tokyo: Rikkyō University Centre for Asian Area Studies, 2006.

Iwamoto Hiromitsu. 'Taiheiyō Sensō-ki ni okeru Nihon-gun no Rabauru senryō tōchi: Nihon gawa no ninshiki to sono jittai'. *Shien* 63, no. 1 (2011): 6–41.

Jansen-Verbeke, Myriam, and Wanda George. 'Reflections on the Great War Centenary: From Warscapes to Memoryscapes in 100 Years'. In *Tourism and War*. Edited by Richard Bulter and Wantanee Suntikul, 273–87. Abingdon: Routledge, 2013.

Kanaoka Shūyū. *Hannya shingyō*. 1973. Reprint. Tokyo: Kōdansha, 2001.

Kanetaka Kaoru. *Watakushi ga tabikara mananda koto: 80 sugitemo 'Sekai no tabi' wa keizokuchū desu noyo!* Tokyo: Shōgakukan, 2010.

Karatani Kōjin, Itō Seikō and Nakamori Akio. '*Yukiyukite Shingun*: Okuzaki Kenzō o tanken suru'. *Shokun* 19, no. 11 (1987): 186–96.

Kasuga Taichi. *Nihon no sensō eiga*. Tokyo: Bungei Shunjū, 2020.

Kawaguchi Kizuki. *Papua Nyūginia: seirei no ie, NGO, sensō, ningen moyōni deau tabi*. Tokyo: Kadensha, 2000.

Kawamura Minato. 'Popular Orientalism and Japanese Views of Asia'. Translated by Kota Inoue and Helen J. S. Lee. In *Reading Colonial Japan: Text, Context, and Critique*. Edited by Michele M. Mason and Helen J. S. Lee, 271–98. Stanford: Stanford University Press, 2012.

Kelly, Mark G. E. *Foucault and Politics: A Critical Introduction*. Edinburgh: Edinburgh University Press, 2014.

Kituai, August Ibrum. *My Gun, My Brother: The World of the Papua New Guinea Colonial Police, 1920–1960*. Honolulu: University of Hawai'i Press, 1998.

Kōsei rōdō-shō (Ministry of Health, Labour and Welfare, Japan). 'Chiiki betsu senbotsusha ikotsu shūyō gaikenzu', https://www.mhlw.go.jp/content/12100000/000337565.pdf (accessed 27 January 2021).

Kōsei rōdō-shō. 'Senbotsusha irei jigyō: Minami Taiheiyō senbotsuha no hi'. http://www.mhlw.go.jp/bunya/engo/seido01/ireihi04.html (accessed 6 August 2019).

Landsberg, Alison. *Prosthetic Memory: The Transformation of American Remembrance in the Age of Mass Culture*. New York: Columbia University Press, 2004.

Lennon, John, and Malcolm Foley. *Dark Tourism: The Attraction of Death and Disaster*. London: Continuum, 2000.

Lifton, Robert Jay. *The Broken Connection: On Death and the Continuity of Life*. New York: Simon and Schuster, 1979.

Lisle, Debbie. *The Global Politics of Contemporary Travel Writing*. Cambridge: Cambridge University Press, 2006.

Lowry, Robert. *Fortress Fiji: Holding the Line in the Pacific War, 1939–45*. Sutton, NSW: Self-published, 2006.

Marschall, Sabine. 'Tourism and Remembrance: The Journey into the Self and Its Past'. *Journal of Tourism and Cultural Change* 12, no. 4 (2014): 335–48.

Masubuchi Tsuyoshi. 'Minami-no-shima ni yuki ga furu'. *Kinema Junpō*, no. 1183, (1 February 1996): 171–2.

Mathews, Gordon. 'Can "A Real Man" Live for His Family? *Ikigai* and Masculinity in Today's Japan'. In *Men and Masculinities in Contemporary Japan: Dislocating the Salaryman Doxa*. Edited by James E. Roberson and Nobue Suzuki, 109–25. London: Routledge Curzon, 2003.

McLelland, Mark. *Queer Japan: From the Pacific War to the Internet Age*. Lanham, MD: Rowman & Littlefield, 2005.

Mezur, Katherine. *Beautiful Boys/Outlaw Bodies: Devising Kabuki Female-Likeness*. New York: Palgrave Macmillan, 2005.

Miya Tsugio. 'Nihon no jigoku-e'. In *Zukai jigoku-e o yomu*. Shibusawa Tatsuhiko and Miya Tsugio, 35–126. Tokyo: Kawade Shobō Shinsha, 1999.

Mizuki Shigeru manga daizenshū henshū iinkai, ed. *Mizuki Shigeru manga daizenshū 000: sōsakuin/nenpu hōka*. Tokyo: Kōdansha, 2019.

Mizushima Satoru. 'Masubuchi Tsuyoshi shi *Minami-no-shima ni yuki ga furu* hyō ni taisuru hanron'. *Kinema Junpō*, no. 1188 (15 April 1996): 168–71.

Moore, Aaron W. *Writing War: Soldiers Record the Japanese Empire*. Cambridge, MA: Harvard University Press, 2013.

Morris, Ivan. *The Nobility of Failure: Tragic Heroes in the History of Japan*. eBook. New York: Holt, Rinehart and Winston, 1975.

Morris-Suzuki, Tessa. *The Past within Us: Media, Memory, History*. London: Verso, 2005.

Mura Nunoe. *Gegege no nyōbō*. Tokyo: Jitsugyō no Nihonsha, 2008.

Nagao Toshihiko. *Suterareta Nihonhei no jinnikushoku jiken*. Tokyo: San'ichi Shobo, 1996.

Nakamura Eri. *Sensō to torauma: fukakashi sareta Nihonhei no sensō shinkeishō*. Tokyo: Yoshikawa Kōbunkan, 2018.

Nakayama Kaoru. 'Senbotsusha irei jumpai oboegaki: Chiba-ken Tochigi-ken Gokokujinja shusai senbotsusha irei jumpai no jireikara'. *Kokugakiin Daigaku kenkyū kaihatsu suishinsentā: rekishi kiyō* 2 (2008): 171–215.

Namihira Emiko. *Nihon-jin no shi no katachi: dentō gishiki kara yasukuni made*. Tokyo: Asahi Shinbunsha, 2004.

Narita Ryūichi. *Sengoshi nyūmon*. Tokyo: Kawade Shobō Shinsha, 2015.

Narita Ryūichi. *Zōho 'sensō keiken' no sengoshi: katarareta taiken/shōgen/kioku*. Rev ed. Tokyo: Iwanami Shoten, 2020.

Nelson, Hank. 'The Consolation Unit: Comfort Women in Rabaul'. *Journal of Pacific History* 43, no. 1 (2008): 1–20.

Nelson, Hank. 'Kokoda: and Two National Histories'. *Journal of Pacific History* 42, no. 1 (2007): 73–88.

Nelson, Hank. 'Papua Nyūginia to Ajia-Taiheiyō sensō'. In *Dōin, teikō, yokusan: Iwanami kōza Taiheiyō sensō*. Edited by Kurasawa Aiko, Sugihara Tōru, Narita Ryūchi, Tessa Morris-Suzuki, Yui Daizaburō and Yoshida Yutaka. Translated by Karashima Masato. Tokyo: Iwanami Shoten, 2006. 217–46.

Nelson, Hank. 'The Swinging Index: Capital Punishment and British and Australian Administrations in Papua and New Guinea, 1888–1945'. *Journal of Pacific History* 13, no. 3, (1978): 130–52.

NHK. 'Kakusareta torauma: seishin shōgai heishi 8,000-nin no kiroku', 25 August 2018.

Nichols, Bill. *Introduction to Documentary* (3rd edn). Bloomington: Indiana University Press, 2017.

Nishimura Akira. *Sengo Nihon to sensō shisha irei: shizume to furui no dainamizumu*. Tokyo: Yūshisha, 2006.

Nishino, Ryōta. 'Better Late Than Never? Mizuki Shigeru's Trans-war Reflections on Journeys to New Britain Island'. *Japan Review* 32 (2019), 107–29.

Nishino, Ryōta. 'From Memory Making to Money Making? Japanese Travel Writers' Impressions of Cross-Cultural Interactions in the Southwestern Pacific Islands Battlesites, 1961–2007'. *Pacific Historical Review* 86, no. 3 (2017): 443–71.

Nishino, Ryōta. 'Pacific Islanders Experience the Pacific War: Informants as Historians and Story Tellers'. *Asia-Pacific Journal: Japan Focus* 15, issue 2, no. 2 (15 October 2017): https://apjjf.org/-Ryota-Nishino/5073/article.pdf (accessed 15 October 2017).

Nishino, Ryōta. 'Pacific War Battle Sites through the Eyes of Japanese Travel Writers: Vicarious Consumer Travel and Emotional Performance in Travelogues'. *History and Memory* 32, no. 2 (2020): 146–75.

Nishino, Ryōta. 'War, Trauma, and Humanity in a Japanese Memoir: Ogawa Masatsugu's *"Island of Death"* (1969)'. *Asia-Pacific Journal: Japan Focus* 20, issue 10, no. 4 (15 May 2022) https://apjjf.org/-Ry--ta--Nishino/5702/article.pdf (accessed 16 May 2022).

Niwa Yoshiyuki. *Nihon no terebi dokyumentarī*. Tokyo: Tōkyō Daigaku Shuppankai, 2020.

Noda Masaaki. *Senso to zaiseki*. Tokyo: Iwanami Shoten, 1988.

Norma, Caroline. 'Australian Military Sexual Adventurism in the New Guinean Campaign, 1942–1945'. In *Transpacific Visions: Connected Histories of the Pacific across North and South*. Edited by Yasuko Hassall Kobayashi and Shinnosuke Takahashi, 81–110. Lanham, MD: Rowman & Littlefield, 2021.

Noro Kuninobu. *Ushinawareta heishi tachi*. 1977. Reprint. Tokyo: Bungei Shunjū, 2015.

Oda Makoto. *Nanshi no shiso*. 1969. Reprint. Tokyo: Iwanami Shoten, 2008.

Onda Shigetaka. *Tōbu Nyūginia-sen: kono kiroku o tōbu Nyūginia senjō de shinde itta heishi tachi ni sasageru* (2 vols.). Tokyo: Gendaishi Shuppankai, 1977.

Orr, James. *The Victim as Hero: Ideologies of Peace and National Identity in Postwar Japan*. Honolulu: University of Hawai'i Press, 2001.

Penney, Matthew. 'War and Japan: The Non-Fiction Manga of Mizuki Shigeru'. *Asia-Pacific Journal: Japan Focus* 6, no. 9 (1 September 2008): https://apjjf.org/-Matthew-Penney/2905/article.pdf (accessed 21 August 2017).

Pennington, Lee K. *Casualties of History: Wounded Japanese Servicemen and the Second World War*. Ithaca, NY: Cornell University Press, 2015.

Powell, Alan. *Third Force: ANGAU's New Guinea War, 1942–46*. Melbourne: Oxford University Press, 2003.
Pratt, Mary Louise. *The Imperial Eyes: Travel Writing and Transculturation* (2nd edn) New York: Routledge, 2008.
Radstone, Susannah, and Bill Schwarz, eds. *Memory: Histories, Theories, Debates*. New York: Fordham University Press, 2010.
Reider, Noriko T. *Japanese Demon Lore: Oni from the Ancient Time to the Present*, Logan: Utah State University Press, 2010.
Riseman, Noah J. *Defending Whose Country? Indigenous Soldiers in the Pacific War*. Lincoln: University of Nebraska Press, 2012.
Ritchie, Johnathan. 'Papua New Guineans Reconstructing their Histories: The Pacific War Revisited'. *Oceania*, 87, no. 2 (2017): 124–38.
Robinson, Neville. *Villagers at War: Some Papua New Guinean Experiences in World War II*. Edited by E. Fisk. Canberra: Australian National University, 1981.
Rosenbaum, Roman. 'Mizuki Shigeru's Pacific War'. *International Journal of Comic Arts* 10, no. 2 (2008): 354–79.
Rosenstone, Robert. *History on Film/Film on History*. New York: Pearson, 2006.
Rothberg, Michael. *The Implicated Subject: Beyond Victims and Perpetrators*. Stanford: Stanford University Press, 2019.
Ruoff, Jeffrey, and Kenneth Ruoff. *The Emperor's Naked Army Marches On: Yukiyukite shingun*. Trowbridge: Flicks Books, 1998.
Ryu Yongwook. 'Departing from the Postwar Regime: The Revision of the "Peace Constitution" and Japan's National Identity'. In *Routledge Handbook of Japanese Foreign Policy*. Edited by Mary McCarthy, 41–54. Abingdon: Routledge, 2018.
Sahlins, Marshall. *Stone Age Economics*. London: Aldine-Athlone, 1972.
Saito, Hiro. *The History Problem: The Politics of War Commemoration in East Asia*. Honolulu: University of Hawai'i Press, 2016.
Satō Tadao. *Nihon eigashi: zōho-ban 3, 1960–2005*. Tokyo: Iwanami Shoten, 2006.
Satō Tadao. 'Sensō hanzai no mondai'. In *Nihon no dokyumentari 2: Seiji Shakai hen*. Edited by Satō Tadao, 67–76. Tokyo: Iwanami Shoten, 2010.
Scarry, Elaine. *The Body in Pain: The Making and Unmaking of the World*. New York: Oxford University Press, 1985.
Seaton, Philip. *Japan's Contested War Memories: The 'Memory Rifts' in Historical Consciousness of World War II*. eBook. Abingdon: Routledge, 2007.
Sekiguchi Noriko. *Senjo no onna tachi*. Tokyo: Ritorumoa, 1990.
Senda Kakou. *Shinikuhei no kokuhaku*. Tokyo: Chōbunsha, 1980.
Seraphim, Franziska. *War Memory and Social Politics in Japan, 1945–2005*. Cambridge, MA: Harvard University Asia Center, 2006.
Sharpley, Richard, and Philip R. Stone, eds. *The Darker Side of Travel: The Theory and Practice of Dark Tourism*. Bristol: Channel View Publications, 2009.
Shepard, Ben. *War of Nerves: Soldiers and Psychiatrists in the Twentieth Century*. Cambridge, MA: Harvard University Press, 2001.

Sherman, Nancy. *Afterwar: Healing the Moral Wounds of Our Soldiers*. New York: Oxford University Press, 2015.

Shimada Keizō. 'The Adventure of Dankichi'. Translated by Helen J. S. Lee. In *Reading Colonial Japan: Text, Context, and Critique*. Edited by Michele M. Mason and Helen J. S. Lee, 245–70. Stanford: Stanford University Press, 2012.

Sissons, David C. S. 'Some Observations on Australian War Crime Trials Involving Cannibalism/Mutilation of the Dead'. In *Bridging Australia and Japan. Volume 2: The Writings of David Sissons, Historian and Political Scientist*. Edited by Keiko Tamura and J. A. A. Stockwin, 155–9. Canberra: Australian National University Press, 2020.

Smaill, Belinda. *The Documentary: Politics, Emotion, Culture*. Basingstoke: Palgrave Macmillan, 2015.

Spremberg, Felix. 'The Asia-Pacific War in Japan's New Moral Education Textbooks'. *Asia-Pacific Journal: Japan Focus* 19, issue 18, no. 2 (15 September 2021) https://apjjf.org/-Felix-Spremberg/5632/article.pdf (accessed 28 October 2021).

Stahl, David C. *The Burdens of Survival: Ōoka Shōhei's Writings on the Pacific War*. Honolulu: University of Hawai'i Press, 2003.

Standish, Isolde. *Myth and Masculinity in the Japanese Cinema: Towards a Political Reading of the 'Tragic Hero'*. London: Routledge, 2000.

Standish, Isolde. *A New History of Japanese Cinema: A Century of Narrative Film*. New York: Continuum, 2005.

Stead, Victoria. 'History as Resource: Moral Reckonings with Place and with the Wartime Past in Oro Province, Papua New Guinea'. *Anthropological Forum* 28, no. 1 (2018): 16–31.

Stead, Victoria. 'Violent Histories and the Ambivalences of Recognition in Postcolonial Papua New Guinea', *Postcolonial Studies* 20, no. 1 (2017): 68–85.

Sudo, Naoto. *Nanyō-Orientalism: Japanese Representations of the Pacific*. Amherst, MA: Cambria Press, 2010.

Suzuki, C. J. (Shige). 'Learning from Monsters: Mizuki Shigeru's Yōkai and War Manga'. *Image & Narrative* 12, no. 1 (2011): 229–44.

Suzuki Yoshikazu. *Terebi wa danshi isshō no shigoto: dokyumentaristo Ushiyama Jun'ichi*. Tokyo: Heibonsha, 2016.

Takahashi Hiroki. *Yubi no hone*. Tokyo: Shinchōsha, 2016.

Takahashi Saburō. *Seniki mono o yomu*. Kyoto: Akademia Shuppankai, 1988.

Takahashi, Tetsuya. 'The National Politics of the Yasukuni Shrine'. In *Nationalisms in Japan*. Edited by Naoko Shimazu. Translated by Philip Seaton, 155–80. London: Routledge, 2006.

Takeda Kazuyoshi. *Periryū: rakuen no gerunika* (11 vols.). Tokyo: Hakusensha, 2016–21.

Takenaka, Akiko. 'Japanese Memories of the Asia-Pacific War: Analyzing the Revisionist Turn Post-1995'. *Asia-Pacific Journal: Japan Focus* 14, issue 20, no. 8 (15 October 2016): https://apjjf.org/-Akiko-Takenaka/4967/article.pdf (accessed 26 November 2020).

Takenaka, Akiko. *Yasukuni: History, Memory, and Japan's Unending Postwar*. Honolulu: University of Hawai'i Press, 2015.

Tanaka Hiromi. *Makkāsā to tatakatta Nihon-gun: Nyūginia-sen no kiroku*. Tokyo: Yumani Shobō, 2009.

Tanaka Toshiyuki. *Shirarezaru sensōhanzai: Nihon-gun wa Ōsutoraria-jin ni nani o shitaka*. Tokyo: Ōtsuki Shoten, 1993.

Tanaka, Yuki. *Hidden Horrors: Japanese War Crimes in World War II* (2nd edn). Lanham, MD: Rowman & Littlefield, 2018.

Tanaka, Yuki. '"Yamazaki, Shoot Emperor Hirohito!" Okuzaki Kenzo's Legal Action to Abolish Chapter One (the Emperor) of Japan's Constitution'. *Asia-Pacific Journal: Japan Focus* 17, issue 20, no. 1 (15 October 2019): https://apjjf.org/-Yuki-Tanaka/5318/article.pdf (accessed 24 October 2019).

Tawara Yoshifumi. 'The Abe Government and the 2014 Screening of Japanese Junior High School History Textbooks'. Translated by Sven Saaler, with Introduction by the Asia-Pacific Journal. *Asia-Pacific Journal: Japan Focus* 13, issue 17, no. 2 (27 April 2015) https://apjjf.org/-Tawara-Yoshifumi/4312/article.pdf (accessed 28 October 2021).

Teshima Fusatarō. 'Jobun'. In *Chi no hate ni shisu*. Uematsu Jinsaku, 1–6. Tokyo: Tosho Shuppansha, 1976.

Thompson, Carl. *Travel Writing*. London: Routledge, 2011.

Tierney, Robert Thomas. *Tropics of Savagery: The Culture of Japanese Empire in Comparative Frame*. Berkeley: University of California Press, 2010.

Trefalt, Beatrice. 'Finding the Remains of the Dead: Photographs from a Japanese Mission to New Guinea, 1969–1970'. *Asia-Pacific Journal: Japan Focus* 20, issue 10, no. 4 (15 May 2022) https://apjjf.org/-Beatrice-Trefalt/5700/article.pdf (accessed 16 May 2022).

Tuzin, Donald F. 'Cannibalism and Arapesh Cosmology: A Wartime Incident with the Japanese'. In *The Ethnography of Cannibalism*. Edited by Paula Brown and Donald F. Tuzin 61–71. Washington, DC: Society for Psychological Anthropology, 1983.

Umehara Takeshi. *The Concept of Hell*. Translated by Robert Wargo. Tokyo: Shūeisha, 1996.

Urry, John. *Consuming Places*. London: Routledge, 2000.

Von Goethe, Johann Wolfgang. *Conversations of Goethe, with Eckermann and Soret*. Translated by John Oxenford. New edition. London: G. Bell, 1874.

Watanabe Masaichi. 'Papua-jin daigyakusatsu o meirei shitano wa watashi datta'. *Maru* 25, no. 3 (March 1972): 82–9.

White, Geoffrey, and Eveline Buchheim. 'Traveling War: Memory Practices in Motion'. *History and Memory* 27, no. 2 (2015): 5–19.

White, Hayden. *The Content of the Form: Narrative Discourse and Historical Representation*. Baltimore, MD: Johns Hopkins University Press, 1987.

Whitehead, Anne. *Memory*. London: Routledge, 2009.

Wigmore, Lionel. *The Japanese Thrust: Australia in the War of 1939–1945, IV* (1st edn). Canberra: Australian War Memorial, 1957.

Williams, Peter. *Japan's Pacific War: Personal Accounts of the Emperor's Warriors.* eBook. Barnsley: Pen and Sword, 2021.

Williams, Peter. *The Kokoda Campaign 1942: Myth and Reality.* Port Melbourne: Cambridge University Press, 2012.

Wilson, Sandra. 'Film and Soldier: Japanese War Movies in the 1950s'. *Journal of Contemporary History* 48, no. 3 (2013): 537–55.

Yamaguchi Makoto. *Nippon no kaigai ryokō: wakamono to kankō media no 50 nenshi.* Tokyo: Chikuma Shobō, 2010.

Yano Kanji. *Hansen eiga kara no koe: ano jidai ni modoranai tameni.* Fukuoka: Gen Shobō, 2017.

Yasujima Takayoshi. 'Wakai sedai ni katarutsugu sensō no kioku'. *Shūkan kinyōbi*, no. 810 (6 August 2010): 38–9.

Yomota, Inuhiko. *What Is Japanese Cinema? A History.* Translated by Philip Kaffen. New York: Columbia University Press, 2019.

Yoshida Yatsuo. 'Toyō no jigoku'. In *Shūkyō jigoku-e*. In Yoshida Yatsuo and Tanaka Masashi, 136–91. Tokyo: Daiwa Shobō, 2006.

Yoshida Yutaka. *Nihon-gun heishi: Ajia-Taiheiyō sensō no genjitsu.* Tokyo: Chūōkōronsha, 2017.

Yoshimi Yoshiaki. *Kusanone no fashizumu: Nihon minshū no sensō taiken.* Tokyo: Tokyo Daigaku Shuppankai, 1987. Translated into English as *Grassroots Fascism: The War Experience of the Japanese People.* Translated, edited, and annotated by Ethan Mark. New York: Columbia University Press, 2016.

Yoshimoto Takaaki. '"Hakuriki" ko to "kyōryoku" eiga'. In *Gunron Yukiyukite Shingun.* Edited by Matsuda Masao and Takahashi Taketomo, 271–84. Tokyo: Tōgosha, 1998.

Youngs, Tim. *The Cambridge Introduction to Travel Writing.* Cambridge: Cambridge University Press, 2013.

Index

Note: Tables are indicated by page number followed by "t". Endnotes are indicated by the page number followed by "n" and the endnote number e.g., 20 n.1 refers to endnote 1 on page 20.

Abe Shinzō 1, 190
  'beautiful Japan' 189
  '*sengo* regime' (*sengo rejīmu*) 189
'action documentary' 108–9, 128
Akasaka Mari 191
Amamiya Karin 190
Angels of War: World War II and the People of Papua New Guinea 113
Annamarie 176–8
anti-malarial medication 58–9, 68
Aoki Tōru 73
Aozu, Major General 33
Arapesh 38, 41, 49
army doctors 24
  helplessness 59
  roles 56
  self-discipline 55, 56–8
  sexual desire and appetite 69–73
  on soldiers' mental conditions 62, 63
  on soldiers' physical conditions 58, 60
  status 56
  views of New Guinea as medical crisis zone 58–61
Asia-Pacific War x–xi, 1, 8, 31, 56, 113, 133, 190–1, 197
  Allies' perspectives 19
  cannibalism in 31
  heroic narratives 16
  historical interpretations in Japan 18–20
  perceptions in Japan 187
  perpetrator narrative 17
  victim narratives 16–17
Asō Tetsuo 67, 68
  self-discipline 66, 193
  towards sexual desire 70–1
Assmann, Jan 203n36
Atabrine 58
Australia 1, 3, 6, 119, 165
  Kokoda campaign in 32
  mateship narrative 6

Bal, Mieke 10
Baskett, Michael 86
Battle of Buna-Gona 60
Battle of Finschhafen 35
Battle of Guadalcanal 73
'beautiful Japan' 189
Benedict, Ruth 57
Biak Island 172–3
Biruma no tategoto (The Burmese Harp) 101
Bismarck archipelago 62, 182
Bōken Dankichi (Adventures of Dankichi) 98, 137
Bourke, Joanna 56, 68
Bruzzi, Stella 106
Buchheim, Eveline 164, 182, 184
Buddhism 23, 37, 43, 44, 50
  concepts of 40
  haibutsu-kishaku 47
  in Japan 35
Bullard, Steven 6, 58
Burgoyne, Robert 24, 82

cannibalism 49, 53, 194, 107, 109
  in memoirs of New Guinea campaign 23, 31–54
  soldiers' opposition to 35–41
  survival egoism in 31, 42–6
  and war crime trials 32
Carrier, James G. 156
chikushōdō (realm of beasts) 43, 44, 45, 199
China 17, 31, 62, 66, 70, 137, 153, 175
The Chrysanthemum and the Sword (Benedict, Ruth) 57

commemoration, nationalist and cosmopolitan 18, 179–180, 187
Conversations of Goethe (Goethe, Johann) 137
co-performative partnership documentaries as 105
cyanide 75

Dambui, Cherubim 178
Daniel, Sanguame 124
dark tourism 26–7
Dening, Greg 25, 195
documentaries 2, 9, 22t, 25–6, 105, 112, 120, 194
Dower, John W. 37, 101, 180
Dubnik, James K. 38, 44
Dutch New Guinea 25, 74, 81, 99, 172, 175
Dvorak, Greg 90

eirei (fallen heroes) 16, 182
Ellis, John 106
Emperor Hirohito 105, 107, 108, 149, 151, 191, 194
Epupe 142, 143, 146
Erll, Astrid 2, 3, 10, 11
  see also travelling memory

Fiji 3, 197
film-makers 24, 120, 128, 194
films 24, 32, 82, 102, 105, 116, 118, 128, 187, 190
Foucault, Michel 24, 56, 57
  see also medical gaze and self-discipline
Frühstück, Sabine 70, 134
Fujiwara Akira 5
Fukabori Yūki 92
Fukuma Yoshiaki 83, 190
Furuichi Noritoshi 190
Fuzzy Wuzzy Angels 6, 119

gaki (hungry demons/ghosts) 37, 39, 48, 50, 51, 199
gaki jigoku (hell for jealousy and greed) 37
gakidō (the realm of hungry ghosts) 44, 47–8, 52, 199
Gauguin, Paul 143
Giruwa 60

The Gift (Mauss, Marcel) 148
Goethe, Johann 137
Goffman, Erving 106
gokuraku (paradise) 50
Gotō Yūsaku 116, 117
Graeber, David 152
de Groot, Jerome 9, 13
Guadalcanal 3, 5, 39, 48, 57, 73, 137

Haibutsu-kishaku (persecution of Buddhists) 47
Halbwachs, Maurice 10
Hannya shingyō (the Heart Sutra) 50
Hara Kazuo 26, 105, 108–9, 128, 193
Hashimoto, Akiko 15
Hatano Katsumi 59, 65, 66
heaven (*tengoku*) 135–6, 192
hell (*jigoku*), references to 23, 34, 37–8, 48, 53, 136, 199
  see also Rokudō (Six Realms of Existence)
heroic narratives, of Asia-Pacific War 16, 18, 181, 187
Hirao Masaharu 64
Hirsch, Marianne 11, 13, 175, 179
historical 187
  film 82, 94
  knowledge 8–9
  memory 2, 15, 18
  narratives 15, 119
  representations 11, 191
  research 179
Hokari Minoru 25
Hosaka Masayasu 75
Hulme, Peter 162
hydraulic model 70
Hynes, Samuel 21

Ienaga Saburō 20, 57, 126
Igarashi, Yoshikuni 53, 60, 95, 192
Iijima Wataru 58
ikigai (That which makes life worth living) 25, 83–4, 89, 87, 93, 193, 199
ikotsu shūshū (bone collection) 161
Imai Kazuo 65–6
The Imperial Eyes (Pratt, Mary Louise) 135
implication
  diachronic 7–8

Morris-Suzuki, Tessa 7, 8, 15, 164
　political 171, 187
　Rothberg, Michael 7, 8, 126, 164, 196
　synchronic 8, 20
Inagaki Hiroshi 95
international travel
　in post-war era Japan 143, 161, 165
ireishiki (spirit-consoling services) 161
Iwamoto, Hiromitsu 6, 23

Japan 7, 10, 62, 70, 120, 137–8, 143, 151,
　　165, 167, 170, 171, 191, 194
　Buddhism in 35
　memoirs of New Guinean campaign
　　in 7, 23
　nationalists 19–20
　war memories 19
　war-retro films 82, 83
　wartime cannibalism 32–3
jigoku (hell) *see* hell (*jigoku*)

Kanaka, Joseph 113
kandere (a matrilineal family
　member) 140, 147, 152, 156, 199
Kanetaka Kaoru 162, 163t, 165, 167, 168,
　　173, 174, 184
Karatani Kōjin 107
Katō Daisuke 22, 25, 81, 85, 193
　finds *ikigai* 86–9
　in Manokwari theatre group 84
　memoir and war in Manokwari
　　84–6, 195
　1961 film adaptation *see Minami-no-
　　shima ni yuki ga furu*
Kawaguchi Kizuki 163t, 179–181
kiga jigoku (hell of starvation) 31
Kokoda campaign 3, 6, 42, 55, 60
　in Australian society 32
Kōnodai Psychiatric Hospital 62
Korea 16, 35, 153, 175

Lae 39, 40, 165
Landsberg, Alison 11, 13, 193
Leyte campaign, in Philippines 182
Lifton, Robert Jay 52
Lisle, Debbie 147, 164

Mabuta no haha (The Mother He Never
　Knew) 95–7

MacArthur, Douglas 3
Madang, New Guinea 47, 66
Majima Mitsuru 31, 35, 40, 41, 53
　opposition to cannibalism 39
Makino Hiromichi 163t, 182–4
malaria 58–60, 151
malnutrition 65, 67
　as medical crisis 59–60
　war-related 63–64, 73
Marschall, Sabine
　personal memory tourism 161
Masubuchi Tsuyoshi 94
Mathews, Gordon 84
Mauss, Marcel 148, 149
medical gaze and self-discipline 65–9
　sexual desire and appetite 69–73
medics (*eiseihei*) 58, 64, 73, 75
memory
　cultural 11, 203n36
　historical 2, 11, 12, 18, 28,
　　161, 188
　mnemonic communities, collective
　　memory 10
　personal 134, 147, 154, 161
　postmemory 11–12
　prosthetic 11–12, 193
　rifts 19
　studies 10
　travelling 2, 3, 10–15, 25, 134
mercy killing 73–6, 193
Minami-no-shima ni yuki ga furu (Snow
　Falling in a Southern Island) 81, 193
　television adaptations 81, 84,
　　85–6, 102
　memoir by Katō Daisuke 81–2, 84,
　　85–6, 193
　1961 film adaptation 81–2, 84, 86–93,
　　102–3
　1995 film adaptation 94–103
Mishima Yukio 94–5, 101
Mitsukawa Motoyuki 65, 73, 193
　self-discipline 71–2
Miyakawa Masayo 163t, 174–8, 182,
　　184, 196
Miyoshi Masayuki 73–6
Mizuki Shigeru 27, 136, 143, 147,
　　149–150, 157, 194, 195–6
　Akuma-kun 133
　Gegege no Kitarō 133, 151

Kanzenban Mizuki Shigeru den 138, 139t, 142, 157
Karankoron hyōhakuki 139t, 142
Komikku Shōwa-shi 138, 139t, 149
Mizuki Shigeru no jūgunkōki: Topetoro tono gojū-nen 153, 154–5, 156
Mizuki Shigeru no musume ni kataru otōsan no senki 144–5, 147, 153
Neboke jinsei 141, 142, 144, 146, 147
Sōin gyokusai seyo 138, 143
travelogues, phases of 136t
war and travel-related books 139t
Watashi wa gegege 146
see also *Nanpō-byō* (South Seas syndrome)
Mizushima Satoru 94–5, 99, 101
Moore, Aaron William 57, 68
Morris-Suzuki, Tessa 7, 8, 15, 164
Motoshima Hitoshi 151
Murai 95, 96, 100, 101, 109

Nakamura Eri 62
Nakayama Kaoru 171
Namale village (New Britain Island) 133, 135–6, 140, 142, 158
Namihira Emiko 170
Nankai Shitai (the South Seas Detachment) 55, 62
Nanpō-byō (South Seas syndrome) 133, 134, 146, 152, 159, 199
nanshi (meaningless death) 83–4, 86, 91–2, 98, 100, 102, 199
nanshin-ron (the South Seas advance) 98
Nanyō–Orientalism 134, 135, 137, 147, 155–6, 158
Naoto Sudō 135
Narita Ryūichi 12–13, 145, 188
Nelson, Hank 5, 113
New Britain Island 3, 5, 27, 39, 66, 133, 142–5
New Guinea campaign 1, 15, 39, 42, 49, 64, 77, 82, 105, 112–13, 175, 181, 187, 194
    cannibalism during 23, 31
    death rate of 5
    Japanese cannibalism phases in 32–3, 38
    Japanese strategic interest in 3
    and its legacies 3–7

malnutrition by famine 60
memories in Japan 2, 23
Nishimura Kōkichi 42
Nobi (Fires on the Plain, Ōoka Shōhei) 33
Noda Masaaki 72
Noira, Makunia 113–14
Nora, Pierre 10
Noro Kuninobu 2
Nukuda Ichisuke 42, 49
    'black' and 'white' human flesh 44
Nyūginia ni chitta 16-man no seishun (160,000 adolescents scattered in New Guinea, dir. Ushiyama Jun'ichi) 26, 105, 120–2, 125–7

Oda Makoto 83, 95, 172
Ogawa Masatsugu 35, 36, 40
    opposition to cannibalism 38–9, 41
Ogawa Takemitsu 72–3
Okuzaki Kenzō 107, 108, 110, 111, 112, 194
Onda Shigetaka 204 n.38
oni (demons) 36–7, 46, 199
onnagata (male actors performing female) 85, 91, 97, 199
Ōoka Shōhei 33, 52
Operation Cartwheel 3
Operation FS 3

pacifist anti-war films 82–3
Paivu 157
Papua New Guinea (PNG) ix–x, 5, 6, 7, 21, 43, 57, 115, 119, 121, 134, 156, 162, 171, 177, 179, 181, 187, 195, 196
    and Japan 1, 218–9n35
paradise (*rakuen*) 27, 50, 135–6, 142, 145, 152, 192
Pennington, Lee 57
perpetrator narrative, of Asia-Pacific War 17
personal memory tourism 134
    Marschall, Sabine 161
Philippines 2, 5, 33, 85, 182
photography 172–4
Pirigi, Angela 114–16
Pisikei, Mora 117, 119
'postmemory' 11, 12, 179, 188, 196
post-war Japan 16, 84, 94–5, 112, 143, 192

Pratt, Mary Louise 26–7, 135, 183
    see also 'travellees'
prosthetic memory 11–12, 193

Rabaul 3, 59, 66–7, 70, 112, 116, 137–8, 140–1, 157–8, 165, 174, 179, 180–2
'revisionist' films 83, 93, 190
Rokudō (Six Realms of Existence) 35, 51
Rosenstone, Robert 24, 82
Rothberg, Michael 7, 8, 126, 164, 196
Ruoff, Jeffrey and Kenneth 107

Saito, Hiro 18, 164
Samoa 3
sange (glorious death) 83–4, 91, 94–7, 100, 101, 199
sarariiman (office workers) 86, 87, 179–182
Satō Tadao 112
Scarry, Elaine 192
Seaton, Philip 13, 15, 17, 20
    'memory rifts' 13, 19
Second World War 10, 21, 113, 180
Sekiguchi Noriko 26, 105, 112, 115–19, 193
self-reflexivity 164, 179
sengo (post-war) 153, 188, 189, 191, 194, 199
'*sengo* regime' (*sengo rejīmu*) 189
Senjōno onna tachi/Sensō Daughters (dir. Sekiguchi Noriko) 26, 105, 112–19
'Sensō to Nihon' 152–3
sexual desire and appetite 90, 97
    of army doctors 69–73
Sherman, Nancy 32, 38, 44
Shimada Keizō 98
Shimamoto Iseko 108
Shinozaki 91
Shinto 47, 182, 199
'Shūchō no musume' (Chieftain's Daughter) 89–91, 97, 102, 142
Smaill, Beinda 106
Snowflakes 92–3
soldiers 11, 17, 21, 33, 42, 43, 55, 60, 70, 81, 127, 170, 173
    anti-malarial medication 58–9
    malaria 58, 64
    masturbation 70–1
    mercy killing 73–6
    opposition to cannibalism 35–41
    psychiatric disturbances in 62
    sexual desire and appetite 69–73
    suicide 64
    war neurosis 62
Solomon Islands 64, 182, 197
Southeast Asia 17, 21, 62, 153, 169
Stahl, David C. 32, 52
Standish, Isolde 82
Stevenson, Robert Louis 143
Sukanaivalu, Sefanaia 197
survival egoism 32, 53
    in cannibalism 42–6
    and human civilization 40
Suzuki Masami 66

Takahashi Hiroki 191
Takahashi, Tetsuya 20
Takasago *giyūtai* (volunteers) 38, 41
Takeda Kazuyoshi 191
Tanaka Hiromi 2, 92, 204 n.38
Tanaka, Yuki (Toshiyuki) 33, 38, 111
Tamura, Keiko 6
Tate-no-kai (the Shield Society) 95
Ten Commandments 35
Terebi Asahi (TV Asahi) 120, 121
Tierney, Robert Thomas 31–2, 38
Timbunke Massacre 121, 122, 124, 175–9
Tōhō 86, 87, 91, 93
Tokyo Purizun (Tokyo Prison) 191
Topetoro 136, 139t, 143, 145, 146, 148t, 149, 151–2, 153, 154–5, 156, 157–8
Toyoda, Yukio 6
Toyotani Hidemitsu 46–8, 52, 53
'travellees' 27, 135, 147, 153, 196, 199
travelling memory 2, 3, 10–15, 134, 189, 190, 192, 197
    broadens notion of travel 11–12
    and media 22t
    notion of memory across media 13
    temporal aspect of 12
travelogue 2, 21–2, 26–8, 134, 135, 136, 147–8, 157, 161, 165, 169, 172, 182, 185, 206n72
tsuitaiken (experience in footsteps of someone else) 162, 182, 199
Tsumori Takudō 163t, 169, 170–3, 184–5
Tsutayama 87–8, 89, 93
tumbuan dance 157
Tuzin, Donald F. 38

Uchimura Yūshi 62
Umehara Takeshi 34, 35
United States 1, 3, 167, 172, 191
Urry, John 161
Ushiyama Jun'ichi 105, 120–7, 193, 196
US-Japan Security Treaty (1960) 87, 167
uyoku (extreme nationalists) 19

victim narratives, of Asia-Pacific War 16–18, 51, 59, 67, 107, 120–1, 166, 181, 192–3, 195

war neurosis 62, 64
war-retro films 82–3, 101
wartime 82–4, 87, 95, 109, 117, 171, 180, 188, 191
   end of Mizuki's long wartime 147–155
   generations 14t
   phases of transmission of war stories 14t
   and post-war 12–13
   responsibility 20
Watanabe Masaichi 121, 122, 124–8, 176, 194

Watanabe Susumu 58–9, 64
West Papua *see* Dutch New Guinea
White, Geoffrey 164, 182, 184
White, Hayden 15
Williams, Peter 32–3, 60

Yamada Kichitarō 109, 111
Yamamoto Isoroku 138
Yanagisawa Genichirō 55, 59–60
Yasujima Takayoshi 162, 163t, 172–4, 184–5
Yasukuni shrine 16, 110, 183
yōkai 149, 157, 199
Yomota Inuhiko 83
Yoshida Yutaka 73
Yoshimoto Takaaki 107
Yubi no hone (Bones in Finger) 191–2
Yukiyukite Shingun (The Emperor's Naked Army Marches On, dir. Hara Kazuo) 25–6, 105, 107–112, 128

Zone of absolute national defence (*zettai kokubōken*) 3–4, 187
Zungen Battalion 138, 140, 143

www.ingramcontent.com/pod-product-compliance
Lightning Source LLC
Chambersburg PA
CBHW062130300426
44115CB00012BA/1878